Internet Congestion Control

Internet Congestion Control

Subir Varma

AMSTERDAM • BOSTON • HEIDELBERG • LONDON
NEW YORK • OXFORD • PARIS • SAN DIEGO
SAN FRANCISCO • SINGAPORE • SYDNEY • TOKYO

Morgan Kaufmann is an imprint of Elsevier

Acquiring Editor: Brian Romer
Editorial Project Manager: Amy Invernizzi
Project Manager: Punithavathy Govindaradjane
Designer: Mark Rogers

Morgan Kaufmann is an imprint of Elsevier
225 Wyman Street, Waltham, MA 02451, USA

Notices
Knowledge and best practice in this field are constantly changing. As new research and experience broaden our understanding, changes in research methods, professional practices, or medical treatment may become necessary.

Practitioners and researchers must always rely on their own experience and knowledge in evaluating and using any information, methods, compounds, or experiments described herein. In using such information or methods they should be mindful of their own safety and the safety of others, including parties for whom they have a professional responsibility.

To the fullest extent of the law, neither the Publisher nor the authors, contributors, or editors, assume any liability for any injury and/or damage to persons or property as a matter of products liability, negligence or otherwise, or from any use or operation of any methods, products, instructions, or ideas contained in the material herein.

ISBN: 978-0-12-803583-2

British Library Cataloguing-in-Publication Data
A catalogue record for this book is available from the British Library

Library of Congress Cataloging-in-Publication Data
A catalog record for this book is available from the Library of Congress

For Information on all Morgan Kaufmann publications
visit our website at www.mkp.com

Working together
to grow libraries in
developing countries

www.elsevier.com • www.bookaid.org

Dedicated to my wife Sangeeta
and children Rohan, Anuj, Gaurav, and Trisha.

The Modeler's Creed:
Everything should be made as simple as possible
but not simpler.

—Attributed to Albert Einstein

Contents

Preface

Traffic congestion is a ubiquitous fact of modern life. Unbeknown to most people, the networks that constitute the Internet are also subject to congestion, albeit caused by data packets rather than autos. The distributed algorithms that keep this congestion under control form the subject matter of this book. Without these algorithms, the network can stop functioning altogether, a phenomenon known as congestion collapse, which is familiar to most people who are stuck in rush hour traffic.

The field of congestion control has seen many notable advances in recent years, but there is a lack of current books on this topic. The purpose of this book, which is targeted toward advanced and intermediate readers, is to inform about the most important developments in this area in the past 20 + years, with special emphasis on analytical modeling of congestion control systems. The book should also enable readers to gain a good understanding of the application of congestion control theory to a number of domains such as data center networks, video streaming, high-speed links, and broadband wireless networks. When seen through the lens of analytical modeling, a number of common threads run through the design and analysis of congestion control protocols in all these different areas, which to my knowledge have not been bought together in a single book before. I also hope this book will lead to a greater degree of cross-fertilization of ideas from these different application areas. By collecting the most significant results in the area of congestion control algorithms in one place, this book can serve as an impetus to new discoveries. For students, it cuts a path through the profusion of algorithms in the literature and puts the topic on a systematic and logical footing.

Some of the important features in the book include:

- A current and concise exposition of some of the most important topics in the area of congestion control for computer networks, with special emphasis on analytical modeling of congestion control systems
- Accessible coverage of the advanced topics of optimization and control theory as applied to congestion control systems
- Application of the theory to the problem of congestion control in a number of areas such as data center networks, video streaming, high-speed links, and broadband wireless networks

The book is primarily directed toward the following audiences:

- Engineers and researchers working in the area of computing systems and computer networking from companies in the computer networking, telecommunications (both wired and wireless) and video streaming industries and from companies that operate large data centers.
- Advanced to intermediate undergraduate and graduate students in electrical engineering and computer science. The book can be used for a graduate-level course on advanced topics in computer networking.
- A secondary audience is engineers, students, and researchers in related fields such as information sciences, operations research, traffic engineering, and manufacturing who also have an interest in congestion control.

The common mathematical framework that underlies most of the work in this book is that of "fluid flow" models of packet data networks. These average out the short-term stochastic fluctuations in quantities of interest such queue sizes and result in ordinary differential equations as a description of the system dynamics. This simplifies the analysis considerably while retaining the essential aspects of the system behavior. As a result, most of the book can be read with only knowledge of freshman-level calculus and some basic probability theory. Knowledge of control theory is needed to understand the results in Chapter 3 and sections of Part 2 of the book that delve into questions of system stability, and I have tried to cover the basics of control theory needed for the book in the Appendices.

Congestion control, along with packet scheduling, mobility, and medium access control, has dominated the work that I have been engaged in during the course of my professional career. Similar to many other authors, I started writing this book as a way of bringing myself up to date with the work in this field, and it has been a wonderful learning experience. The book has evolved over the past year as my own understanding of the subject increased, and this has considerably improved the material that is presented here. I have had the vantage point of surveying the past almost 30 years of work in this area and have chosen the results that have withstood the test of time. But as with any other author, the choice of topics is idiosyncratic, and in my case, biased toward work that can be put into an elegant theoretical framework. Most of the work has appeared in research publications, but in places, I have filled in gaps that I found, resulting in some new material.

About the Author

Subir has more than 20 years of experience in the technology industry, during which he has held leadership positions for large companies such as IBM and Sprint, as well several Silicon Valley—based start-ups. At IBM, he was part of the design team for IBM's next-generation broadband architecture, and his contribution to improving the performance of IBM's host-based protocol stack led to an IBM Outstanding Innovation Award. He served as director of systems architecture at cable modem pioneer Hybrid Networks, where his design for the Medium Access Control protocol enabled the company to establish an early lead in the MMDS metro area wireless space. While at Hybrid, he also took part in the drafting of the DOCSIS Cable Model specification. He was the co-founder and CTO/VP of engineering at Aperto Networks, a pioneer in the broadband wireless space, where he was the chief designer of its Packetwave line of products. His work at Aperto led to the creation of the industry's leading wireless access system, which was 5+ years ahead of the rest of the competition. Subsequently, through his chairing of the IEEE 802.16 MAC standards group, this design had a big influence on the WiMAX specification, which in turn influenced the design of LTE, which is the leading cellular wireless protocol in use today. Most recently, Subir was part of the Office of the CTO at Tellabs, where he led the company's architectural efforts in the area of broadband wireless gateways. The projects that he contributed to included a design for an LTE WiFi Gateway and a Software-Defined Networking—based architecture for the LTE packet core.

Subir holds 45 patents, which along with his other publications, have been cited more than 800 times. His most cited works are in the areas of congestion control, packet scheduling/BW management, mobility, and Medium Access Control. His graduate work on fork-join and resequencing queuing systems has found recent applications in the areas of RAID systems, vertical search engines, and parallel databases. Subir holds a PhD in electrical engineering from the University of Maryland, College Park, and a BTech. in electrical engineering from IIT Kanpur, India.

Acknowledgments

Work on this book has taken me away from my family for almost every weekend and most evenings over the past year. This book is dedicated to them for their love and understanding: my beloved wife Sangeeta and wonderful children, Rohan, Anuj, Gaurav, and Trisha.

I have worked with many talented individuals during the course of my career. At Aperto Networks, where I served as co-founder and Head of Technology, some of the theories from this book pertaining to broadband wireless networks were successfully put into practice. I would like to acknowledge Paul Truong and Tassos Michail from Aperto in helping me understand the intricacies of applying mathematical results to systems operating in the real world. Charlie Perkins and Dr. Mustafa Ergen at Wichorus have played a big role in my thinking on the modeling of complex systems that occur in the cellular wireless context. I would also like to thank Prof. Armand Makowski, my advisor from my PhD days at the University of Maryland, for instilling the love of mathematical modeling and being a good friend over the ensuing decades; Prof. Anujan Varma from the University of California at Santa Cruz and Dr. Leandros Tassiulas from Yale University for serving as my brilliant collaborators during my early years in Silicon Valley; and Prof. Yannis Viniotis from North Carolina State University, with whom I go back more than 30 years, for helping me understand high-speed networking concepts, during my time with IBM's Networking Division in the 1990s. Prof. Viniotis also served as a reviewer for this book, and the content is immeasurably improved as a result.

Subir Varma
Almaden Valley, California
April 2015

List of Abbreviations

AA	Application Specific IP Address
ABE	Available Bandwidth Estimate
ABR	Adaptive Bit Rate (in the context of video streaming)
	Available Bit Rate (in the context of ATM networks)
ADSL	Asymmetric Digital Subscriber Loop
AI	Additive Increase
	Artificial Intelligence
AIAD	Additive Increase Additive Decrease
AIMD	Additive Increase Multiplicative Decrease
AP	Averaging Principle
AQM	Active Queue Management
APPN	Advanced Peer to Peer Networking
AR	Auto Regressive
	Aggregation Router
ARED	Adaptive Random Early Detection
ARIMA	Auto Regressive Integrated Moving Average
ARMA	Auto Regressive Moving Average
ARP	Address Resolution Protocol
ARQ	Automatic Repeat reQuest
AS	Aggregation Switch
ASN	Ack'd Sequence Number
ATB	AIMD based HAS Algorithm
ATM	Asynchronous Transfer Mode
BBRS	Buffer Based Rate Selection
BIC	Binary Increase Congestion Control
CA	Congestion Avoidance
CBR	Constant Bit Rate
CC	Congestion Control
CDN	Content Delivery Network
CoDel	Controlled Delay
CP	Control Point
CR	Core Router
CTB	Control Theory Based ABR Algorithm
CTCP	Compound TCP
DASH	Dynamic Adaptive Streaming over HTTP
DCB	Data Center Bridging
DCN	Data Center Network
DCT	Discrete Cosine Transform
DCTCP	Data Center TCP
D^2TCP	Deadline Aware Data Center TCP
DHFT	Dual Homed Fat Tree
EC	Efficiency Controller
ECMP	Equal Cost Multi Path

ECN	Explicit Congestion Notification
EDF	Earliest Deadline First
EERC	End-to-End Rate based flow Control
FARIMA	Fractional Auto Regressive Integrated Moving Average
FC	Fairness Controller
	Fiber Channel
FCFS	First Come First Served
FCOE	Fiber Channel Over Ethernet
FCT	Flow Completion Time
FEC	Forward Error Correction
FIFO	First In First Out
FPGA	Field Programmable Gate Array
FPS	Frames Per Second
FR	Fast Recovery
GAIMD	Generalized Additive Increase Multiplicative Decrease
GBN	Go Back N
GCC	Google Congestion Control
GGSN	Gateway GPRS Support Node
GPRS	General Packet Radio Service
HARQ	Hybrid ARQ
HAI	Hyper Active Increase
HAS	HTTP Adaptive Streaming
HDS	HTTP Dynamic Streaming (Adobe)
HDTV	High Definition Television
HFC	Hybrid Fiber Coax
HLS	HTTP Live Streaming (Apple)
HSS	HTTP Smooth Streaming (Microsoft)
HSTCP	High Speed TCP
HTTP	Hyper Text Transport Protocol
HULL	High Bandwidth Ultra Low Latency
IEEE	Institute of Electrical and Electronic Engineers
IETF	Internet Engineering Taskforce
IntServ	Integrated Services
IP	Internet Protocol
IS	Intermediate Switches
I-TCP	Indirect TCP
ITU	International Telecommunications Union
LA	Link specific IP Address
LAN	Local Area Network
LB	Load Balancing
LBE	Less than Best Effort
LEDBAT	Low Extra Delay Background Transport
LDA	Loss Discrimination Algorithm
LHS	Left Hand Side
LL PDU	Link Layer Packet Data Unit
LTE	Long Term Evolution
MAC	Medium Access Control
MIAD	Multiplicative Increase Additive Decrease

MIMD	Multiplicative Increase Multiplicative Decrease
ML	Machine Learning
MPC	Model Predictive Control
MPTCP	Multi Path TCP
MPEG	Moving Pictures Experts Group
MSS	Maximum Segment Size
M-TCP	Mobile TCP
MVA	Mean Value Analysis
NAT	Network Address Translation
NIC	Network Interface Card
NSN	Next Sequence Number
NOS	Network Operating System
NTB	Network Throughput Based HAS Algorithm
OFDMA	Orthogonal Frequency Division Multiple Access
PD	Progressive Download
PDQ	Preemptive Distributed Quick Flow Control
PD-BR	Progressive Download with Byte Ranges
PDSN	Packet Data Serving Node
PDU	Packet Data Unit
PGW	Packet Gateway
PI	Proportional + Integral AQM Controller
PM	Phase Margin
PQ	Phantom Queue
PS	Processor Sharing
QAM	Quadrature Amplitude Modulation
QCN	Quantum Congestion Notification
QoE	Quality of Experience
QoS	Quality of Service
QPSK	Quadrature Phase Shift Queueing
RAP	Rate Adaptive Protocol
RED	Random Early Detection
RCP	Rate Control Protocol
RHS	Right Hand Side
RP	Reaction Point
RS	Reed Solomon
RR	RTCP Receiver Report
RSVP	ReSerVation Protocol
RTO	Re-transmission Time Out
RTCP	Real Time Control Protocol
RTP	Real Time Transport Protocol
RTSP	Real Time Streaming Protocol
RTT	Round Trip Time
RW	Receive Window
SAN	Storage Area Network
SDN	Software Defined Network
SJF	Shortest Job First
SN	Sequence Number
SR	Selective Repeat

SRAM	Static Random Access Memory
SS	Slow Start
STB	Smoothed Throughput Based HAS Algorithm
TBB	Threshold Based Buffer HAS Algorithm
TCP	Transmission Control Protocol
TFRC	TCP Friendly Rate Control
TM	Traffic Management
ToR	Top of Rack
TRILL	Transparent Interconnection of Lots of Links
TSN	Transmit Sequence Number
TSW	Time Sliding Window
UDP	User Datagram Protocol
VBR	Variable Bit Rate
VLAN	Virtual Local Area Network
VLB	Valiant Load Balancing
VM	Virtual Machine
VoD	Video on Demand
VoQ	Virtual output Queue
VxLAN	Virtual extensible Local Area Network
WAN	Wide Area Network
WebRTC	Web Real Time Communications Protocol
WFQ	Weighted Fair Queueing
WLAN	Wireless Local Area Network
XCP	Express Control Protocol
ZRW	Zero Receive Window
ZWP	Zero Window Probe

INTRODUCTION

1.1 INTRODUCTION

The Transmission Control Protocol (TCP) is one of the pillars of the global Internet. One of TCP's critical functions is congestion control, and the objective of this book is to provide an overview of this topic, with special emphasis on analytical modeling of congestion control protocols.

TCP's congestion control algorithm has been described as the largest human-made feedback-controlled system in the world. It enables hundreds of millions of devices, ranging from huge servers to the smallest PDA, to coexist together and make efficient use of existing bandwidth resources. It does so over link speeds that vary from a few kilobits per second to tens of gigabits per second. How it is able to accomplish this task in a fully distributed manner forms the subject matter of this book.

Starting from its origins as a simple static-window−controlled algorithm, TCP congestion control went through several important enhancements in the years since 1986, starting with Van Jacobsen's invention of the Slow Start and Congestion Avoidance algorithms, described in his seminal paper [1]. In addition to significant developments in the area of new congestion control algorithms and enhancements to existing ones, we have seen a big increase in our theoretical understanding of congestion control. Several new important application areas, such as video streaming and data center networks (DCNs), have appeared in recent years, which have kept the pace of innovation in this subject area humming.

The objective of this book is twofold: Part 1 provides an accessible overview of the main theoretical developments in the area of modeling of congestion control systems. Not only have these models helped our understanding of existing algorithms, but they have also played an essential role in the discovery of newer algorithms. They have also helped us explore the limits of stability of congestion control algorithms. Part 2 discusses the application of congestion control to some important areas that have arisen in the past 10 to 15 years, namely Wireless Access Networks, DCNs, high-speed links, and Packet Video Transport. Each of these applications comes with its own unique characteristics that has resulted in new requirements from the congestion control point of view and has led to a proliferation of new algorithms in recent years. Several of these are now as widely deployed as the legacy TCP congestion control algorithm. The strong theoretical underpinning that has been established for this subject has helped us greatly in understanding the behavior of these new algorithms.

The rest of this chapter is organized as follows: Section 1.2 provides an introduction to the topic of congestion control in data networks and introduces the idea of additive increase/multiplicative decrease (AIMD) algorithms. Section 1.3 provides a description of the TCP Reno algorithm, and Section 1.4 discusses Active Queue Management (AQM). TCP Vegas is described in Section 1.5, and Section 1.6 provides an overview of the rest of the chapters in this book.

1.2 BASICS OF CONGESTION CONTROL

The problem of congestion control arises whenever multiple distributed agents try to make use of shared resources (Figure 1.1). It arises widely in different scenarios, including traffic control on highways or air traffic control. This book focuses on the specific case of packet data networks, where the high-level objective of congestion control is to provide good utilization of network resources and at the same time provide acceptable performance for the users of the network.

The theory and practice of congestion control for data networks have evolved in the past 3 decades to the system that we use today. The early Internet had very rudimentary congestion control, which led to a series of network collapses in 1986. As a result, a congestion control algorithm called TCP Slow Start (also sometimes called TCP Tahoe) was put into place in 1987 and 1988, which, in its current incarnation as TCP Reno, remains one of the dominant algorithms used in the Internet today. Since then, the Internet has evolved and now features transmissions over wireless media, link speeds that are several orders of magnitudes faster, widespread transmission of video streams, and the recent rise of massive data centers. The congestion control research and development community has successfully met the challenge of modifying the original congestion control algorithm and has come up with newer algorithms to address these new types of networks.

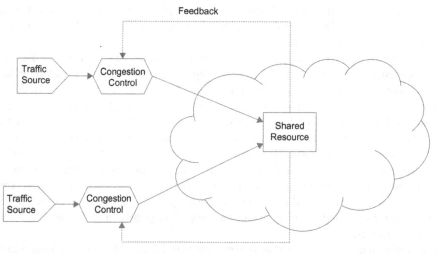

FIGURE 1.1

The congestion control problem.

1.2.1 THE CONGESTION CONTROL PROBLEM DEFINITION

To define the congestion control problem more formally, consider the graph in Figure 1.2 in which the throughput of a data source has been plotted on the y-axis and the network traffic load from the source has been plotted on the x-axis. We observe the following:

- If the load is small, the throughput keeps up with the increasing load. After the load reaches the network capacity, at the "knee" of the curve, the throughput stops increasing. Beyond the knee, as the load increases, queues start to build up in the network, thus increasing the end-to-end latency without adding to the throughput. The network is then said to be in a state of congestion.
- If the traffic load increases even further and gets to the "cliff" part of the curve, then the throughput experiences a rather drastic reduction. This is because queues within the network have increased to the point that packets are being dropped. If the sources choose to retransmit to recover from losses, then this adds further to the total load, resulting in a positive feedback loop that sends the network into congestion collapse.

To avoid congestion collapse, each data source should try to maintain the load it is sending into the network in the neighborhood of the knee. An algorithm that accomplishes this objective is known as a congestion avoidance algorithm; a congestion control algorithm tries to prevent the system from going over the cliff. This task is easier said than done and runs into the following challenge: The location of the knee is not known and in fact changes with total network load and traffic patterns. Hence, the problem of congestion control is inherently a distributed optimization problem in which each source has to constantly adapt its traffic load as a function of feedback information it is receiving from the network as it tries to stay near the knee of the curve.

The original TCP Tahoe algorithm and its descendants fall into the congestion control category because in the absence of support from the network nodes, the only way they can detect congestion is by filling up the network buffers and then detecting the subsequent packet drops as a sign of congestion. Many routers today implement a more sophisticated form of buffer management called Random Early Detection (RED) that provides early warnings of a congestive situation. TCP in

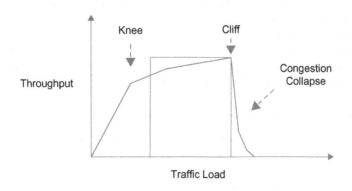

FIGURE 1.2

Throughput versus load.

combination with RED then qualifies as a congestion avoidance algorithm. Algorithms such as TCP Vegas operate the system around the knee without requiring special support in the network nodes.

Some of the questions that need to be answered in the design of a congestion control algorithm include the following (all of the new terms used below are defined in this chapter):

- Should the congestion control be implemented on an end-to-end or on a hop-by-hop basis?
- Should the traffic control be exercised using a windows-based mechanism or a rate-based mechanism?
- How does the network signal to the end points that it is congested (or conversely, not congested)?
- What is the best Traffic Rate Increment rule in the absence of congestion?
- What is the best Traffic Rate Decrement rule in the presence of congestion?
- How can the algorithm ensure fairness among all connections sharing a link, and what measure of fairness should be used?
- Should the congestion control algorithm prioritize high link utilization of low end-to-end latency?

There is a function closely related to congestion control, called flow control, and often the two terms are used interchangeably. For the purposes of this book, *flow control* is defined as a function that is used at the destination node to prevent its receive buffers from overflowing. It is implemented by providing feedback to the sender, usually in the form of window-size constraints. Later in this book, we will discuss the case of video streaming in which the objective is to prevent the receive buffer from underflowing. We classify the algorithm used to accomplish this objective also in the flow control category.

1.2.2 OPTIMIZATION CRITERIA FOR CONGESTION CONTROL

This section and the next are based on some pioneering work by Chiu and Jain [2] in the congestion control area. They defined optimization criteria that the congestion control algorithms should satisfy, and then they showed that there is a class of controls called AIMD that satisfies many of these criteria. We start by enunciating the Chiu-Jain optimization criteria in this section.

Consider a network with N data sources and define $r_i(t)$ to be the data rate (i.e., load) of the ith data source. Also assume that the system is operating near the knee of the curve from Figure 1.2 so that the network rate allocation to the ith source after congestion control is also given by $r_i(t)$. We assume that the system operation is synchronized and happens in discrete time so that the rate at time $(t+1)$ is a function of the rate at time t, and the network feedback received at time t. We will also assume that the network congestion feedback is received at the sources instantaneously without any delay.

Define the following optimization criteria for selecting the best control:

- Efficiency: Every source has a bottleneck node, which is the node where it gets the least throughput among all the nodes along its path. Let A_i be the set of other sources that also pass through this bottleneck node; then the efficiency criterion states that $\sum_{j \in A_i} r_i(n)$ should be as close as possible to C, where C is the capacity of the bottleneck node.
- Fairness: The efficiency criterion does not put any constraints on how the data rates are distributed among the various sources. A fair allocation is when all the sources that share a

bottleneck node get an equal allocation of the bottleneck link capacity. The Jain fairness index defined below quantifies this notion of fairness.

$$F(r_1, \ldots, r_N) = \frac{\left(\sum r_i\right)^2}{N\left(\sum r_i^2\right)}$$
(1)

Note that this index is bounded between 0 and 1, so that a totally fair allocation (with all r_i's equal) has an index of 1, but a totally unfair allocation (in which the entire capacity is given to one user) has an index of 1/N.

• Convergence: There are two aspects to convergence. The first aspect is the speed with which the rate $r_i(t)$ gets to its equilibrium rate at the knee after starting from zero (called responsiveness). The second aspect is the magnitude of its oscillations around the equilibrium value while in steady state (called smoothness).

1.2.3 OPTIMALITY OF ADDITIVE INCREASE MULTIPLICATIVE DECREASE CONGESTION CONTROL

In this section, we restrict ourselves to a two-source network that shares a bottleneck link with capacity C. As shown in Figure 1.3, any rate allocation (r_1, r_2) can be represented by a point in a two-dimensional space. The objective of the optimal congestion control algorithm is to bring the system close to the optimal point (C/2, C/2) irrespective of the starting position.

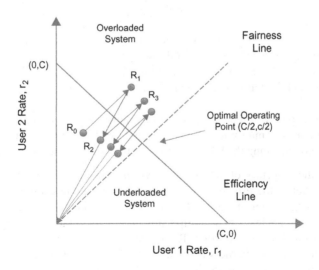

FIGURE 1.3

Additive Increase and Multiplicative Decrease Congestion Control.

We assume that the system evolves in discrete time, such that at the nth step the following linear controls are used:

Rate Increase Rule

$$r_i(n+1) = a_I + b_I r_i(n) \quad i = 1, 2 \text{ if the bottleneck is not congested} \tag{2}$$

Rate Decrease Rule

$$r_i(n+1) = a_D + b_D r_i(n) \quad i = 1, 2 \text{ if the bottleneck is congested} \tag{3}$$

Note the following special cases:

- $a_I = a_D = 0$, $b_I > 1$ and $0 < b_D < 1$ corresponds to multiplicative increase/multiplicative decrease (MIMD) controls.
- $b_I = b_D = 1$ corresponds to additive increase/additive decrease (AIAD) controls.
- $b_I = 1$, $a_D = 0$ and $0 < b_D < 1$ corresponds to AIMD controls.
- $a_I = 0$, $b_D = 1$ corresponds to multiplicative increase/additive decrease (MIAD) controls.

With reference to Figure 1.3, note the following:

- All allocations for which $r_1 + r_2 = C$ are efficient allocations, which correspond to points on the "efficiency line" in Figure 1.3. All points below the efficiency line represent underloaded systems, and the correct control decision in this region is to increase the rates. Conversely, all points above the efficiency line represent overloaded systems, and the correct control decision in this region is to decrease the rates.
- All allocations for which $r_1 = r_2$ are fair allocations, which corresponds to points on the "fairness line" in Figure 1.3. Also note that because the fairness at any point (r_1, r_2) is given by

$$F(r_1, r_2) = \frac{(r_1 + r_2)^2}{2(r_1^2 + r_2^2)},$$

multiplying both the rates by a factor b does not change the fairness, that is, (br_1, br_2) has the same fairness as (r_1, r_2). Hence all points on the straight line joining (r_1, r_2) to the origin have the same fairness and such a line is called an "equi-fairness" line.
- The efficiency line and the fairness line intersect at the point (C/2, C/2), which is the optimal operating point.
- The additive increase policy of increasing both users' allocations by a_I corresponds to moving up along a 45-degree line. The multiplicative decrease policy of increasing both users' allocations by b_I corresponds to moving along the line that connects the origin to the current operating point.

Figure 1.3 shows the trajectory of the two-user system starting from point a R_0 using an AIMD policy. Because R_0 is below the efficiency line, the policy causes an additive increase along a 45-degree line that moves the system to point R_1 (assuming a big enough increment value), which is above the efficiency line. This leads to a multiplicative decrease in the next step by moving to point R_2 toward the origin on the line that joins R_1 to the origin (assuming a big enough decrement value). Note that R_2 has a higher fairness index than R_0. This increase–decrease cycle repeats over and over until the system converges to the optimal state (C/2, C/2).

Using similar reasoning, it can be easily seen that with both the MIMD or the AIAD policies, the system never converges toward the optimal point but keeps oscillating back and forth across the efficiency line. Hence, these systems achieve efficiency but not fairness. The MIAD system, on the other hand, is not stable and causes one of the rates to blow up over time.

These informal arguments can be made more rigorous [2] to show that the AIMD policy given by

$$r_i(n+1) = a_I + r_i(n) \quad i = 1,2 \tag{4}$$

$$r_i(n+1) = b_D r_i(n) \quad i = 1,2 \tag{5}$$

is the optimal policy to achieve the criteria defined in Section 1.2.2. Indeed, most of the algorithms for congestion control that are described in this book adhere to the AIMD policy. This analysis framework can also be extended to nonlinear increase−decrease algorithms of the type

$$r_i(n+1) = r_i(n) + \alpha(r_i(n))^k \tag{6}$$

Nonlinear algorithms have proven to be especially useful in the congestion control of high-speed links over large propagation delays, and several examples of this type of algorithm are presented in Chapter 5 of this book.

Two assumptions were made in this analysis that greatly simplified it: (1) the network feedback is instantaneous, and (2) the sources are synchronized with each other and operate in discrete time. More realistic models of the network that are introduced in later chapters relax these assumptions; as a result, the analysis requires more sophisticated tools. The simple equations 2 and 3 for the evolution of the transmit rates have to be replaced by nonlinear delay-differential equations, and the proof of system stability and convergence requires sophisticated techniques from control theory such as the Nyquist criterion.

1.2.4 WINDOW-BASED CONGESTION CONTROL

Window-based congestion control schemes have historically preceded rate-based schemes and, thanks to the popularity of TCP, constitute the most popular type of congestion control scheme in use today. As shown in Figure 1.4, a window whose size can be set either in bytes or in multiples of the packet size drives the basic operation. Assuming the latter and a window size of N packets, the system operates as follows:

- Assume that the packets are numbered sequentially from 1 and up. When a packet gets to the destination, an ACK is generated and sent back to the source. The ACK carries the sequence number (SN) of packet that it is acknowledging.
- The source maintains two counters, Ack'd and Sent. Whenever a packet is transmitted, the Sent counter is incremented by 1, and when an ACK arrives from the destination, the Ack'd counter is incremented by 1. Because the window size is N packets, the difference un_ackd = (Sent−Ack'd) is not allowed to exceed N. When unAck'd = N, then the source stops transmitting and waits for more ACKs to arrive.
- ACKs can be of two types: An ACK can either acknowledge individual packets, which is known as Selective Repeat ARQ, or it can carry a single SN that acknowledges multiple packets with lower SNs. The latter strategy is called Go Back N.

This simple windowing scheme with the Go Back N Acking strategy is basically the way in which TCP congestion control operated before 1988.

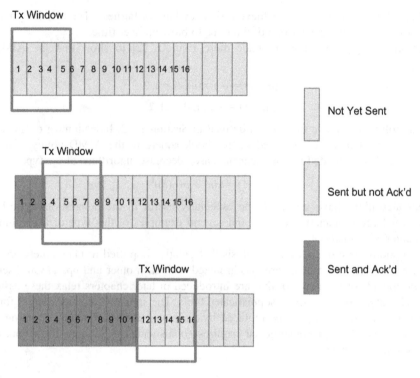

FIGURE 1.4

Transmit window operation. *Tx*, Transmit.

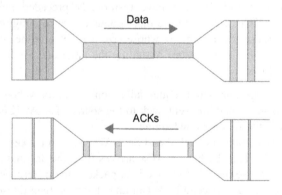

FIGURE 1.5

Self-clocking property.

Figure 1.5 illustrates the mechanism by which a simple static window scheme is able to react to congestion in the network. This served as the primary means of congestion control in the Internet before the introduction of the TCP Slow Start algorithm. As shown, if a node is congested, then the rate at which ACKs are sent back is precisely equal to the rate at which the congested node is able to serve the packets in its queue. As a result, the source sending rate gets autoregulated to the rate at which the bottleneck node can serve the packets from that source. This is also known as the "self-clocking" property and is one of the benefits of the window-based congestion control over the rate-based schemes.

The window-based scheme also functions as an effective flow control algorithm because if the destination is running out of buffers, then it can withhold sending ACKs and thereby reduce the rate at which packets are being transmitted in the forward direction.

Readers will notice that there are a number of potential problems with the static window congestion control algorithm. In particular:

1. When the algorithm is started, there is no mechanism to regulate the rate at which the source sends packets into the network. Indeed, the source may send a whole windowfull of packets back to back, thus overwhelming nodes along the route and leading to lost packets. When the ACKs start to flow back, the sending rate settles down to the self-clocked rate.
2. Given a window size of W and a round trip time of T, the average throughput R is given by the formula $R = W/T$ in steady state (this is explained in Chapter 2). If the network is congested at a node, then the only way to clear it is by having the sources traversing that node reduce their sending rate. However, there is no way this can be done without reducing the corresponding window sizes. If we do introduce a mechanism to reduce window sizes in response to congestion, then we also need to introduce a complementary mechanism to increase window sizes after the congestion goes away.
3. If the source were to vary its window size in response to congestion, then there needs to be a mechanism by which the network can signal the presence of congestion back to the source.

Partially as a result of a lack of mechanism to address the first two issues, the Internet suffered a so-called "congestion collapse" in 1986, during which all traffic ground to a halt. As a result, a number of proposals made by Van Jacobsen and Karels [1] were adopted that addressed these shortcomings. These are described in detail in Section 1.3.

1.2.5 RATE-BASED CONGESTION CONTROL

Instead of using a window to regulate the rate at which the source is sending packets into the network, the congestion control algorithm may alternatively release packets using a packet rate control mechanism. This can be implemented by using a timer to time the interpacket intervals. In practice, the end-to-end rate-based flow control (EERC) algorithm, which was part of the Asynchronous Transfer Mode (ATM) Forum Available Bit Rate (ABR) traffic management scheme, was one instance when a rate-based control was actually put into practice [3]. However, because ABR was not widely implemented in even ATM networks, there is less practical experience with rate-based schemes than with dynamic window schemes. More recently, rate-based control has been used for the TCP Friendly Rate Control (TFRC) algorithm, which is used for streaming applications. Video streaming was thought to be an area in which rate-based control fits in more naturally than window-based control. However, even for video, the industry has settled on a scheme that uses TCP for congestion control for reasons that are explained in Chapter 6. Rate control has been used in recent years in non-TCP contexts, and a couple of examples of this are provided in this book: The IEEE802.1Qau algorithm, also known as Quantum Congestion Notification (QCN;

see Chapter 8), uses rate-based control, and so does the Google Congestion Control (GCC; see Chapter 9) algorithm that is used for real-time interbrowser communications.

Compared with window-based schemes, rate-based schemes have the following disadvantages:

- Window-based schemes have a built-in choke-off mechanism in the presence of extreme congestion when the ACKs stop coming back. However, in rate-based schemes, there is no such cut-off, and the source can potentially keep pumping data into the network.
- Rate-based schemes require a more complex implementation at both the end nodes and in the network nodes. For example, at the end node, the system requires a fine-grained timer mechanism to control the rates.

1.2.6 END-TO-END VERSUS HOP-BY-HOP CONGESTION CONTROL

In the discussion thus far, we have implicitly assumed that the congestion control mechanism exists on an end-to-end basis (i.e., other than providing congestion feedback, the network nodes do not take any other action to relieve the congestion). However, there exists an alternate design called hop-by-hop congestion control, which operates on a node-by-node basis. Such a scheme was actually implemented as part of the IBM Advanced Peer to Peer Network (APPN) architecture [4] and was one of the two competing proposals for the ATM ABR congestion control algorithm [3].

Hop-by-hop congestion control typically uses a window-based congestion control scheme at each hop and operates as follows: If the congestion occurs at the nth node along the route and its buffers fill up, then that node stops sending ACKs to the $(n-1)^{rst}$ node. Because the $(n-1)^{rst}$ node can no longer transmit, its buffers will start to fill up and consequently will stop sending ACKs to the $(n-2)^{nd}$ node. This process continues until the backpressure signal reaches the source node. Some of the benefits of hop-by-hop congestion control are:

- Hop-by-hop schemes can do congestion control without letting the congestion deteriorate to the extent that packets are being dropped.
- Individual connections can be controlled using hop-by-hop schemes because the window scheme described earlier operated on a connection-by-connection basis. Hence, only the connections that are causing congestion need be controlled, as opposed to all the connections originating at the source node or traversing a congested link.

Note that these benefits require that the hop-by-hop window be controlled on a per-connection basis. This can lead to greater complexity of the routing nodes within the network, which is the reason why hop-by-hop schemes have not found much favor in the Internet community, whose design philosophy has been to push all complexity to the end nodes and keep the network nodes as simple as possible.

The big benefit of hop-by-hop schemes is that they react to congestion much faster than end-to-end schemes, which typically take a round trip of latency or longer. The rise of DCNs, which are very latency sensitive, has made this feature more attractive, and as seen in Chapter 7, some recent data center–oriented congestion control protocols feature hop-by-hop congestion control. Also, hop-by-hop schemes are attractive for systems that cannot tolerate any packet loss. An example of this is the Fiber Channel protocol used in Storage Area Networks (SAN), which is a user of hop-by-hop congestion control.

1.2.7 IMPLICIT VERSUS EXPLICIT INDICATION OF NETWORK CONGESTION

The source can either implicitly infer the existence of network congestion, or the network can send it explicit signals that it is congested. Both of these mechanisms are used in the Internet. Regular TCP is an example of a protocol that implicitly infers network congestion by using the information contained in the ACKs coming back from the destination, and TCP Explicit Congestion Notification (ECN) is an example of a protocol in which the network nodes explicitly signal congestion.

1.3 DESCRIPTION OF TCP RENO

Using the taxonomy from Section 1.2, TCP congestion control can be classified as a window-based algorithm that operates on an end-to-end basis and uses implicit feedback from the network to detect congestion. The initial design was a simple fixed window scheme that is described in Sections 1.3.1 and 1.3.2. This was found to be inadequate as the Internet grew, and a number of enhancements were made in the late 1980s and early 1990s (described in Sections 1.3.3 and 1.3.4), which culminated in a protocol called TCP Reno, which still remains one of the most widely implemented congestion control algorithms today.

1.3.1 BASIC TCP WINDOWING OPERATIONS

TCP uses byte-based sequence numbering at the transport layer. The sender maintains two counters:

- Transmit Sequence Number (TSN) is the SN of the next byte to be transmitted. When a data packet is created, the SN field in the TCP header is filled with the current value of the TSN, and the sender then increments the TSN counter by the number of bytes in the data portion of the packet. The number of bytes in a packet is equal to Maximum Segment Size (MSS) and can be smaller if the application runs out of bytes to send.
- Ack'd Sequence Number (ASN) is the SN of the next byte that the receiver is expecting. The ASN is copied from the ACK field of the last packet that is received.

To maintain the window operation, the sender enforces the following rule:

$$(SN - ASN) \leq W \tag{7}$$

where W is the transmit window size in bytes and SN is the sequence number of the next packet that sender wishes to transmit. If the inequality is not satisfied, then the transmit window is full, and no more packets can be transmitted.

The receiver maintains a single counter:

- Next Sequence Number (NSN): This is the SN of the next byte that the receiver is expecting. If the SN field of the next packet matches the NSN value, then the NSN is incremented by the number of bytes in the packet. If the SN field in the received packet does not match the NSN value, then the NSN is left unchanged. This event typically happens if a packet is lost in transmission and one of the following packets makes it to the receiver.

The receiver inserts the NSN value into the ACK field of the next packet that is being sent back. Note that ACKs are cumulative, so that if one of them is lost, then the next ACK makes up for it. Also, an ACK is always generated even if SN of a received packet does not match the NSN. In this case, the ACK field will be set to the old NSN again. This is a so-called Duplicate ACK, and as discussed in Section 1.3.4, the presence of Duplicate ACKs can be used by the transmitter as an indicator of lost packets, and indirectly, network congestion.

ACKs are usually piggybacked on the data flowing back in the opposite direction, but if there is no data flowing back, then the receiver generates a special ACK packet with an empty data field. To reduce the number of ACK packets flowing back, most receiver implementations start a 200-msec timer on receipt of a packet, and if another packet arrives within that period, then a single ACK is generated. This rule, which is called Delayed ACKs, cuts down the number of ACKs flowing back by half.

The receiver also implements a receive window (RW), whose value is initially set to the number of bytes in the receive buffer. If the receiver has one or more packets in the receive buffer whose total size is B bytes, then it reduces the RW size to RW = (RW − B). All ACKs generated at the receiver carry the current RW value, and on receipt of the ACK, the sender sets the transmit window to W = min(W, RW). This mechanism, which was referred to as flow control in Section 1.2.1, allows the receiver with insufficient available buffer capacity to throttle the sender.

Note that even though TCP maintains byte counters to keep track of the window sizes, the congestion control algorithms to be described next are often specified in terms of packet sizes. The packet that is used in these calculations is of size equal to the TCP packet size.

1.3.2 WINDOW SIZE DECREMENTS, PART 1: TIMER OPERATION AND TIMEOUTS

The original TCP congestion control algorithm used a retransmit timer as the sole mechanism to detect packet losses and as an indicator of congestion. This timer counts in ticks of 500-msec increments, and the sender keeps track of the number of ticks between when a packet is transmitted and when its gets ACKed. If the value of the timer exceeds the value of the retransmission timeout (RTO), then the sender assumes that the packet has been lost and retransmits it. The sender also takes two other actions on retransmitting a packet:

- The sender doubles the value of RTO and keeps doubling if there are subsequent timeouts for the same packet until it is delivered to the destination.
- The sender reduces the TCP window size to 1 packet (i.e., W = 1).

Choosing an appropriate value for RTO is critical because if the value is too low, then it can cause unnecessary timeouts, and if the value is too high, then the sender will take too long to react to network congestion. The current algorithm for RTO estimation was suggested by Jacobsen and Karels [1] and works as follows:

Define the following:

M: Latest measurement of the round trip latency value (RTT). The sender only measures the RTT for one packet at a time. When a timeout and retransmission occur on the packet being used for measurement, then the RTT estimators are not updated for that packet.

A: The smoothed RTT estimator

D: The smoothed mean deviation of the RTT

g, h: Smoothing constants used in the estimate of A and D, respectively. g is set to 0.125 and h to 0.25.

The calculations are as follows:

$$Err = M - A$$
$$A \leftarrow A + gErr$$
$$D \leftarrow D + h(|Err| - D)$$
$$RTO = A + 4D$$

(8)

Before Jacobsen and Karels' [1] work, the RTO value was set to a multiple of A alone, which underestimated the timeout value, thus leading to unnecessary retransmissions.

1.3.3 WINDOW SIZE INCREMENTS: SLOW START AND CONGESTION AVOIDANCE

1.3.3.1 Slow Start

The windowing algorithm described in Section 1.3.1 assumed static windows. Among other problems, this led to the scenario whereby on session start-up, a whole window full of packets would be injected at back to back into the network at full speed. This led to packet drops as buffers became overwhelmed. To correct this problem, Jacobsen and Karels [1] proposed the Slow Start algorithm, which operates as follows:

- At the start of a new session, set the TCP transmit window size to $W = 1$ packet (i.e., equal to MSS bytes). The sender sends a packet and waits for its ACK.
- Every time an ACK is received, increase the window size by one packet (i.e., $W \leftarrow W + 1$).

Even though the algorithm is called Slow Start, it actually increases the window size quite rapidly: $W = 1$ when the first packet is sent. When the ACK for that packet comes back, W is doubled to 2, and two packets are sent out. When the ACK for the second packet arrives, then W is set to 3, and the ACK for the third packet causes W to increase to 4. Hence, during the Slow Start phase, the correct reception of each windowfull of packets causes the W to double (i.e., the increase is exponential) (Figure 1.6). The rapid increase is intentional because it enables the sender to quickly increase its bandwidth to the value of the bottleneck capacity along its path, assuming that the maximum window size is large enough to achieve the bottleneck capacity. If the maximum window size is not large enough to enable to connection to get to the bottleneck capacity, then the window stops incrementing when the maximum window size is reached. Also note that during the Slow Start phase, the receipt of every ACK causes the sender to inject two packets into the network, the first packet because of the ACK itself and second packet because the window has increased by 1.

1.3.3.2 Congestion Avoidance

During normal operation, the Slow Start algorithm described in Section 1.3.3.1 is too aggressive with its exponential window increase, and something more gradual is needed. The congestion

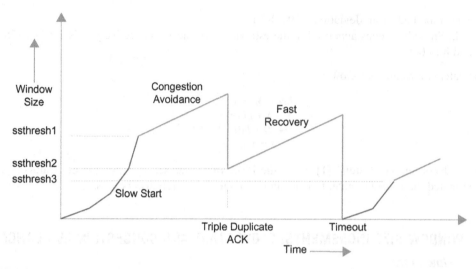

FIGURE 1.6

Phases of TCP Congestion Control.

avoidance algorithm, which was also part of Van Jacobsen and Karels' [1] 1988 paper, leads to a linear increase in window size and hence is more suitable. It operates as follows:

1. Define a new sender counter called ssthresh. At the start of the TCP session, ssthresh is initialized to large value, usually 64 KBytes.
2. Use the Slow Start algorithm at session start, which will lead to an exponential window increase, until the bottleneck node gets to the point where a packet gets dropped (assuming that there are enough packets being transmitted for the system to get to this point). Let's assume that this happens at $W = W_f$.
3. Assuming that the packet loss is detected because of a timer expiry, then the sender resets the window to $W = 1$ packet (i.e., MSS bytes) and sets ssthresh $= W_f/2$ bytes.
4. After the session successfully retransmits the lost packet, the Slow Start algorithm is used to increment the window size until $W \geq$ ssthresh bytes. Beyond this value, the window is increased using the following rule on the receipt of every ACK packet:

$$W \leftarrow W + 1/W \text{ in units of packets} \qquad (9)$$

5. In step 3, if the packet gets dropped because of Duplicate ACKs (these are explained in Section 1.3.4) rather than a timer expiry, then a slightly different rule is used. In this case, the sender sets $W = W_f/2$ as well as ssthresh $= W_f/2$. After the lost packet is recovered, the sender directly transitions to the congestion avoidance phase (because $W =$ ssthresh) and uses equation 9 to increment its windows.

Note that as a result of the window increment rule (equation 9), the receipt of ACKs for an entire window full of packets leads to an increase in W by just one packet. Typically, it takes a round trip or more to transmit a window of packets and receive their ACKs; hence, under the congestion avoidance phase, the window increases by at most one packet in every round trip (i.e., a linear increase) (see Figure 1.6) This allows the sender to probe whether the bottleneck node is getting close to its buffer capacity one packet at a time, and indeed if the extra packet causes the buffer to overflow, then at most one packet is lost, which is easier to recover from.

1.3.4 WINDOW SIZE DECREMENTS, PART 2: FAST RETRANSMIT AND FAST RECOVERY

Section 1.3.3 discusses the rules that TCP Reno uses to increment its window in the absence of network congestion. This section discusses the rules that apply to decrementing the window size in the presence of congestion. TCP uses the design philosophy that dropped packets are the best indicator of network congestion, which falls within the implicit congestion indicator category from Section 1.2.4. When TCP Slow Start was first designed, this was the only feedback that could be expected from the simpler routers that existed at that time. In retrospect, this decision came with a few issues: The only way that the algorithm can detect congestion is by driving the system into a congestive state (i.e., near the cliff of the curve in Figure 1.2). Also, if the packet losses are because of a reason other than congestion (e.g., link errors), then this may lead to unnecessary rate decreases and hence performance loss. This problem is particularly acute for error-prone wireless links, as explained in Chapter 4.

As alluded to in Section 1.3.3.2, TCP uses two different mechanisms to detect packet loss. The first technique uses the retransmit timer RTO and is discussed in Section 1.3.2. The second technique is known as Fast Retransmit (Figure 1.7) and tries to make the system more responsive to packet losses. It works as follows:

- If the SN field in a packet at the receiver does not match the NSN counter, then the receiver immediately sends an ACK packet, with the ACK field set to NSN. The receiver continues to do this on subsequent packets until SN matches NSN (i.e., the missing packet is received).
- As a result of this, the sender begins to receive more than one ACK with the same ACK number; these are known as duplicate ACKs. The sender does not immediately jump to the conclusion that the duplicate ACKs are caused by a missing packet because in some cases, they may be caused by packets getting reordered before reception. However, if the number of duplicate ACKs reaches three, then the sender concludes that the packet has indeed been dropped, and it goes ahead and retransmits the packet (whose SN = duplicate ACK value) without waiting for the retransmission timer to expire. This action is known as Fast Retransmit.
- Just before the retransmission, the sender sets the ssthresh value to half the current window size W, and after the retransmission, it sets W ← ssthresh + 3.MSS. Each time another duplicate ACK arrives, the sender increases W by the packet size, and if the new value of W allows, it goes ahead and transmits a new packet. This action is known as Fast Recovery.

The justification for this is the following: When the receiver finally receives the missing packet, the next ACK acknowledges all the other packets that it has received in the window, which on the average can be half the transmit window size. When the sender receives this ACK, it is allowed to transmit up to half a window of back-to-back packets (because W is now at half the previous value), which can potentially overwhelm the buffers in the bottleneck node. However, by doing FAST Recovery, the sender keeps sending additional packets while it waits for the ACK for the missing packet to arrive, and this prevents the sudden onslaught of new packets into the network. When the ACK for the missing packet arrives, W is set back to the ssthresh value in the previous step. This behavior can be seen in Figure 1.8; note that the window size shows a spike of 3 MSS on error detection and falls back to W/2 after the missing packet is received.

The Fast Retransmit mechanism is able to efficiently recover from packet losses as long as no more than one packet is lost in the window. If more than one packet is lost, then usually the retransmit timer for the second or later expires, which triggers the more drastic step of resetting W back to one packet.

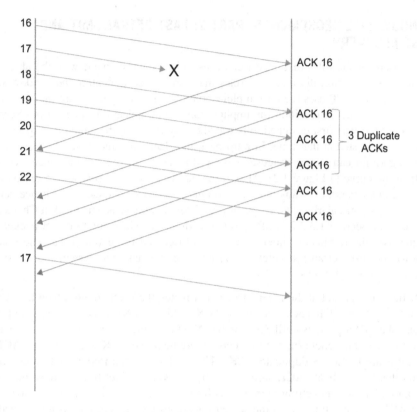

FIGURE 1.7

Illustration of fast retransmit via duplicate ACKs.

1.3.5 TCP NEW RENO

Not long after the introduction of TCP Reno, it was discovered that it is possible to improve its performance significantly by making the following change to the Fast Recovery phase of the algorithm: If a Partial ACK is received during the Fast Recovery period that acknowledges some but not all of the packets that were outstanding at the start of the Fast Recovery period, then this is treated as an indication that the packet immediately following the acknowledged packet has also been lost and should be retransmitted. Thus, if multiple packets are lost within a single window, then New Reno can recover without a retransmission timeout by retransmitting one lost packet per round trip until all the lost packets from the window have been retransmitted. New Reno remains in Fast Recovery until all data outstanding at the start of the Fast Recovery phase has been acknowledged.

In this book, we will assume that legacy TCP implies Reno, with the understanding that the system has also implemented the New Reno changes.

1.3.6 TCP RENO AND AIMD

Even though it may not be very clear from the description of TCP Reno in the last few subsections, this algorithm does indeed fall into the class of AIMD congestion control algorithms. This can be most clearly seen by writing down the equations for the time evolution of the window size.

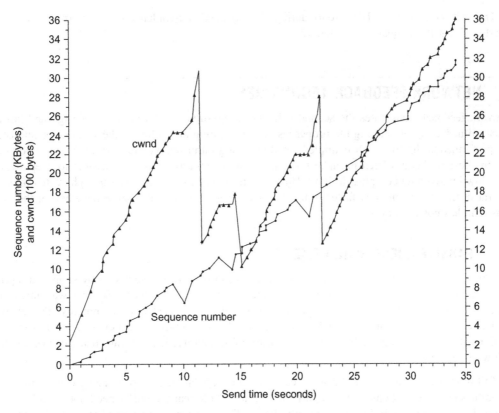

FIGURE 1.8

Illustration of Fast Recovery.

In the Slow Start phase, as per the description in Section 1.3.3.1, the window size after n round trip times is given by

$$W(nT) = 2^n W_0 \tag{10}$$

where W_0 is the initial window size. This equation clearly captures the exponential increase in window size during this phase.

During the Congestion Avoidance phase (Section 1.3.3.2), the window size evolution is given by

$$W \leftarrow W + 1 \text{ per round trip delay} \tag{11}$$

because each returning ACK causes the window size to increase by 1/W, and equation 11 follows from the fact that there are W returning ACKs for a window of size W.

Detection of a lost packet at time t because of Duplicate ACKs causes a reduction in window size by half, so that

$$W \leftarrow \frac{W}{2} \tag{12}$$

Note that with New Reno, multiple packet losses within a window result in a single reduction in the window size.

The AIMD nature of TCP Reno during the congestion avoidance/fast retransmit phases is clearly evident from equations 11 and 12.

1.4 NETWORK FEEDBACK TECHNIQUES

Network feedback constitutes the second half of a congestion control algorithm design and has as much influence in determining the properties of the resulting algorithm as the window or rate control performed at the source. It is implemented using algorithms at a switch or router, and traditionally the design bias has been to make this part of the system as simple as possible to keep switch costs low by avoiding complex designs. This bias still exists today, and even though switch logic is several orders of magnitudes faster, link speeds have increased at the same rate; hence, the cost constraint has not gone away.

1.4.1 PASSIVE QUEUE MANAGEMENT

The simplest congestion feedback that a switch can send back to the source is by simply dropping a packet when it runs out of buffers, which is referred to as tail-drop feedback. This was how most routers and switches operated originally, and even today it is used quite commonly. Packet loss triggers congestion avoidance at the TCP source, which takes action by reducing its window size.

Even though tail-drop feedback has the virtue of simplicity, it is not an ideal scheme for the following reasons:

- Tail-drop—based congestion signaling can lead to excess latencies across the network if the bottleneck node happens to have a large buffer size. Note that the buffer need not be full for the session to attain full link capacity; hence, the excess packets queued at the node add to the latency without improving the throughput (this claim is proven in Chapter 2).
- If multiple TCP sessions are sharing the buffer at the bottleneck node, then the algorithm can cause synchronized packet drops across sessions. This causes all the affected sessions to reduce their throughput, which leads to a periodic pattern, resulting in underutilization of the link capacity.
- Even for a single session, tail-drop feedback tends to drop multiple packets at a time, which can trigger the TCP RTO—based retransmission mechanism, with its attendant drop in window size to one packet.

An attempt to improve on this led to the invention of RED-based queue management, which is described in the next section.

1.4.2 ACTIVE QUEUE MANAGEMENT (AQM)

To correct the problems with tail-drop buffer management, Floyd and Jacobsen [5] introduced the concept of AQM, in which the routing nodes use a more sophisticated algorithm called RED to manage their queues. The main objectives of RED are the following:

- Provide congestion avoidance by controlling the average queue size at a network node.
- Avoid global synchronization and a bias against bursty traffic sources.

- Maintain the network in a region of low delay and high throughput by keeping the average queue size low while fluctuations in the instantaneous queue size are allowed to accommodate bursty traffic and transient congestion.

As explained later, RED provides congestion feedback to the source when the average queue size exceeds some threshold, either by randomly dropping a packet or by randomly marking the ECN bit in a packet. Furthermore, the packet dropping probability is a function of the average queue size, as shown in Figure 1.9.
The RED algorithm operates as follows:
  For each packet arrival,

1. Calculate the average queue size avg as $avg \leftarrow (1 - w_q)avg + w_q q$, where q is the current queue size. The smoothing constant w_q determines the time constant of this low-pass filter. This average is computed every time a packet arrives at the node.
2. Define constants min_{th} and max_{th}, such that min_{th} is the minimum threshold for the average queue size and max_{th} is the maximum threshold for the average queue size (see Figure 1.9). If $min_{th} \leq avg \leq max_{th}$, then on packet arrival, calculate the probability p_b and p_a as

$$p_b \leftarrow \frac{max_p(avg - min_{th})}{(max_{th} - min_{th})}$$
$$p_a \leftarrow \frac{p_b}{(1 - count \cdot p_b)} \tag{13}$$

where max_p is the maximum value for p_b and *count* is the number of packets received since the last dropped packet. Drop the arriving packet with probability p_a. Note that p_a is computed such that after each drop, the algorithm uniformly chooses one of the next $1/p_b$ packets to drop next.

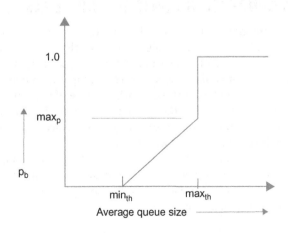

FIGURE 1.9

Packet discard probability in Random Early Detection (RED).

This randomized selection of packets to be dropped is designed to avoid the problem of synchronized losses that is seen in tail-drop queues.

3. If $avg \geq \max_{th}$, then drop the arriving packet.

RED has been heavily analyzed, with the objective of estimating the optimal queue thresholds and other parameters. Some of this work is covered in Chapter 3, where tools from optimal control theory are brought to bear on the problem. In general, researchers have discovered that RED is not an ideal AQM scheme because there are issues with its responsiveness and ability to suppress queue size oscillations as the link capacity or the end-to-end latency increases. Choosing a set of RED parameters that work well across a wide range of network conditions is also a nontrivial problem, which has led to proposals that adapt the parameters as network conditions change.

However, it is widely implemented in routers today, and furthermore, all the analysis work done on RED has led to the discovery of other more effective AQM schemes. More recent AQM algorithms that build off the ideas in RED include the Data Center Congestion Control Protocol (DCTCP) (see Chapter 7), the IEEE 802.1Qau QCN algorithm (see Chapter 8), and an influential protocol designed for high-speed networks called eXpress Control Protocol (XCP) (see Chapter 5).

Floyd [6] also went on to design a follow on enhancement to RED called ECN. In ECN systems, the queue does not discard the packet but instead marks the ECN bits in TCP packet header. The receiver then receives the marked packets and in turn marks the ECN bit in the returning ACK packet. When the sender receives ACKs with marked packets, then it reacts to them in the same way as if it had detected a lost packet using the duplicate ACK mechanism and proceeds to reduce its window size. This avoids unnecessary packet drops and thus unnecessary delays for packets. It also increases the responsiveness of the algorithm because the sender does not have to wait for three duplicate ACKs before it can react to congestion.

1.5 DELAY-BASED CONGESTION CONTROL: TCP VEGAS

Brakmo and Peterson [7] proposed a fundamentally different solution to the congestion control problem compared with TCP Reno. Their algorithm, which they called TCP Vegas, uses end-to-end packet delay as a measure of congestion rather than packet drops. This idea has proven to be very influential and has inspired the design of several congestion control protocols that are in wide use today, including Compound TCP (CTCP), which is the default protocol on all Windows servers (see Chapter 5); Low Extra Delay Background Transport (LEDBAT), which is used for background data transfers by the Bit-Torrent file sharing service (see Chapter 4); and FAST TCP, which was designed for high-speed networks (see Chapter 5).

TCP Vegas estimates the level of congestion in the network by calculating the difference in the expected and actual data rates, which it then uses to adjust the TCP window size. Assuming a window size of W and a minimum round trip latency of T seconds, the source computes an expected throughput R_E once per round trip delay, by

$$R_E = \frac{W}{T} \tag{14}$$

The source also estimates the current throughput R by using the actual round trip time T_s according to

$$R = \frac{W}{T_s} \tag{15}$$

The source then computes the quantity *Diff* given by

$$Diff = T(R_E - R) \tag{16}$$

Note that Diff can also be written as

$$Diff = \frac{W}{T_s}(T_s - T) = R(T_s - T) \tag{17}$$

By Little's law [8], the expression on the RHS equals the number of packets belonging to the connection that are queued in the network and hence serves as a measure of congestion.

Define two thresholds α and β such that $\alpha < \beta$. The window increase decrease rules are given by:

- When $\alpha \leq Diff \leq \beta$, then leave W unchanged.
- When $Diff > \beta$, decrease W by 1 for the next RTT. This condition implies that congestion is beginning to build up the network; hence, the sending rate should be reduced.
- When $Diff < \alpha$, increase W by 1 for the next RTT. This condition implies the actual throughput is less than the expected throughput; hence, there is some danger that the connection may not use the full network bandwidth.

TCP Vegas tries to maintain the "right" amount of queued data in the network. Too much queued data will cause congestion, and too little queued data will prevent the connection from rapidly taking advantage of transient increases in available network bandwidth. Note that this mechanism also eliminates the oscillatory behavior of TCP Reno while reducing the end-to-end latency and jitter because each connection tends to keep only a few packets in the network.

A few issues with TCP Vegas were pointed out by Mo and colleagues [9], among them the fact that when TCP Vegas and Reno compete for bandwidth on the same link, then Reno ends with a greater share because it is more aggressive in grabbing buffers, but Vegas is conservative and tries to occupy as little space as it can. Also, if the connection's route changes (e.g., because of mobility), then this causes problems with Vegas' round trip latency estimates and leads to a reduction in throughput. Because of these reasons, especially the first one, Vegas is not widely deployed despite its desirable properties.

1.6 OUTLINE OF THE REST OF THE BOOK

The contents of this book are broadly split in to two parts:

Part 1 is devoted to the analysis of models of congestion control systems.

Chapter 2 has a detailed discussion of TCP models, starting from simple models using fluid approximations to more sophisticated models using stochastic theory. The well-known "square root" formula for the throughput of a TCP connection is derived and is further generalized to AIMD congestion control schemes. These formulae have proven to be very useful over the years and have formed an integral part of the discovery of new congestion control protocols, as shown in Part 2. For example, several high-speed protocols discussed in Chapter 5 use techniques from Chapter 2 to analyze their algorithms. Chapter 2 also analyzes systems with multiple parallel TCP connections and derives expressions for the throughput ratio as a function of the round trip latencies.

Chapter 3 has more advanced material in which optimization theory and optimal control theory are applied to a differential equation–based fluid flow model of the packet network. This results in the decomposition of the global optimization problem into independent optimizations at each source node and the explicit derivation of the optimal source rate control rules as a function of a network wide utility function. In the case of TCP Reno, the source rate control rules are known, but then the theory can be used to derive the network utility function that Reno optimizes. In addition to the mathematical elegance of these results, the results of this theory have been used recently to obtain optimal congestion control algorithms using machine learning techniques (see discussion of Project Remy in Chapter 9). The system stability analysis techniques using the Nyquist criterion introduced in Chapter 3 have become an essential tool in the study of congestion control algorithms and are used several times in Part 2 of this book. By using a linear approximation to the delay-differential equation describing the system dynamics, this technique enables us to derive explicit conditions on system parameters to achieve a stable system.

Part 2 of the book describes congestion control protocols used in five different application area, namely broadband wireless access networks, high-speed networks with large latencies, video transmission networks, DCNs, and Ethernet networks.

Chapter 4 discusses congestion control in broadband wireless networks. This work was motivated by finding solutions to the performance problems that TCP Reno has with wireless links. Because the algorithm cannot differentiate between congestion losses and losses caused by link errors, decreasing the window size whenever a packet is lost has a very detrimental effect on performance. The chapter describes TCP Westwood, which solved this problem by keeping an estimate of the data rate of the connection at the bottleneck node. Thus, when Duplicate ACKs are received, the sender reduces its window size to the transmit rate at the bottleneck node (rather than blindly cutting the window size by half, as in Reno). This works well for wireless links because if the packet was lost because of wireless errors, then the bottleneck rate my still be high, and this is reflected in the new window size. The chapter also describes techniques, such as Split-Connection TCP and Loss Discrimination Algorithms, that are widely used in wireless networks today. The combination of TCP at the end-to-end transport layer and link layer retransmissions (ARQ) or forward error correction (FEC) coding on the wireless link is also analyzed using the results from Chapter 2. The large variation in link capacity that is observed in cellular networks has led to a problem called bufferbloat. Chapter 4 describes techniques using AQM at the nodes as well as end-to-end algorithms to solve this problem.

Chapter 5 explores congestion control in high-speed networks with long latencies. One of the consequences of the application of control theory to TCP congestion control, described in Chapter 3, was the realization that TCP Reno was inherently unstable as the delay-bandwidth product of the network became large or even for very large bandwidths. As a result of this, a number of new congestion control designs were suggested with the objective of solving this problem such as

High Speed TCP (HSTCP), TCP BIC, TCP CUBIC, and Compound TCP (CTCP), which are described in the chapter. Currently, TCP CUBIC serves as the default congestion control algorithm for Linux servers and as a result is as widely deployed as TCP Reno. CTCP is used as the default option for Windows servers and is also very widely deployed. The chapter also describes the XCP and RCP algorithms that have been very influential in the design of high-speed congestion control protocols. Finally, the chapter makes connections between the algorithms in this chapter and the stability theory from Chapter 3 and gives some general guidelines to be used in the design of high-speed congestion control algorithms.

Chapter 6 covers congestion control for video streaming applications. With the explosion in video streaming traffic in recent years, there arose a need to protect the network from congestion from these types of sources and at the same time ensure good video performance at the client end. The industry has settled on the use of TCP for transmitting video even though at first cut, it seems to be an unlikely match for video's real-time needs. This problem was solved by a combination of large receive playout buffers, which can smoothen out the fluctuations caused by TCP rate control, and an ingenious algorithm called HTTP Adaptive Streaming (HAS). HAS runs at the client end and controls the rate at which "chunks" of video data are sent from the server, such that the sending rate closely matches the rate at which the video is being consumed by the decoder. Chapter 6 describes the work in this area, including several ingenious HAS algorithms for controlling the video transmission rate.

Chapter 7 discusses congestion control in DCNs. This is the most current, and still rapidly evolving, area because of the enormous importance of DCNs in running the data centers that underlie the modern Internet economy. Because DCNs can form a relatively autonomous region, there is also the possibility of doing a significant departure from the norm of congestion control algorithms if the resulting performance is worth it. This has resulted in innovations in congestion control such as the application of ideas from Earliest Deadline First (EDF) scheduling and even in-network congestion control techniques. All of these are driven by the need to keep the end-to-end latency between two servers in a DCN to values that are in the tens of milliseconds or smaller to satisfy the real-time needs of applications such as web searching and social networking.

Chapter 8 covers the topic of congestion control in Ethernet networks. Traditionally, Ethernet, which operates at Layer 2, has left the task of congestion control to the TCP layer. However recent developments such as the spread of Ethernet use in applications such as SANs has led the networking community to revisit this design because SANs have a very strict requirement that no packets be dropped. As a result, the IEEE 802.1 Standards group has recently proposed a congestion control algorithm called IEEE802.1Qau or QCN for use in Ethernet networks. This algorithm uses several advances in congestion control techniques described in the previous chapters, such as the use of rate averaging at the sender, as well as AQM feedback, which takes the occupancy as well as the rate of change of the buffer size into account.

Chapter 9 discusses three different topics that are at the frontiers of research into congestion control: (1) We describe a project from MIT called Remy, that applies techniques from Machine Learning to congestion control. It discovers the optimal congestion control rules for a specific (but partially observed) state of the network, by doing an extensive simulation based optimization of network wide utility functions that were introduced in Chapter 3. This is done offline, as part of the learning phase, and then the resulting algorithm is applied to the operating network. Remy has been shown to out-perform human designed algorithms by a wide margin in preliminary tests.

(2) Software Defined Networks or SDNs have been one of the most exciting developments in networking in recent years. Most of their applications have been in the area of algorithms and rules that are used to control the route that a packet takes through the network. However we describe a couple of instances in which ideas from SDNs can also be used to improve network congestion control. In the first case SDNs are used to choose the most appropriate AQM algorithm at a node, while in the other case they are used to select the best AQM parameters as a function of changing network state. (3) Lastly we describe an algorithm called Google Congestion Control (GCC), that is part of the WebRTC project in the IETF, and is used for controlling real time in-browser communications. This algorithm has some interesting features such as a unique use of Kalman Filtering at the receiver, to estimate whether the congestion state at the bottleneck queue in the face of a channel capacity that is widely varying.

1.7 FURTHER READING

The books by Comer [10] and Fall and Stevens [11] are standard references for TCP from the protocol point of view. The book by Srikant [12] discusses congestion control from the optimization and control theory point of view, and Hassan and Jain [13] provide a good overview of applications of congestion control to various domains.

REFERENCES

[1] Jacobsen V, Karels MJ. Congestion avoidance and control. ACM CCR 1988;18(4);314–29.
[2] Chiu DM, Jain R. Analysis of increase and decrease algorithms for congestion avoidance in computer networks. Comput Netw ISDN Syst 1989;17(1).
[3] Jain R. Congestion control and traffic management in ATM networks: recent advances and a survey. Comput Netw ISDN Syst 1995;28(13):1723–38.
[4] Bird R, Brotman C, Case R, Dudley G. Advances in APPN architecture. IBM Syst J 1995;34 (3):430–51.
[5] Floyd S, Jacobsen V. Random early detection gateways for congestion avoidance. IEEE/ACM Trans Netw 1993;1:397–413.
[6] Floyd S. TCP and explicit congestion notification. ACM SIGCOMM 1994;24(5):8–23.
[7] Brakmo LS, Peterson LL. End-to-end congestion avoidance on a global Internet. IEEE JSAC 1995;13:1465–80.
[8] Little JDC. A proof of the queueing formula $L = \lambda W$. Oper Res 1961;9(3):383–7.
[9] Mo J, La RJ, Anantharam V, Walrand J. Analysis and comparison of TCP Reno and Vegas. IEEE INFOCOM 1999;3:1556–63.
[10] Comer DE. Internetworking with TCP/IP. Upper Saddle River, NJ: Pearson Prentice Hall; 2006.
[11] Fall K, Stevens WR. TCP/IP illustrated, volume 1: the protocols. Boston, MA: Addison-Wesley; 2011.
[12] Srikant R. The mathematics of internet congestion control. Reinach: Birkhauser; 2004.
[13] Hassan M, Jain R. High performance TCP/IP networking: concepts, issues and solutions. Upper Saddle River, NJ: Pearson Prentice Hall; 2004.

THEORY

ANALYTIC MODELING OF CONGESTION CONTROL

2.1 INTRODUCTION

The past 2 decades have witnessed a great deal of progress in the area of analytic modeling of congestion control algorithms, and this chapter is devoted to this topic. This work has led to explicit formulae for the average throughput or window Size of a TCP connection as a function of parameters such as the delay-bandwidth product, node buffer capacity, and packet drop rate. More advanced models, which are discussed in Chapter 3, can also be used to analyze congestion control and Active Queue Management (AQM) algorithms using tools from optimization and control theories. This type of analysis useful for a number of reasons:

- By explicitly describing the dependence of congestion control performance on a few key system parameters, they provide valuable guidelines on ways the congestion control algorithm can be improved or adapted to different network conditions. We will come across several examples in Part 2 of this book, where the analytic techniques and formulae developed in this chapter are used to design and analyze congestion control algorithms that scale up to very high speeds (see Chapter 5) or are able to work over high error rate wireless links (see Chapter 4) or satisfy the low latency requirements in modern data center networks (see Chapter 7).
- The analysis of congestion control algorithms provides fundamental insight into their ultimate performance limits. For example, the development of the theory led to the realization that TCP becomes unstable if the link speed or the round trip delay becomes very large. This has resulted in innovations in mechanisms that can be used to stabilize the system under these conditions.

A lot of the early work in congestion control modeling was inspired by the team working at the Lawrence Berkeley Lab, who published a number of very influential papers on the simulation-based analysis of TCP congestion control [1–3]. A number of more theoretical papers [4–6] followed their work and led to the development of the theory described here. One of the key insights that came out of this work is the discovery that at lower packet drop rates, TCP Reno's throughput is inversely proportional to the square root of the drop rate (also known as the square-root formula). This formula was independently arrived at by several researchers [2,4,7], and it was later extended by Padhye and colleagues [5], who showed that at higher packet drop rates, the throughput is inversely proportional to the drop rate.

TCP models can be classified into single connection models and models for a multinode network. This chapter mostly discusses single connection models, but toward the end of the chapter, the text also touches on models of multiple connections passing through a common bottleneck node. Chapter 3 introduces models for congestion control in the network context.

The rest of this chapter is organized as follows: In Section 2.2, we derive formulae for TCP throughput as a function of various system parameters. In particular, we consider of influence of the delay-bandwidth product, window size, node buffer size, packet drop rates, and so on. We consider the case of connections with no packet drops (Section 2.2.1), connections in which all packet drops are attributable to buffer overflow (Section 2.2.2), and connections in which packet drops are attributable to random link errors (Section 2.2.3). In Section 2.3, we develop a fluid-flow model based technique for computing the throughput that is used several times later in this book. We also generalize TCP's window increment rules to come up with an additive increase/multiplicative decrease (AIMD) system and analyze its system throughput in Section 2.3.1. Section 2.4 analyzes a more sophisticated model in which the packet loss process features correlated losses. In Section 2.6, we consider the case of multiple TCP connections that share a common bottleneck and analyze its performance. The analysis of AQM schemes such as Random Early Detection (RED) is best pursued using tools from optimal control theory, and this is done in Chapter 3.

An initial reading of this chapter can be done in the following sequence: $2.1 \rightarrow 2.2$ (2.2.1 and 2.2.2) $\rightarrow 2.3$, which covers the basic results needed to understand the material in Part 2 of the book. The results in Section 2.3 are used extensively in the rest of the book, especially the general procedure for deriving formulae for the throughput of congestion control algorithms. More advanced readers can venture into Sections 2.2.3, 2.4, 2.5, and 2.6, which cover the topics of mean value analysis, stochastic analysis, and multiple parallel connections.

2.2 TCP THROUGHPUT ANALYSIS

2.2.1 THROUGHPUT AS A FUNCTION OF WINDOW SIZE

Consider the model shown in Figure 2.1, with a single TCP Reno controlled traffic source passing through a single bottleneck node. Even though this is a very simplified picture of an actual

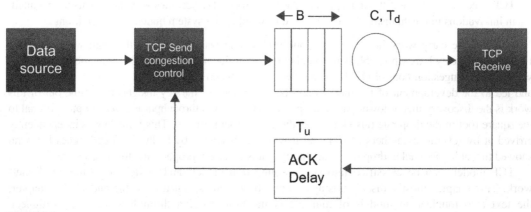

FIGURE 2.1

Model for a TCP connection.

network, Low and Varaiya [8] have shown that there is no loss of generality in replacing all the nodes along the path by a single bottleneck node. Define the following:

W(t): TCP window size in packets at time t
W_{max}: Maximum TCP window size
W_f: Window size at which a packet is lost
MSS: TCP packet size in bytes
C: The bottleneck node capacity in packets/sec
B: Buffer count at the bottleneck node in packets
T_d: Propagation delay in the forward (or downstream) direction in seconds
T_u: Propagation delay in the backward (or upstream) direction in seconds
T: Total propagation + Transmission delay for a segment
b_{max}: The maximum buffer occupancy at the bottleneck node in packets
R(t): Throughput of the connection in packets/sec at time t
R_{avg}: Average throughput of a connection in packets/sec

Note that T, which is the fixed part of the round trip latency for a connection, is given by

$$T = T_d + T_u + \frac{1}{C}$$

We first consider the simplest case when the window size is in equilibrium with size W_{max}, there is sufficient buffering at the bottleneck node, so no packets get dropped because of overflows, and the link is error free. These assumptions are relaxed in the following sections as the sophistication of the model increases.

Consider the case when $T > W_{max}/C$, or $W_{max}/T < C$ (Figure 2.2). The diagram illustrates the fact that in this case the sender transmits the entire window full of packets before it receives the ACK for first packet back. Hence, the average connection throughput R_{avg} is limited by the window size and is given by

$$R_{avg} = \frac{W_{max}}{T} \quad \text{when } W_{max} < CT \tag{1}$$

Because the rate at which the bottleneck node is transmitting packets is greater than or equal to the rate at which the source is sending packets into the network, the bottleneck node queue size is zero. Hence, at any instant in time, all the packets are in one of two places: either in the process of being transmitted in the downstream direction ($= R_{avg}.T_d$ packets), or their ACKs are in the process of being transmitted in the upstream direction ($= R_{avg}.T_u$ ACKs).

In Figure 2.3, we consider the case when $T < W_{max}/C$, i.e., $W_{max}/T > C$. As the figure illustrates, the ACKs for the first packet in the window arrive at the sender before it has finished transmitting the last packet in that window. As a result, unlike in Figure 2.2, the sender is continuously transmitting. The system throughput is no longer limited by the window size, and is able to attain the full value of the link capacity, that is,

$$R_{avg} = C \quad \text{when } W_{max} > CT \tag{2}$$

Combining equations 1 and 2, we get

$$R_{avg} = \min\left(\frac{W_{max}}{T}, c\right) \tag{3}$$

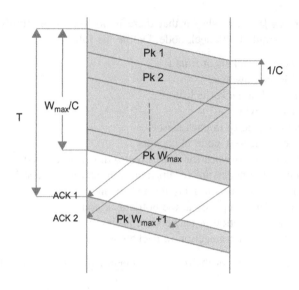

FIGURE 2.2

Packet (Pk) transmissions with $T > W_{max}/C$.

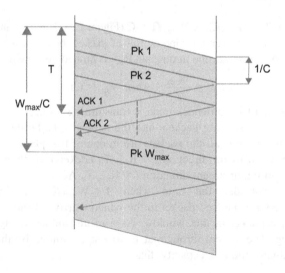

FIGURE 2.3

Packet transmissions with $T < W_{max}/C$.

In this case, $C.T_d$ packets are the process of being transmitted in the downstream direction, and $C.T_u$ ACKs are in the process of being transmitted in the upstream direction, for a total of $C.(T_d + T_u) = CT$ packets and ACKs. Because $CT < W_{max}$, this leaves $(W_{max} - CT)$ packets from the TCP window unaccounted for, and indeed they are to be found queued up in the bottleneck node! Hence, in equilibrium, the maximum buffer occupancy at the bottleneck node is given by

$$b_{max} = \max(W_{max} - CT, 0) \tag{4}$$

Using equations 3 and 4, R_{avg} can also be written as

$$R_{avg} = \frac{W_{max}}{T + \frac{b_{max}}{C}} \tag{5}$$

This shows that the average throughput is given by the window size divided by the total round trip latency, including the queuing delay.

This discussion illustrates the rule of thumb that the optimum maximum window size is given by $W_{max} = CT$, i.e., it should equal the delay-bandwidth product for the connection because at this point the connection achieves its full bandwidth (equal to the link rate). Any increase in W_{max} beyond CT increases the length of the bottleneck queue and hence end-to-end delay, without doing anything to increase the throughput.

Figure 2.4 plots R_{avg} vs W_{max} based on equation 3, and as the graph shows, there a knee at $W_{max} = CT$, which is the ideal operating point for the system.

Figure 2.5 plots the maximum buffer occupancy b_{max} as a function of W_{max} based on equation 4. When W_{max} increases to $B + CT$, then $b_{max} = B$, and any increase of W_{max} beyond this value will cause the buffer to overflow. Note that until this point, we have made no assumptions about the specific rules used to control the window size. Hence, all the formulae in this section apply to any window-based congestion control scheme in the absence of packet drops.

In Section 2.2.2, we continue the analysis for TCP Reno for the case $W_{max} > B + CT$, when packets get dropped because of buffer overflows.

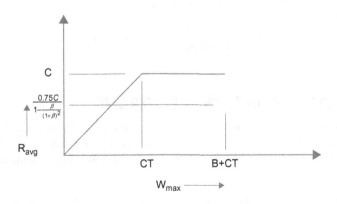

FIGURE 2.4

Average TCP throughput R_{avg} as a function of the window size W_{max}.

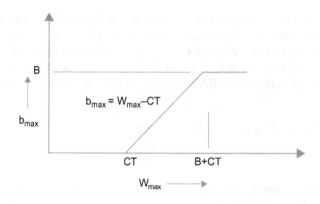

FIGURE 2.5

Maximum buffer occupancy as a function of W_{max}.

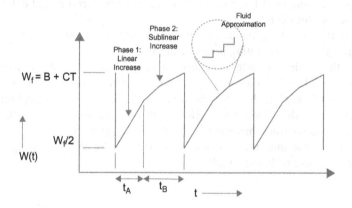

FIGURE 2.6

Variation of window size in steady state for TCP Reno.

2.2.2 THROUGHPUT AS A FUNCTION OF BUFFER SIZE

In Section 2.2.1, we found out that if $W_{max} > B + CT$, then it results in packet drops because of buffer overflows. In the presence of overflows, the variation of the window size $W(t)$ as a function of time is shown in Figure 2.6 for TCP Reno. We made the following assumptions in coming up with this figure:

1. Comparing Figure 2.6 with Figure 1.6 in Chapter 1, we assume that we are in the steady phase of a long file transfer, during which the system spends all its time in the congestion avoidance phase, i.e., the initial Slow-Start phase is ignored, and all packet losses are recovered using duplicates ACKs (i.e., without using timeouts).

2. We also ignore the Fast Recovery phase because it has a negligible effect on the overall throughput, and including it considerably complicates the analysis.

3. Even though the window size W increases and decreases in discrete quantities, we replace it by a continuous variable W(t), thus resulting in what is known as a fluid approximation. This simplifies the analysis of the system considerably while adding only a small error term to the final results.

We now define two additional continuous time variables b(t) and T(t), where b(t) is the fluid approximation to the buffer occupancy process at time t, given by

$$b(t) = W(t) - CT$$

and T(t) is the total round trip latency at time t, given by

$$T(t) = T + \frac{b(t)}{C}$$

The throughput R(t) at time t is defined by

$$R(t) = \frac{W(t)}{T(t)}$$

and the average throughput is given by

$$R_{avg} = \lim_{t \to \infty} \frac{1}{t} \int_0^t R(t)dt$$

As shown in Figure 2.7, W(t) increases up to a maximum value of $W_f = (B + CT)$ and is accompanied by an increase in buffer size to B, at which point a packet is lost at the bottleneck node because of buffer overflow. TCP Reno then goes into the congestion recovery mode, during which it retransmits the missing packet and then reduces the window size to $W_f/2$. Using equation 2, if $W_f/2$ exceeds the delay-bandwidth product for the connection, then $R_{avg} = C$. Note that $\frac{W_f}{2} \geq CT$ implies that

$$\frac{B + CT}{2} \geq CT$$

which leads to the condition

$$B \geq CT \qquad (6)$$

Hence, if the number of buffers exceeds the delay-bandwidth product of the connection, then the periodic packet loss caused by buffer overflows does not result in a reduction in TCP throughput, which stays at the link capacity C. Combining this with the condition for buffer overflow, we get

$$W_{max} - CT \geq B \geq CT$$

as the conditions that cause a buffer overflow but do not result in a reduction in throughput. Equation 6 is a well-known rule of thumb that is used in sizing up buffers in routers and switches. Later in this chapter, we show that equation 6 is also a necessary condition for full link utilization in the presence of multiple connections passing through the link, provided the connections are all synchronized and have the same round trip latency.

When $B < CT$, then the reduction in window size to $W_f/2$ on packet loss leads to the situation where all the packets are either in transmission or being ACK'd, thus emptying the buffer periodically, as a result of which the system throughput falls below C (Figure 2.8). An analysis of this scenario is carried out next.

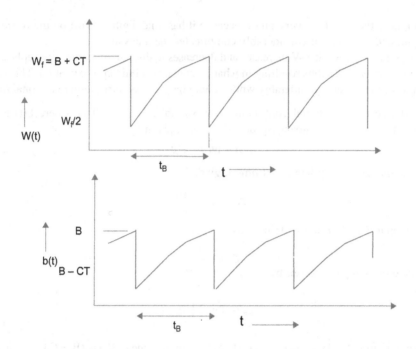

FIGURE 2.7

Window and buffer occupancy evolution for B > CT.

We compute the throughput by obtaining the duration and the number of packets transmitted during each cycle. The increase of the TCP window size happens in two phases, as shown in Figure 2.8:

In phase 1, W(t) < CT, which implies that the queue at the bottleneck node is empty during this phase. Hence, the rate at which ACKs are returning to the sender is equal to the TCP throughput R(t) = W(t)/T. This implies that the rate at which the window is increasing is given by

$$\frac{dW(t)}{dt} = \frac{dW}{da} \cdot \frac{da}{dt} = \frac{1}{W(t)} \cdot \frac{W(t)}{T} = \frac{1}{T} \tag{7}$$

where a(t) is the number of ACKs received in time t and da/dt is the rate at which ACKs are being received.

Hence,

$$W(t) - \frac{W_f}{2} = \int_0^t \frac{dt}{T} = \frac{t}{T}$$

This results in a linear increase in the window size during phase 1, as shown in Figure 2.6. This phase ends when $W = W_f = CT$, so if t_A is the duration of this phase, then

$$CT - \frac{W_f}{2} = \frac{t_A}{T},$$

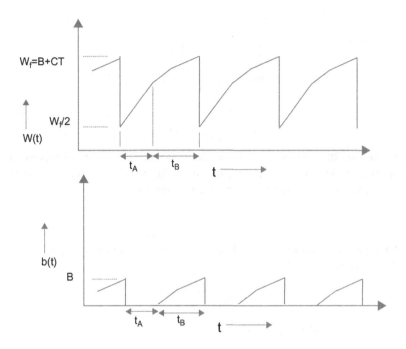

FIGURE 2.8

Window and buffer occupancy evolution for $B < CT$.

so that

$$t_A = T\left(CT - \frac{W_f}{2}\right). \tag{8}$$

The number of packets n_A transmitted during phase 1 is given by

$$
\begin{aligned}
n_A &= \int_0^{t_A} R(t)dt = \int_0^{t_A} \frac{W(t)}{T} dt \\
&= \frac{1}{T}\int_0^{t_A}\left(\frac{W_f}{2} + \frac{t}{T}\right)dt \\
&= \frac{1}{T}\left(\frac{W_f \cdot t_A}{2} + \frac{t_A^2}{2T}\right)
\end{aligned} \tag{9}
$$

In phase 2, $W(t) > CT$ so that the bottleneck node has a persistent backlog. Hence, the rate at which ACKs are returning back to the sender is given by C. It follows that the rate of increase of the window is given by

$$\frac{dW(t)}{dt} = \frac{dW(t)}{da} \cdot \frac{da}{dt} = \frac{C}{W(t)} \tag{10}$$

Hence,

$$\int_{CT}^{W} W(t) \cdot dW = \int_{0}^{t} C \cdot dt$$
$$W^2(t) - (CT)^2 = 2Ct$$

so that

$$W(t) = \sqrt{2Ct + (CT)^2} \tag{11}$$

Equation 11 implies that the increase in window size during phase 2 happens in a sublinear fashion, as illustrated in Figure 2.6. During this phase, the window increases until it reaches W_f, and by equation 11, the time required to do this, t_B, is given by

$$t_B = \frac{W_f^2 - (CT)^2}{2C} \tag{12}$$

Because of the persistent backlog at the bottleneck node, the number of packets n_B transmitted during phase 2 is given by

$$n_B = Ct_B = \frac{W_f^2 - (CT)^2}{2} \tag{13}$$

The average TCP throughput is given by

$$R_{avg} = \frac{n_A + n_B}{t_A + t_B} \tag{14}$$

From equations 9 and 13, it follows that

$$n_A + n_B = \frac{1}{T}\left(\frac{W_f \cdot t_A}{2} + \frac{t_A^2}{2T}\right) + \frac{W_f^2 - (CT)^2}{2}$$

Substituting for t_A from equation 8, and after some simplifications, we get

$$n_A + n_B = \frac{3W_f^2}{8} \tag{15}$$

Thus, the number of packets transmitted during a cycle is proportional to the square of the maximum window size, which is an interesting result in itself and is used several times in Part 2 of this book. Later in this chapter, we will see that this relation continues to hold even for the case when the packet losses are because of random link errors.

Similarly, from equations 8 and 12, we obtain

$$t_A + t_B = T\left(CT - \frac{W_f}{2}\right) + \frac{W_f^2 - (CT)^2}{2C}$$

which after some simplifications becomes

$$t_A + t_B = \frac{W_f^2 + (CT)^2 - CTW_f}{2C} \tag{16}$$

Substituting equations 15 and 16 back into equation 14, we obtain

$$R_{avg} = \frac{\frac{3}{4}W_f^2 C}{W_f^2 + (CT)^2 - CTW_f} \tag{17}$$

Note that $W_f = B + CT$, so that (17) simplifies to

$$R_{avg} = \frac{0.75}{\left[1 - \frac{B \cdot CT}{(B+CT)^2}\right]} C \tag{18}$$

Define $\beta = \frac{B}{CT} \leq 1$, so that

$$R_{avg} = \frac{0.75}{\left[1 - \frac{\beta}{(1+\beta)^2}\right]} C \tag{19}$$

Define f

$$f = \frac{0.75}{\left[1 - \frac{\beta}{(1+\beta)^2}\right]} \tag{20}$$

and note that

$$\lim_{\beta \to 0} f = 0.75 \quad \text{and} \quad \lim_{\beta \to 1} f = 1$$

As shown in Figure 2.9, f monotonically increases from 0.75 to 1 as β increases from 0 to 1, so that $R_{avg} \leq C$.

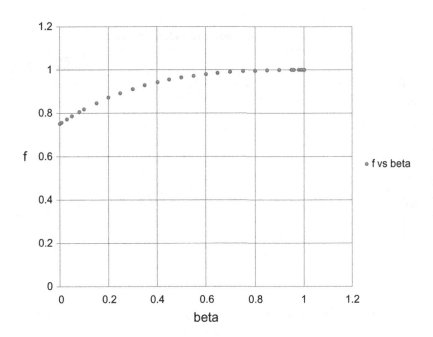

FIGURE 2.9

Plot of f vs beta.

Equations 19 to 21 imply that in a network with a large delay bandwidth product (relative to the buffer size), a TCP Reno–controlled connection is not able to attain its full throughput C. Instead, the throughput maxes out at 0.75C because of the lack of buffering at the bottleneck node. If B exceeds CT, then the throughput converges to C as expected. However, the fact that the throughput is able to get up to 0.75C even for very small buffer sizes is interesting and has been recently used in the design of the CoDel AQM Scheme (see Chapter 4).

2.2.3 THROUGHPUT AS A FUNCTION OF LINK ERROR RATE

In the presence of random link errors, TCP may no longer be able to attain the maximum window size of B + CT; instead, the window increases to some value that is now a random variable. This is clearly illustrated in Figure 2.10, with the maximum window and consequently the starting window varying randomly. To analyze this case, we have to resort to probabilistic reasoning and find the expected value of the throughput. In Section 2.2.3.1, we consider the case when the lost packets are recovered using the duplicate ACKs mechanism, and in Section 2.2.3.2, we consider the more complex case when packet losses result in timeouts.

To take the random losses into account, we need to introduce a second model in to the system, that of the packet loss process. The simplest case is when packet losses occur independently of one another with a loss probability p; this is the most common loss process used in the literature.

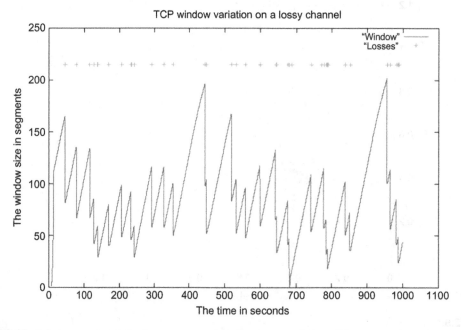

FIGURE 2.10

Evolution of TCP window size with random link errors.

Wireless links lead to losses that tend to bunch together because of a phenomenon known as fading. In Section 2.4, we analyze a system in which the packet loss intervals are correlated, which can be used to model such a system.

The type of analysis that is carried out in the next section is known as mean value analysis (MVA) in which we work with the expectations of the random variables. This allows us to obtain closed form expressions for the quantities of interest. There are three other alternative models that have been used to analyze this system:

- Fluid flow models: The fluid flow model that is introduced in Section 2.2.2 can also be extended to analyze the system in the presence of random losses, and this is discussed in Section 2.3.
- Markov chain models [9,10]: These work by defining a state for the system that evolves according to a Markov process, with the state transition probabilities derived as a function of the link error rate. The advantage of this approach is that it is possible to obtain the full distribution of the TCP window size, as opposed to just the mean value. However, it is not possible to get closed form solutions for the Markov chain, which has to be solved numerically.
- Stochastic models [6]: These models replace the simple iid model for packet loss by a more sophisticated stochastic process model. As a result, more realistic packet loss models, such as bursty losses, can also be analyzed. We describe such a model in Section 2.4.

2.2.3.1 Link Errors Recovered by Duplicate ACKs

The TCP model used in this section uses discrete states for the window size, as opposed to the fluid model used in Section 2.2.2 [5]. We define a cycle as the time between two loss events (Figure 2.11) and a subcycle as the time required to transmit a single window of packets followed by reception of their ACKs.

In addition to assumptions 1 and 2 from Section 2.2.2, we make the following additional assumptions:

4. All the packets in a window are transmitted back to back at the start of a subcycle, and no other packets are sent until the ACK for the first packet is received, which marks the end of the subcycle and the start of the next one.
5. The time needed to send all the packets in a window is smaller than the round trip time. This assumption is equivalent to stating that the round trip time $T(t)$ is fixed at $T(t) = T$ and equals the length of a subcycle. This is clearly an approximation because we observed in Section 2.2.2 that the $T(t)$ increases linearly after the window size exceeds CT because of queuing at the bottleneck node.

   Another consequence of this assumption is that the window increase process stays linear throughout, so we are approximating the sublinear increase for larger window sizes shown in Figure 2.6 (which is caused by the increase in $T(t)$), by a straight line.

6. Packet losses between cycles are independent, but within a cycle when a packet is lost, then all the remaining packets transmitted until the end of the cycle are also lost. This assumption can be justified on the basis of the back-to-back transmission assumption and the drop-tail behavior of the bottleneck queue.

Define the following:

W_i: TCP window size at the end of the i_{th} cycle
A_i: Duration of the ith cycle
X_i: Number of subcycles in the i_{th} cycle
Y_i: Number of packets transmitted in the i_{th} cycle
R_{avg}: Average TCP throughput
p: Probability that a packet is lost because of random link error given that it is either the first packet in its round or the preceding packet in its round is not lost.

As shown in Figure 2.11, cycles are indexed using the variable i, and in the ith cycle, the initial TCP window is given by the random variable $W_{i-1}/2$, and the final value at the time of packet loss is given by W_i. Within the ith cycle, the sender transmits up to X_i windows of packets, and the time required to transmit a single window of packets is constant and is equal to the duration of the (constant) round trip latency T, so that there are X_i subcycles in the ith cycle. Within each subcycle, the window size increases by one packet as TCP goes through the congestion avoidance phase, so that by the end of the cycle, the window size increases by X_i packets.

We will assume that the system has reached a stationary state, so that the sequences of random variables $\{W_i\}$, $\{A_i\}$, $\{X_i\}$ and $\{Y_i\}$ converge in distribution to the random variables W, A, X and Y, respectively. We further define the expected values of these stationary random variables as E(W), E(A), E(X), and E(Y), so that:

E(W): Expected TCP window size at time of packet loss
E(Y): Expected number of packets transmitted during a single cycle
E(X): Expected number of subcycles within a cycle
E(A): Expected duration of a cycle

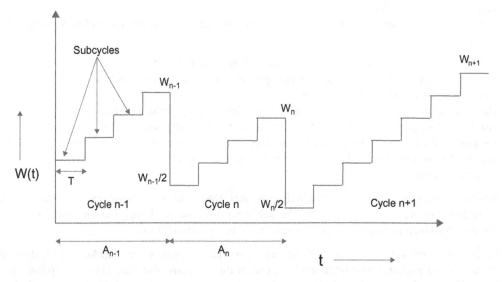

FIGURE 2.11

Evolution of TCP window size under random losses.

Our objective is to compute R_{avg}, the average throughput. From the theory of Markov regenerative processes, it follows that

$$R_{avg} = \frac{E(Y)}{E(A)} \tag{21}$$

We now proceed to compute E(Y), followed by E(A).

After a packet is lost, $W_i - 1$ additional packets are transmitted before the cycle ends. We will ignore these packets, so that Y_i equals the number packets transmitted until the first drop occurs. Under this assumption, the computation of E(Y) is straightforward, given that the number of packets transmitted during a cycle is distributed according to the Bernoulli distribution, that is,

$$P(Y_i = k) = (1-p)^{k-1}p, \quad k = 1, 2, \ldots \tag{22}$$

Hence,

$$E(Y) = \frac{1}{p} \tag{23}$$

Next, note that E(A) is given by

$$E(A) = E(X) \cdot T \tag{24}$$

where T is the fixed round trip delay for the system. Furthermore, because

$$W_i = \frac{W_{i-1}}{2} + X_i, \forall i \tag{25}$$

it follows by taking expectations on both sides, that the average number of subcycles E(X) is given by

$$E(X) = \frac{E(W)}{2} \tag{26}$$

To compute E(W), note that in each subcycle, the TCP window size increases by 1; hence, if we ignore the packets transmitted in the last subcycle, we get

$$
\begin{aligned}
Y_i &= \sum_{k=0}^{X_i-1} \left(\frac{W_{i-1}}{2} + k \right) \\
&= \frac{X_i}{2} W_{i-1} + \frac{(X_i - 1)X_i}{2} \\
&= \frac{X_i}{2} \left(W_{i-1} + W_i - \frac{W_{i-1}}{2} - 1 \right) \\
&= \frac{X_i}{2} \left(W_i + \frac{W_{i-1}}{2} - 1 \right)
\end{aligned}
\tag{27}
$$

Assuming that $\{X_i\}$ and $\{W_i\}$ are mutually independent sequences of iid random variables and taking the expectation on both sides, we obtain

$$E(Y) = \frac{E(X)}{2}\left(E(W) + \frac{E(W)}{2} - 1\right) = \frac{E(X)}{2}\left(\frac{3E(W)}{2} - 1\right) \tag{28}$$

Substituting the value of $E(X)$ from (27) and using the fact that $E(Y) = 1/p$, we obtain

$$\frac{3(E(W))^2}{8} - \frac{E(W)}{4} - \frac{1}{p} = 0 \tag{29}$$

Solving this quadratic equation yields

$$E(W) = \frac{1 + \sqrt{1 + \frac{24}{p}}}{3} \quad \text{packets} \tag{30a}$$

This is approximately equal to

$$E(W) \approx \sqrt{\frac{8}{3p}} \quad \text{packets,} \tag{30b}$$

and from equation 26, we conclude

$$E(X) \approx \sqrt{\frac{2}{3p}} \tag{31}$$

Finally, it follows from equations 21, 23, 24, and 31 that

$$R_{avg} \approx \frac{1/p}{T\sqrt{2/3p}} = \frac{1}{T}\sqrt{\frac{3}{2p}} \quad \text{packets/sec} \tag{32}$$

Equation 32 is the well-known "square root" law for the expected throughput of a TCP connection in the presence of random link errors that was first derived by Mathis and colleagues [7]. Our derivation is a simplified version of the proof given by Padhye et al. [5]

2.2.3.2 Link Errors Recovered by Duplicate ACKs and Timeouts

In this section, we derive an expression for the average TCP throughput in the presence of duplicate ACK as well as *timeouts*. As in the previous section, we present a simplified version of the analysis in the paper by Padhye and colleagues [5].

As illustrated in Figure 2.12, we now consider a supercycle that consists of a random number of cycles (recall that cycles terminate with a duplicate ACK−based packet recovery) and a single timeout interval.

Define the following random variables:

Z_i^{DA}: Time duration during which missing packets are recovered using duplicate ACK triggered retransmissions in the ith supercycle. This interval is made of several cycles, as defined in the previous section.

n_i: Number of cycles within a single interval of length Z_i^{DA} in the ith supercycle

Y_{ij}: Number of packets sent in the jth cycle of the ith supercycle

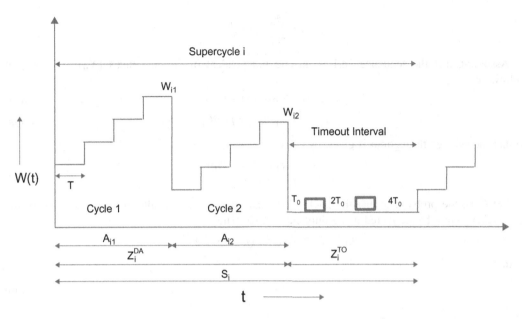

FIGURE 2.12

Evolution of TCP window size in the presence of duplicate ACKs and timeouts.

X_{ij}: Number of subcycles in the jth cycle of the ith supercycle
A_{ij}: Duration of the jth cycle of the ith supercycle
Z_i^{TO}: Time duration during which a missing packet is recovered using TCP timeouts
M_i: Number of packets transmitted in the i_{th} supercycle
P_i: Number of packets transmitted during the timeout interval Z_i^{TO}
S_i: Time duration of a complete supercycle, such that

$$S_i = Z_i^{DA} + Z_i^{TO} \qquad (33)$$

As in the previous section, we assume that the system is operating in a steady state in which all the random variables defined above have converged in distribution. We will denote the expected value of these random variables with respect to their limit distribution by appending an E before the variable name as before.

Note that the average value of the system throughput R_{avg}, is given by

$$R_{avg} = \frac{E(M)}{E(S)} \qquad (34)$$

We now proceed to compute the expected values $E(M)$ and $E(S)$. By their definitions, we have

$$M_i = \sum_{j=1}^{n_i} Y_{ij} + P_i \qquad (35)$$

$$S_i = \sum_{j=1}^{n_i} A_{ij} + Z_i^{TO} \tag{36}$$

Assuming that the sequence $\{n_i\}$ is iid and independent of the sequences $\{Y_{ij}\}$ and $\{A_{ij}\}$, it follows that

$$E(M) = E(n) \cdot E(Y) + E(P) \tag{37}$$

$$E(S) = E(n) \cdot E(A) + E(Z^{TO}) \tag{38}$$

so that the average throughput is given by

$$R_{avg} = \frac{E(Y) + E(P)/E(n)}{E(A) + E(Z^{TO})/E(n)} \tag{39}$$

Let Q be the probability that the packet loss that ends a cycle results in a timeout, that is, the lost packet cannot be recovered using duplicate ACKs. Then

$$\Pr(n = k) = (1 - Q)^{k-1}Q, \quad k = 1, 2, \dots$$

so that

$$E(n) = \frac{1}{Q} \tag{40}$$

which results in the following expression for R_{avg}

$$R_{avg} = \frac{E(Y) + QE(P)}{E(A) + QE(Z^{TO})} \tag{41}$$

We derived expressions for E(Y) and E(A) in the last section, namely

$$E(Y) = \frac{1}{p} \quad \text{and} \tag{42}$$

$$E(A) = T\sqrt{\frac{2}{3p}} \tag{43}$$

and we now obtain formulae for E(P), $E(Z^{TO})$ and Q.

1. **E(P)**

   The same packet is transmitted one or more times during the timeout interval Z^{TO}. Hence a sequence of k TOs occurs when there are $(k-1)$ consecutive losses followed by a successful transmission. Hence,

   $$\Pr(P = k) = p^{k-1}(1 - p), \quad k = 1, 2, \dots$$

   from which it follows that

   $$E(P) = \frac{1}{1-p}. \tag{44}$$

2. **E(Z^{TO})**

   Note that the time duration for Z^{TO} with k timeouts are given by

   $$Z^{TO}(k) = \begin{cases} (2^k - 1)T_0, & \text{for } k \le 6 \\ [63 + 64(k - 6)]T_0, & \text{for } k \ge 7 \end{cases} \tag{45}$$

This formula follows from the fact that the value of the timeout is doubled for the first six timer expiries and then kept fixed at $64T_0$ for further expirations. It follows that

$$
\begin{aligned}
E(Z^{TO}) &= \sum_{k=1}^{\infty} Z^{TO}(k) \cdot \Pr(P=k) \\
&= T_0 \frac{1+p+2p^2+4p^3+8p^4+16p^5+32p^6}{1-p}
\end{aligned}
\tag{46}
$$

Define f(p) as

$$
f(p) = 1 + p + 2p^2 + 4p^3 + 8p^4 + 16p^5 + 32p^6
\tag{47}
$$

so that

$$
E(Z^{TO}) = T_0 \frac{f(p)}{1-p}
\tag{48}
$$

3. Q

Q is approximated by the formula (see Appendix 2.A for details)

$$
Q = \min\left(1, \frac{3}{E(W)}\right) = \min\left(1, 3\sqrt{\frac{3p}{8}}\right)
\tag{49}
$$

From equations 41 to 44, 48, and 49, it follows that

$$
R_{avg} = \frac{\frac{1}{p} + \frac{1}{1-p} \min\left(1, 3\sqrt{\frac{3p}{8}}\right)}{T\sqrt{\frac{2}{3p}} + \frac{T_0 f(p)}{1-p} \min\left(1, 3\sqrt{\frac{3p}{8}}\right)}
\tag{50}
$$

which after some simplification results in

$$
R_{avg} = \frac{1 - p + p \min\left(1, 3\sqrt{\frac{3p}{8}}\right)}{T(1-p)\sqrt{\frac{2}{3p}} + T_0 p f(p) \min\left(1, 3\sqrt{\frac{3p}{8}}\right)}
\tag{51}
$$

For smaller values of p, this can be approximated as

$$
R_{avg} = \frac{1}{T\sqrt{\frac{2}{3p}} + T_0 p (1 + 32p^2) \min\left(1, 3\sqrt{\frac{3p}{8}}\right)}
\tag{52}
$$

This formula was empirically validated by Padhye et al. [5] and was found to give very good agreement with observed values for links in which a significant portion of the packet losses are attributable to timeouts.

2.3 A FLUID FLOW MODEL FOR CONGESTION CONTROL

Some of the early analysis work for TCP throughput in the presence of packet drops was done by Floyd [2] and Mathis et al. [7], using a simple heuristic model based on the fluid flow model of the

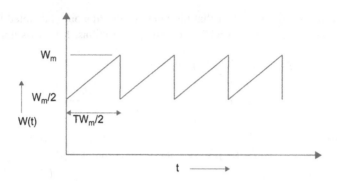

FIGURE 2.13

Fluid model for Reno in the congestion avoidance phase.

window size evolution (Figure 2.13). This is a simplification of the fluid flow model used in Section 2.2.2 (see Figure 2.6) because the model assumes that the window growth is strictly linear within each cycle.

With reference to Figure 2.13, consider a single sample path $W(t)$ of the window size process, such that the value of the maximum window size is W_m, so that the value of the window after a packet loss is $W_m/2$. During the period in which the window size increases from $W_m/2$ to W_m (called a cycle), it increases by 1 for every round trip duration T; hence, it takes $W_m/2$ round trips to increase from $W_m/2$ to W_m. This implies that the length of a cycle is given by $TW_m/2$ seconds.

Note that the number of packets that are transmitted during a cycle is given by

$$Y = \int_0^{TW_m/2} R(t)dt$$

and after substituting $R(t) = W(t)/T$, we get

$$
\begin{aligned}
Y &= \int_0^{TW_m/2} \frac{W(t)}{T} dt \\
&= \frac{1}{T}\left[T\left(\frac{W_m}{2}\right)^2 + \frac{T}{2}\left(\frac{W_m}{2}\right)^2 \right] \\
&= \frac{3}{8}W_m^2
\end{aligned}
\tag{53}
$$

It is an interesting coincidence that this formula for the number of packets transmitted in a cycle is identical to the one derived in Section 2.2.2 (see equation 15) because in the earlier case, the derivation took the nonlinear evolution of the window size into account, but in the current case, we made a simplifying linear approximation.

It follows that the throughput for a single cycle of the sample path is given by

$$R = \frac{Y}{TW_m/2} = \frac{3}{4}\frac{W_m}{T}$$

This expression can also be formulated in terms of Y, as

$$R = \frac{3}{4T}\sqrt{\frac{8Y}{3}} = \frac{1}{T}\sqrt{\frac{3Y}{2}} \tag{54}$$

Taking the expectations on both sides, it follows that

$$R_{avg} = \frac{1}{T}\sqrt{\frac{3}{2}}E\left(\sqrt{Y}\right) \tag{55}$$

The usual way of analyzing this system implicitly makes this assumption that the expectation and the square root operations can be interchanged. Note that this can be done only if Y is a constant, say Y = N, and under this assumption, equation 55 reduces to

$$R_{avg} = \frac{1}{T}\sqrt{\frac{3}{2}}\sqrt{E(Y)} = \frac{1}{T}\sqrt{\frac{3N}{2}} \tag{56}$$

Because the system drops one packet of every N that are transmitted, the packet drop rate p is given by p = 1/N. Substituting this in equation 56, we obtain

$$R_{avg} = \frac{1}{T}\sqrt{\frac{3}{2p}} \tag{57}$$

and we have recovered the square-root formula. However, this analysis makes it clear that this equation only holds for the case of deterministic number of packets per cycle and is referred to as the "deterministic approximation" in the rest of this book.

If we do not make the deterministic approximation, then for the case when the packet drop variables are iid with probability p, the number of packets per cycle follows the following geometric distribution.

$$P(Y = n) = (1-p)^{n-1}p \quad n = 1, 2, \ldots \quad \text{so that} \tag{58}$$

$$E\left(\sqrt{Y}\right) = \sum_{n=1}^{\infty}\sqrt{n}(1-p)^{n-1}p \tag{59}$$

In the absence of a closed form expression for this sum, the final expression for the iid packet loss case is given by

$$R_{avg} = \frac{1}{T}\sqrt{\frac{3p}{2}}\sum_{n=1}^{\infty}\sqrt{n}(1-p)^{n-1} \tag{60}$$

If we approximate the geometric distribution (equation 58) by an exponential distribution with density function given by

$$f_Y(y) = \lambda e^{-\lambda y} \quad y \geq 0 \tag{61}$$

and to match the two distributions, we set $\lambda = p$.

Define a random variable X given by

$$X = \sqrt{Y}$$

Then it can shown that the density function for X is given by

$$f_X(x) = 2\lambda x e^{-\lambda x^2} \quad x \geq 0 \tag{62}$$

so that

$$
\begin{aligned}
E(X) &= 2\lambda \int_0^\infty x^2 e^{-\lambda x^2} dx \\
&= 2\lambda \lim_{x \to \infty} \left[\frac{\sqrt{\pi}}{4\lambda^{3/2}} erf\left(\sqrt{\lambda}x\right) - \frac{xe^{-\lambda x^2}}{2\lambda} \right] \\
&= \lim_{x \to \infty} \left[\frac{1}{2}\sqrt{\frac{\pi}{\lambda}} erf\left(\sqrt{\lambda}x\right) - xe^{-\lambda x^2} \right] \\
&= \frac{1}{2}\sqrt{\frac{\pi}{\lambda}}
\end{aligned}
\tag{63}
$$

where erf is the standard error function. From equations 55 and 63, it follows that

$$
R_{avg} = \frac{1}{T}\sqrt{\frac{3\pi}{8p}}
\tag{64}
$$

where we substituted p back into the equation. Hence, we have succeeded in recovering the square-root formula using the more exact calculation. The constant in equation 64 computes to 1.08, as opposed to 1.22 in equation 57, so it results in a slightly lower average throughput.

In the calculation done in Section 2.2.3.1, the assumption following equation 28 that the $\{X_i\}$ and $\{W_i\}$ sequences are independent also results in implicitly introducing the deterministic assumption into the computation, so that the final result coincides with that of the deterministic case.

As we will see later in Part 2, the most important information in the formula for the average throughput is not the constant but the nature of the functional dependence on p and T. Because the deterministic approximation gives the correct functional dependence while using fairly straightforward computations, we will follow the rest of the research community in relying on this technique in the rest of this book.

Equation 53 can be used to derive an expression of the distribution of the maximum TCP window size W_m, and this is done next. Because $W_m = \sqrt{\frac{8Y}{3}}$, it follows that

$$
P(W_m \le x) = P\left(Y \le \frac{3x^2}{8}\right)
$$

Again, using the exponential distribution (equation 61) for the number of packets per cycle, it follows that

$$
P(W_m \le x) = 1 - e^{-\frac{3px^2}{8}}
$$

so that the density function for W_m is given by

$$
f_{W_m}(x) = \frac{3px}{4} e^{-\frac{3px^2}{8}} \quad x \ge 0.
$$

A GENERAL PROCEDURE FOR COMPUTING THE AVERAGE THROUGHPUT

Basing on the deterministic approximation, we provide a procedure for computing the average throughput for a congestion control algorithm with window increase function given by W(t) and maximum window size W_m. This procedure is used in the next section as well as several times in Part 2 of this book:

1. Compute the number of packets Y transmitted per cycle by the formula

$$Y_\alpha(W_m) = \frac{1}{T} \int_0^T W(t, \alpha) dt$$

In this equation, T is the round trip latency, and α represents other parameters that govern the window size evolution.

2. Equate the packet drop rate p to Y, using the formula

$$Y_\alpha(W_m) = \frac{1}{p}$$

If this equation can be inverted, then it leads to a formula for W_m as a function of p, that is,

$$W_m = Y_\alpha^{-1}\left(\frac{1}{p}\right)$$

3. Compute the cycle duration $\tau(W_m)$ for a cycle as a function of the maximum window size.
4. The average throughput is then given by

$$R_{avg} = \frac{1/p}{\tau(W_m)} = \frac{1/p}{\tau(Y_\alpha^{-1}(\frac{1}{p}))}$$

The formula for the window increase function $W(t, \alpha)$ can usually be derived from the window increase-decrease rules. Note that there are algorithms in which the inversion in step 2 is not feasible, in which case we will have to resort to approximations. There are several examples of this in Chapter 5.

2.3.1 THROUGHPUT FOR GENERAL ADDITIVE INCREASE/MULTIPLICATIVE DECREASE (AIMD) CONGESTION CONTROL

Recall that the window increase−decrease rules for TCP Reno can be written as:

$$W \leftarrow \begin{cases} W + 1 & per \quad RTT \quad on \quad ACK \quad receipt \\ \dfrac{W}{2} & on \quad packet \quad loss \end{cases} \tag{65}$$

This rule can be generalized so that the window size increases by a packets per RTT in the absence of loss, and it is reduced by a fraction bW on loss. This results in the following rules:

$$W \leftarrow \begin{cases} W + a & per \quad RTT \quad on \quad ACK \quad receipt \\ (1 - b)W & on \quad packet \quad loss \end{cases} \tag{66}$$

This is referred to as an AIMD congestion control [11], and has proven to be very useful in exploring new algorithms; indeed, most of the algorithms in this book fall within this framework. In general, some of the most effective algorithms combine AIMD with increase decrease parameters (a,b) that are allowed to vary as a function of either the congestion feedback or the window size itself. Here are some examples from later chapters:

- By choosing the value of a, the designer can make the congestion control more aggressive (if a > 1) or less aggressive (if a < 1) than TCP Reno. The choice a > 1 is used in high-speed

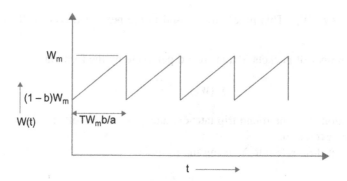

FIGURE 2.14

Window variation with additive increase/multiplicative decrease (AIMD) congestion control.

networks because it causes the window to increase faster to take advantage of the available bandwidth. Protocols such as High Speed TCP (HSTCP), TCP BIC, TCP FAST and TCP LEDBAT use an adaptive scheme in which they vary the value of a depending on the current window size, the congestion feedback, or both.

- The value of b influences how readily the connection gives up its bandwidth during congestion. TCP Reno uses a rather aggressive reduction of window size by half, which causes problems in higher speed links. By choosing $b < 0.5$, the reduction in window size is smaller on each loss, which leads to a more stable congestion control algorithm. But this can lead to fairness issues because existing connections don't give up their bandwidth as readily. Protocols such as Westwood, Data Center TCP (DCTCP) and HSTCP vary b as a function of the congestion feedback (Westwood, DCTCP) or the window size (HSTCP).

Using the deterministic approximation technique from the previous section, we derive an expression for the throughput of AIMD congestion control.

With reference to Figure 2.14, the TCP window size reduces from W_m to $(1-b)W_m$ on packet loss (i.e., a reduction of bW_m packets). On each round trip, the window size increases by a packets, so that it takes bW_m/a round trips for the window to get back to W_m. This implies that the length of a cycle is given by

$$\tau = TW_m \frac{b}{a} \text{ seconds.}$$

The average number of packets transmitted over a single cycle is then given by:

$$
\begin{aligned}
Y &= \int_0^{TW_m b/a} \frac{W(t)}{T} dt \\
&= \frac{1}{T}\left[T\frac{W_m b}{a}(1-b)W_m + \frac{T}{2}\frac{W_m b}{2 a}W_m \right] \\
&= \left(\frac{2b - b^2}{2a}\right) W_m^2
\end{aligned}
\tag{67}
$$

By step 2 of the deterministic approximation procedure, equating Y to 1/p leads to

$$\frac{1}{p} = \left(\frac{2b - b^2}{2a}\right) W_m^2$$

so that

$$W_m = \sqrt{\frac{2a}{(2b - b^2)}\frac{1}{p}} \tag{68}$$

The average response time R_{avg} is then given by

$$R_{avg} = \frac{1/p}{TW_m\, b/a} = \frac{1}{T}\sqrt{\frac{a(2 - b)}{2bp}} \tag{69}$$

Comparing equation 69 with the equivalent formula for TCP Reno (equation 57), it follows that an AIMD congestion control algorithm with parameters (a,b) has the same average throughput performance as TCP Reno if the following equation is satisfied:

$$a = \frac{3b}{2 - b}. \tag{70}$$

In Chapter 3, we generalize the notion of AIMD congestion control by introducing nonlinearities in the window increase–decrease rules, which is called generalized AIMD or GAIMD congestion control. Note that equation 69 holds only for the case when the parameters a and b are constants. If either of them is a function of the congestion feedback or the current window size, it leads to a nonlinear evolution of the window size for which this analysis does not hold.

2.3.2 DIFFERENTIATING BUFFER OVERFLOWS FROM LINK ERRORS

The theory developed in Sections 2.2 and 2.3 can be used to derive a useful criterion to ascertain whether the packet drops on a TCP connection are being caused because of buffer overflows or because of link errors.

When buffer overflows are solely responsible for packet drops, then N packets are transmitted per window cycle, where N is given by equation 15

$$N = \frac{3W_f^2}{8}.$$

Because one packet is dropped per cycle, it follows that packet drop rate is given by

$$p = \frac{1}{N} = \frac{8}{3W_f^2}. \tag{71}$$

Because $W_f \approx CT$ (ignoring the contribution of the buffer size to W_f), it follows that

$$p(CT)^2 \approx \frac{8}{3} \tag{72}$$

when buffer overflows account for most packet drops.

On the other hand, when link errors are the predominant cause of packet drops, then the maximum window size W_m achieved during a cycle may be much smaller than W_f. It follows that with high link error rate,

$$W_m^2 \ll W_f^2$$

so that by equation 53,

$$p = \frac{1}{E(Y)} = \frac{8}{3E(W_m^2)} \gg \frac{8}{3W_f^2}.$$

It follows that if

$$p(CT)^2 \gg \frac{8}{3} \tag{73}$$

then link errors are the predominant cause of packet drops. This criterion was first proposed by Lakshman and Madhow [4] and serves as a useful test for the prevalence of link errors on a connection with known values for p, C, and T.

2.4 A STOCHASTIC MODEL FOR CONGESTION CONTROL

In this section, following Altman and colleagues [6], we replace the simple packet loss model that we have been using with a more sophisticated loss model with correlations among interloss intervals. Define the following model for the packet loss process:

$\{\tau_n\}_{n=-\infty}^{+\infty}$: Sequence of time instants at which packets are lost
$S_n = \tau_{n+1} - \tau_n$: Sequence of intervals between loss instants
$d = E(S_n)$: The average interloss interval
$U(k) = E[S_n S_{n+k}]$: The correlation function for the interloss interval process.
R_n: Value of the TCP throughput just before n^{th} packet loss at T_n

Recall that the throughput at time t is given by

$$R(t) = \frac{W(t)}{T} \quad \text{so that} \quad \frac{dR}{dt} = \frac{1}{T}\frac{dW}{dt} \tag{74}$$

For TCP Reno, dW/dt = 1/T under the assumption that the round trip delay remains constant during a cycle, so that

$$\frac{dR}{dt} = \frac{1}{T^2} \tag{75}$$

so that R(t) increases linearly with slope $1/T^2$. From equation 75, it follows that

$$R_{n+1} = (1-b)R_n + \frac{S_n}{T^2} \tag{76}$$

where $(1-b)$ is the window decrease factor on packet loss (i.e., we are using the AIMD window rules in equation 66 with b < 1 and a = 1).

Equation 76 is a stochastic linear differential equation, with a solution given by Brandt [12].

$$R_n^* = \frac{1}{T^2}\sum_{k=0}^{\infty}(1-b)^k S_{n-1-k} \tag{77}$$

To compute the average throughput R_{avg}, we start with its definition given by

$$R_{avg} = \lim_{t \to \infty}\frac{1}{t}\int_0^t R(t)dt$$

Using the inversion formula from Palm calculus [13] and substituting from equations 76 and 77, it follows that

$$
\begin{aligned}
R_{avg} &= \frac{1}{d} E^0 \left[\int_0^{\tau_1} \left[(1-b)R_0 + \frac{t}{T^2} \right] dt \right] = \frac{1}{d} E^0 \left[(1-b)R_0 S_0 + \frac{S_0^2}{2T^2} \right] \\
&= \frac{1}{d} E^0 \left[\frac{1-b}{T} \sum_{k=0}^{\infty} (1-b)^k S_{-1-k} S_0 \right] + \frac{1}{2dT^2} E^0 \left[S_0^2 \right] \\
&= \frac{1}{dT^2} \left[\frac{1}{2} U(0) + \sum_{k=1}^{\infty} (1-b)^k U(k) \right]
\end{aligned}
\tag{78}
$$

Note that in this formula, we have used the fact that $\tau_0 = 0$ so that $S_0 = \tau_1$. The expectation E^0 is with respect to the Palm measure P^0 that is conditioned on sample paths for which $\tau_0 = 0$.

To express this formula as a function of the packet loss probability p, note that if A(t) is the number of packets transmitted and L(t) is the number of loss events until time t, then

$$
p = \lim_{t \to \infty} \frac{L(t)}{A(t)} = \lim_{t \to \infty} \frac{t/d}{\int_0^t R(s) ds} = \frac{1}{dE[R(t)]}
\tag{79}
$$

Define the normalized correlation function as

$$
\hat{U}(k) = \frac{U(k)}{d^2}
$$

Substituting the value of d from (79) into (78), it follows that

$$
R_{avg} = \frac{1}{T} \sqrt{\frac{1}{p} \left[\frac{\hat{U}(0)}{2} + \sum_{k=1}^{\infty} (1-b)^k \hat{U}(k) \right]}
\tag{80}
$$

For the case of deterministic interpacket loss intervals, it follows that

$$
\hat{U}(k) = 1 \quad k = 0, 1, 2, \ldots
$$

so that

$$
R_{avg} = \frac{1}{T} \sqrt{\frac{1}{p} \frac{2-b}{2b}}
\tag{81}
$$

which coincides with equation 72 in the previous section. Substituting $b = \frac{1}{2}$, we again recover the square-root formula.

Equation 80 implies that a correlation between packet loss intervals leads to an increase in the average throughput.

2.5 WHY DOES THE SQUARE-ROOT FORMULA WORK WELL?

From equation 80 in the previous section, it follows that increasing the variance or the presence of correlation between the interpacket loss intervals increases the average throughput. Because in

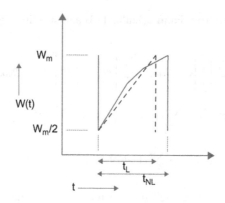

FIGURE 2.15

Comparison of fluid models.

practice, interpacket loss intervals have a finite variance and probably are correlated as well, it begs the question of why equation 60 work so well in practice even though it was derived under the assumption of deterministic interloss intervals.

Recall that we made the assumption in Section 2.2.3.1 that the rate of increase of the congestion window is linear, as shown in the dashed curve in Figure 2.15. This is equivalent to assuming that the round trip latency remains constant over the course of the window increase. This is clearly not the case in reality because the latency increases with increasing window size attributable to increasing congestion in the network. Hence, the actual increase in window size becomes sublinear as shown in the solid curve in Figure 2.15; indeed, we analyzed this model in Section 2.2.2.

We will assume that the bottleneck node for both cases has the same buffer size, so that both of these windows increase to the same value W_m at the end of their cycles. Let R_L be the throughput of the linear model and let R_{NL} be the throughput of the nonlinear model. It follows that

$$R_L = \frac{N_L}{t_L} \quad \text{and} \quad R_{NL} = \frac{N_{NL}}{t_{NL}}.$$

where N_L is the number of packets transmitted in the linear model and N_{NL} is the number for the nonlinear model. In equations 15 and 53, we computed N_{NL} and N_L, respectively, and it turns out that $N_{NL} = N_L$. However because $t_L < t_{NL}$, it follows that $R_L > R_{NL}$. Hence, the reason why the linear model with deterministic number of packets per cycle works well is because of the cancellation of the following two error sources:

- $R_L > R_{NL}$ due to the linear increase assumption, as explained earlier
- From the discussion in the previous section, the presence of interloss interval variance and correlation increases the throughput for R_{NL} relative to R_{NL}.

2.6 THE CASE OF MULTIPLE PARALLEL TCP CONNECTIONS

In this section, following Bonald [14], we extend the analysis in Section 2.2 to the case when there are multiple TCP connections passing through a single bottleneck node (Figure 2.16). We will consider two cases:

- In Section 2.6.1, we discuss the homogeneous case when all connections have the same round trip latency.
- In Section 2.6.2, we discuss the heterogeneous case in which the round trip latencies are different.

In general, the presence of multiple connections increases the complexity of the model considerably, and in most cases, we will have to resort to approximate solutions after making simplifying assumptions. However, this exercise is well worth the effort because it provides several new insights in the way TCP functions in real-world environments. The analysis in this section assumes that there are no packet drops due to link errors so that all losses are attributable to buffer overflows.

Consider the following system: There are K TCP connections passing through the bottleneck link.

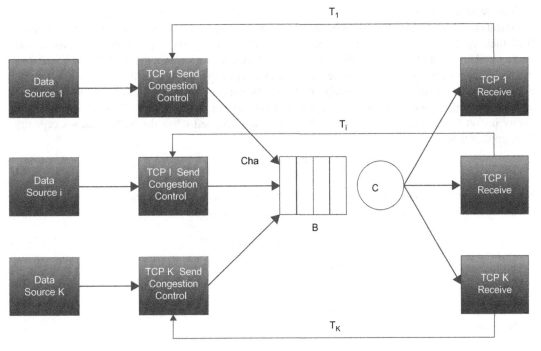

FIGURE 2.16

Multiple parallel TCP connections passing through a bottleneck.

Define the following:

$W_i(t)$ TCP window size for the ith session, $i = 1, 2, \ldots, K$

$W(t) = W_1(t) + W_2(t) + \ldots + W_K(t)$ The total window size attributable to all the K sessions.

T_i^d: Propagation delay in the forward (or downstream) direction in seconds for the ith session, $i = 1, 2, \ldots, K$

T_i^u: Propagation delay in the backward (or upstream) direction in seconds for the ith session, $i = 1, 2, \ldots, K$

T_i: Total propagation + Transmission delay for a segment, $i = 1, 2, \ldots, K$

$R_i(t)$, R_i^{avg}: Instantaneous throughput and the average throughput of the ith session, $i = 1, 2, \ldots, K$

$R(t)$, R^{avg}: Instantaneous total throughput and average total throughput attributable to all the K sessions.

The constants W_{max}, C, and B and the variable $b(t)$ are defined as in Section 2.2.1.

2.6.1 HOMOGENEOUS CASE

We will initially consider the homogeneous case in which the propagation + transmission delays for all the sessions are equal (i.e., $T = T_i = T_j$, $i, j = 1, 2, \ldots, K$).

The basic assumption that is used to simplify the analysis of this model is that of session synchronization. This means that the window size variations for all the K sessions happen together (i.e., their cycles start and end at the same time). This assumption is justified from observations made by Shenker et al. [3] in which they observed that tail drop causes the packet loss to get synchronized across all sessions. This is because packets get dropped because of buffer overflow at the bottleneck node; hence, because typically multiple sessions encounter the buffer overflow condition at the same time, their window size evolution tends to get synchronized. This also results in a bursty packet loss pattern in which up to K packets are dropped when the buffer reaches capacity. This implies that

$$\frac{dW_i(t)}{dt} = \frac{dW_j(t)}{dt} \quad \forall i, j \tag{82}$$

because the rate at which a window increases is determined by the (equal) round trp latencies. From the definition of $W(t)$ and equations 7 and 82, it follows that

$$\frac{dW(t)}{dt} = \frac{K}{T} \quad \text{when } W(t) \leq CT \tag{83}$$

From equations 10 and 82, we obtain

$$\frac{dW(t)}{dt} = \frac{KC}{W(t)} \quad \text{when } W(t) > CT \tag{84}$$

Note that

$$R_i(t) = \frac{R(t)}{K} \quad i = 1, 2, \ldots, K \tag{85}$$

so that it is sufficient to find an expression for total throughput $R(t)$.

As in Section 2.2.2, the time evolution of the total window W(t) shows the characteristic saw-tooth pattern, with the sum of the window sizes W(t) increasing until it reaches the value $W_f = B + CT$. This results in synchronized packet losses at all the K connections and causes W(t) to decrease by half to $W_f/2$. When this happens, there are two cases:

1. $W_f/2 > CT$ (i.e., $B > CT$)

This condition holds for a network with a small delay-bandwidth product. In this case, the bottleneck queue is always occupied, hence

$$R(t) = C \quad \text{and} \quad R_i(t) = \frac{C}{K} \quad i = 1, 2, \ldots, K \tag{86}$$

2. $W_f/2 < CT$ (i.e., $B < CT$)

This condition holds for a network with a large delay-bandwidth product. In this case, there are two phases with $W(t) < CT$ in phase 1 and $W(t) > CT$ in phase 2. The calculations are exactly the same as in Section 2.2.2, and they lead to the following formula for the average total throughput R^{avg}

$$R^{avg} = \frac{0.75}{\left[1 - \frac{\beta}{(1+\beta)^2}\right]} C, \quad \text{where} \quad \beta = \frac{B}{CT} \tag{87}$$

which leads to

$$R_i^{avg} = \frac{0.75}{\left[1 - \frac{\beta}{(1+\beta)^2}\right]} \frac{C}{K} \quad i = 1, 2, \ldots, K \tag{88}$$

Note that the total throughput R^{avg} is independent of the number of connections K. Equation 87 also implies that as a result of the lack of buffers in the system and the synchronization of the TCP sessions, the link does not get fully used even with a large number of sessions. Case 1 also leads to the interesting result that for the fully synchronized case, the amount of buffering required to keep the link continuously occupied is given by CT and is independent of the number of connections passing through the link.

2.6.2 HETEROGENEOUS CASE

In this case, the session propagation delays T_i, $i = 1, 2, \ldots, K$ may be different.

Recall that the throughput $R_i(t)$ for session i is defined by the formula

$$R_i(t) = \frac{W_i(t)}{T_i + \frac{b(t)}{C}} \quad i = 1, 2, \ldots, K \tag{89}$$

Hence, for the case when the bottleneck link is fully used, we have

$$\sum_{i=1}^{K} R_i(t) = C,$$

so that

$$\sum_{i=1}^{K} \frac{W_i(t)}{b(t) + CT_i} = 1 \tag{90}$$

The following equation follows by reasoning similar to that used to derive equation 7.

$$\frac{dW_i(t)}{dt} = \frac{1}{T_i + \frac{b(t)}{C}} \qquad i = 1, 2, \ldots, K \tag{91}$$

Following the analysis in Section 2.2.2, the average throughput for the ith session is given by

$$R_i^{avg} = \frac{\frac{3}{8}(W_i^f)^2}{t_i^A + t_i^B} \qquad i = 1, 2, \ldots, K \tag{92}$$

where, as before, t_i^A is the average time interval after a packet loss when the buffer is empty, and t_i^B is the average time interval required for the buffer to fill up.

In general, it is difficult to find closed form solutions for $W_i(t)$ and an expression for W_i^f from these equations, even if synchronization among sessions is assumed. Hence, following Bonald [14], we do an asymptotic analysis, which provides some good insights into the problem.

1. The case of large buffers

    Define $\beta_i = \frac{B}{CT_i}$, $i = 1, 2, \ldots, K$ and assume that β_i is very large, that is, the delay bandwidth product for all sessions is negligible compared with the number of buffers in the bottleneck node. This means that the bottleneck buffer is continuously occupied, so that $t_i^A = 0$. Using equation 91, this leads to

$$\frac{dW_i(t)}{dt} \approx \frac{C}{b(t)}, \qquad i = 1, 2, \ldots, K \tag{93}$$

    Equation 93 implies that all the K windows increase at the same rate; hence, the maximum window sizes are also approximately equal, so that $W_i^f \approx W_j^f$, and $t_i^B \approx t_j^B$ for all i,j. From equation 92, it then follows that

$$R_i^{avg} \approx R_j^{avg} \qquad i, j = 1, 2, \ldots, K \tag{94}$$

    Hence, when the number of buffers in the bottleneck node is large, each connection gets a fair share of the capacity despite any differences in propagation delays.

2. The case of large delay-bandwidth product

    We assume that β_i, $i = 1, 2, \ldots, K$ is very small, that is, the delay-bandwidth product for each session is very large compared with the number of buffers in the bottleneck node. We also make the assumption that the K connections are synchronized, so that they drop their packets at the bottleneck node at the same time.

    From equation 91, it follows that

$$\frac{dW_i(t)}{dt} \approx \frac{1}{T_i}$$

so that

$$\frac{W_i(t)}{W_j(t)} \approx \frac{T_j}{T_i} \qquad i, j = 1, 2, \ldots, K \tag{95}$$

and from equations 63 and 69, it follows that

$$\frac{R_i(t)}{R_j(t)} \approx \frac{W_i/T_i}{W_j/T_j} \approx \left(\frac{T_j}{T_i}\right)^2 \qquad i, j = 1, 2, \ldots, K \tag{96}$$

Hence, for large delay-bandwidth products, TCP Reno with tail drop has a very significant bias against connections with larger propagation delays. At first glance, it may seem that equation 96 contradicts the formula for the average throughput (60) because the latter shows only an inverse relationship with the round trip latency T. However, note that by making the assumption that the K sessions are synchronized, their packet drop probabilities p become a function of T as well, as shown next. We have

$$\frac{R^i_{avg}}{R^j_{avg}} = \frac{T_j}{T_i} \sqrt{\frac{p_j}{p_i}} \quad \text{and furthermore} \tag{97}$$

$$p_i \approx \frac{1}{E(W_i)(t/T_i)} \tag{98}$$

where t is common cycle time for all the K connections and $E(W_i)t/T_i$ is expected number of packets transmitted per cycle. Substituting $E(W_i) = \sqrt{\frac{8}{3p}}$ from equation 30b, it follows that $p_i = \frac{3}{8}(\frac{T_i}{t})^2$. Substituting this expression into equation 97, we obtain

$$\frac{R^i_{avg}}{R^j_{avg}} = \left(\frac{T_j}{T_i}\right)^2. \tag{99}$$

Using heuristic agreements, equation 99 can be extended to the case when the average throughput is given by the formula:

$$R_{avg} = \frac{h}{T^e p^d} \tag{100}$$

where h, e, and d are constants. Equations such as equation 100 for the average throughput arise commonly when we analyze congestion control algorithms in which the window increase is no longer linear (see Chapter 5 for several examples of this). For example, for TCP CUBIC, e = 0.25, and d = 0.75.

It can be shown that the throughput ratio between synchronized connections with differing round trip latencies is given by

$$\frac{R^i_{avg}}{R^j_{avg}} = \left(\frac{T_j}{T_i}\right)^{\frac{e}{1-d}} \tag{101}$$

To prove equation 101, we start with equation 100 so that

$$\frac{R^i_{avg}}{R^j_{avg}} = \left(\frac{T_j}{T_i}\right)^e \left(\frac{p_j}{p_i}\right)^d \tag{102}$$

Because the probability of a packet loss is the inverse of the number of packets transmitted during a cycle and t/T_i is the number of round trips in t seconds, it follows that

$$p_i = \frac{1}{E(W_i)(t/T_i)} = \frac{T^e_i p^d}{th} \tag{103}$$

where we have used the formula

$$E(W) = R_{avg}T = \frac{h}{T^{e-1}p^d}$$

From equation 103, it follows that

$$p_i = \left(\frac{T_i^e}{th'}\right)^{1/1-d} \tag{104}$$

Substituting equation 104 into equation 102 leads to equation 101. This equation was earlier derived by Xu et al. [15] for the special case when $e = 1$. It has proven to be very useful in analyzing the intraprotocol fairness properties of congestion protocols, as shown in Chapter 5.

Equation 101 is critically dependent on the assumption that the packet drops are synchronized among all connections, which is true for tail-drop queues. A buffer management policy that breaks this synchronization leads to a fairer sharing of capacity among connections with unequal latencies. One of the objectives of RED buffer management was to break the synchronization in packet drops by randomizing individual packet drop decisions. Simulations have shown that RED indeed achieves this objective, and as a result, the ratio of the throughputs of TCP connections using RED varies as the first power of their round trip latencies rather than the square.

2.7 FURTHER READING

TCP can also be analyzed by embedding a Markov chain at various points in the window size evolution and by using the packet loss probability to control the state transitions. The stationary distribution of the window size can then be obtained by numerically solving the resulting equations. This program has been carried out by Casetti and Meo [9], Hasegawa and Murata [16], and Kumar [10]. Because this technique does not result in closed form expressions, the impact of various parameters on the performance measure of interest are not explicitly laid out.

Tinnakornsrisuphap and Makowski [17] carry out an analysis of the congestion control system with multiple connections and RED by setting up a discrete time recursion equation between quantities of interest and then show that by using limit theorems the equations converge to a simpler more robust form. Budhiraja et al. [18] analyze the system by directly solving a stochastic differential equation for the window size and thereby derive the distribution of the window size in steady state.

APPENDIX 2.A DERIVATION OF Q = min(1,3/E(W))

Recall that Q is the probability that a packet loss that ends a cycle results in a timeout. Note that the timeout happens in the last cycle of the supercycle (see Figure 2.9). We will focus on the last subcycle of the last cycle, which ends in a timeout, as well as the subcycle just before it, which will be referred to as the "penultimate" subcycle.

Let w be the window size during the penultimate subcycle and assume that packets $f_1,\ldots,f_w$ are transmitted during the penultimate subcycle. Of these packets, $f_1,\ldots,f_k$ are ACKed, and the remaining packets $f_{k+1},\ldots,f_w$ are dropped (using assumption 6). Because $f_1,\ldots,f_k$ are ACKed, this will result in the transmission of k packets in the last subcycle, say $s_1,\ldots,s_k$. Assume that packet s_{m+1} is dropped in the last round; this will result in the dropping of packets $s_{m+2},\ldots,s_k$. Note that packets

$s_1,\ldots,s_m$ that are successfully transmitted in the last round will result in the reception of m duplicate ACKs at the sender. Hence, a TCP timeout will result if m = 0,1, or 2 because in this case, there are not enough ACKs received to trigger a duplicate ACK−based retransmission.
Define the following:

A(w,k): The probability that the first k packets are ACK'd in a subcycle of w packets given that there is a loss of one or more packets during the subcycle

D(n,m): The probability that m packets are ACK'd in sequence in the last subcycle (where n packets are sent) and the rest of the packets in the round, if any, are lost.

$\hat{Q}(w)$: The probability that a packet loss in a penultimate subcycle with window size w results in a timeout in the last subcycle.

Then

$$A(w,k) = \frac{(1-p)^k p}{1 - (1-p)^w} \tag{A1}$$

$$D(n,m) = \begin{cases} (1-p)^m p & \text{if } m \le n-1 \\ (1-p)^n & \text{if } m = n \end{cases} \tag{A2}$$

From the discussion above, the last subcycle will result in a timeout if (1) the window size in the penultimate subcycle is 3 or less; (2) if the window size in the penultimate round is greater than 3 but only two or fewer packets are transmitted successfully; or (3) if the window size in the penultimate round is greater than 3 and the number of packets that are successfully transmitted is 3 or greater but only 0, 1, or 2 of the packets in the last round are transmitted successfully.

In all the three cases above, not enough duplicate ACKs are generated in the last subcycle to trigger a retransmission. It follows that $\hat{Q}(w)$ is given by

$$\hat{Q}(w) = \begin{cases} 1 & \text{if } w \le 3 \\ \sum_{k=0}^{2} A(w,k) + \sum_{k=3}^{w} A(w,k) \sum_{m=0}^{2} D(k,m) & \text{otherwise} \end{cases} \tag{A3}$$

Substituting equations A1 and A2 into equation A3, it follows that

$$\hat{Q}(w) = \min\left(1, \frac{(1-(1-p)^3)(1+(1-p)^3(1-(1-p)^{w-3}))}{1-(1-p)^w}\right) \tag{A4}$$

Using L'Hopital's rule, it follows that

$$\lim_{p \to 0} \hat{Q}(w) = \frac{3}{w}$$

A very good approximation to Q(w) is given by

$$\hat{Q}(w) \approx \min\left(1, \frac{3}{w}\right) \tag{A5}$$

Note that

$$Q = \sum_{w=1}^{\infty} Q(w)P(W=w) = E[\hat{Q}]$$

Making the approximation

$$Q \approx \hat{Q}(E(W))$$

we finally obtain

$$Q \approx \min\left(1, \frac{3}{E(W)}\right). \tag{A6}$$

REFERENCES

[1] Jacobsen V, Karels MJ. Congestion avoidance and control. ACM CCR 1988;18(4);314−29.

[2] Floyd S. Connections with multiple congested gateways in packet switched networks. Part 1: one-way traffic. ACM CCR 1991;21(5):30−47.

[3] Shenker S, Zhang L, Clark DD. Some observations on the dynamics of a congestion control algorithm. ACM CCR 1991;20(5):30−9.

[4] Lakshman TV, Madhow U. The performance of TCP/IP for networks with high bandwidth-delay products and random loss. IEEE/ACM Trans Netw 1997;5(3):336−50.

[5] Padhye J, Firoiu V, Towsley D, Kurose J. Modeling TCP throughput: a simple model and its empirical validation. ACM SIGCOMM 1998.

[6] Altman E, Avrachenkov K, Barakat C. A stochastic model of TCP/IP with stationary random losses. ACM SIGCOMM 2000.

[7] Mathis M, Semke J, Mahdavi J, Ott T. The macroscopic behavior of the TCP congestion avoidance algorithm. ACM CCR 1997;27(3):67−82.

[8] Low S, Varaiya P. A simple theory of traffic and resource allocation in ATM. GLOBECOM 1991;3:1633−7.

[9] Casetti C, Meo M. A new approach to model the stationary behavior of TCP connections. IEEE INFOCOM 2000;1:367−75.

[10] Kumar A. Comparative performance analysis of versions of TCP in a local network with a lossy link. IEEE/ACM Trans Netw 1998;6(4):485−98.

[11] Floyd S, Handley M, Padhye J. A comparison of equation based and AIMD congestion control. ICIR Tech Rep 2000.

[12] Brandt A. The stochastic equation $Y_{n+1} = A_n Y_n + B_n$ with stationary coefficients. Adv Appl Prob 1986;18:211−20.

[13] Baccelli F, Bremaud P. Elements of queueing theory: palm-martingale calculus and stochastic recurrences. Berlin: Springer-Verlag; 1994.

[14] Bonald T. Comparison of TCP Reno and TCP Vegas via fluid approximations. RR- 3563, 1998; <inria-00073120>.

[15] Xu L, Harfoush K, Rhee I. Binary increase congestion control (BIC) for fast long distance networks. IEEE INFOCOM 2004;4:2514−24.

[16] Hasegawa G, Murata M. Analysis of dynamic behaviors of many TCP connections sharing tail-drop/RED routers. IEEE GLOBECOM 2001;3:1811−15.

[17] Tinnakornsrisuphap P, Makowski AM. TCP traffic modeling via limit theorems. UMD ISR; TR 2002−23, 2002.

[18] Budhiraja A, Hernandez-Cmpos F, Kulkarni VG, Smith FD. Stochastic differential equation for TCP window size. Prob Eng Info Sci 2004;18(1):111−40.

SUGGESTED READING

Appenzeller G. Sizing router buffers. PhD thesis, Stanford University, 2005

Barakat C. TCP/IP modeling and validation. IEEE Netw 2001;15(3):38−47.

Brown P. Resource sharing of TCP connections with different round trip times. IEEE INFOCOM 2000;3:1734−41.

Firoiu V, Yeom I, Zhang X. A framework for practical performance evaluation and traffic engineering in IP networks. IEEE ICT 2001.

Floyd S, Fall K. Promoting the use of end-to-end congestion control in the Internet. IEEE/ACM Trans Netw 1999;7(4):458−72.

Misra A, Baras JS, Ott T. The window distribution of multiple TCPs with random loss queues. IEEE GLOBECOM 1999;3:1714−26.

Misra V, Gong W, Towsley D. Fluid based analysis of a network of AQM routers supporting TCP flows with an application to RED. ACM SIGCOMM 2000:151−60.

SUGGESTED READING

OPTIMIZATION AND CONTROL THEORETIC ANALYSIS OF CONGESTION CONTROL

3.1 INTRODUCTION

In this chapter, we introduce a network wide model of congestion control in the fluid limit and use it to ask the following questions: Can the optimal congestion control laws be derived as a solution to an optimization problem? If so, what is the utility function being optimized? What is meant by stability of this system, and what are the conditions under which the system is stable? This line of investigation was pursued by Kelly [1], Kelly et al. [2], Low [3], Low et al. [4], Kunniyur and Srikant [5], and Holot et al. [6,7], among others, and their results form the subject matter of this chapter.

As in Chapter 2, we continue to use fluid flow models for the system. Unlike the models used in Chapter 2, the models in this chapter are used to represent an entire network with multiple connections. These models are analogous to the "mean field" models in physics, in which phenomena such as magnetism are represented using similar ideas. They enable the researcher to capture the most important aspects of the system in a compact manner, such that the impact of important system parameters can be analyzed without worrying about per-packet level details.

It has been shown that by applying Lagrangian optimization theory to a fluid flow model of the network, it is possible to decompose the global optimization problem into independent local optimization problems at each source. Furthermore, the Lagrangian multiplier that appears in the solution can be interpreted as the congestion feedback coming from the network. This is an elegant theoretical result that provides a justification for the way congestion control protocols are designed. Indeed, TCP can be put into this theoretical framework by modeling it in the fluid limit, and then the theory enables us to compute the global utility function that TCP optimizes. Alternately, we can derive new congestion control algorithms by starting from a utility function and then using the theory to compute the optimal rate function at the source nodes.

The fluid flow model can also be used to answer questions about TCP's stability as link speeds and round trip latencies are varied. This is done by applying tools from classical optimal control theory to a linearized version of the differential equations obeyed by the congestion control algorithm. This technique leads to some interesting results, such as the fact that TCP Reno with Active Queue Management (AQM) is inherently unstable, especially when a combination of high bandwidth and large propagation delay is encountered. This analysis has been used to analyze the Random Early Detection (RED) controller and discover suitable parameter settings for it. It has also been used to find other controllers that perform better than RED.

The techniques developed in this chapter for analyzing TCP constitute a useful toolkit that can be used to analyze other congestion control algorithms. In recent years, algorithms such as Data Canter TCP (DCTCP) and the IEEE 802.1 Quantum Congestion Notification (QCN) have been analyzed using these methods. We end the chapter with a discussion of a recent result called the averaging principle (AP), which shows the equivalence of a proportional-integral (PI) type AQM and a special type of rate control rule at the source.

The rest of this chapter is organized as follows: In Section 3.2, we use Lagrangian optimization theory to analyze the congestion control problem and derive an expression for the utility function for TCP Reno. In Section 3.3, we introduce and analyze Generalized additive increase/multiplicative decrease (GAIMD) algorithms, Section 3.4 discusses the application of control theory to the congestion control problem and the derivation of system stability criteria, and Section 3.5 explores a recent result called the AP that has proven to be very useful in designing congestion control algorithms.

An initial reading of this chapter can be done in the following sequence: $3.1 \rightarrow 3.2 \rightarrow 3.4$ (3.4.1 and 3.4.1.1), which covers the basic results needed to understand the material in Part 2 of the book. The most important concepts covered in these sections are that of the formulation of congestion control as the solution to an optimization problem and the application of classical Nyquist stability criteria to congestion control algorithms. More advanced readers can venture into Sections 3.3, 3.4.1.2, 3.4.1.3, and 3.5, which cover the topics of GAIMD algorithms, advanced AQM controllers, and the AP.

3.2 CONGESTION CONTROL USING OPTIMIZATION THEORY

Consider a network with L links and N sources (Figure 3.1).

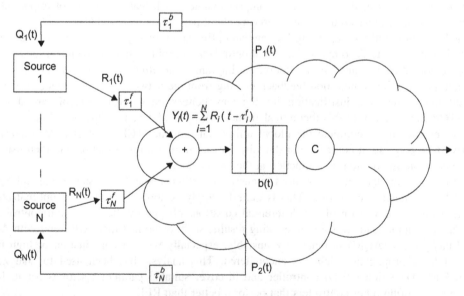

FIGURE 3.1

Illustration of the model for N sources sharing a link.

Define the following:

C_i: Capacity of the ith link, for $1 \le i \le L$, it is the ith element of the column vector C

L_i: Set of links that are used by source i

X_{li}: Element of a routing LXN matrix X, such that $X_{li} = 1$, if $l \in L_i$, and 0 otherwise

$R_i(t)$: Transmission rate of source i, for $1 \le i \le N$

r_i: Steady-state value of $R_i(t)$

$Y_l(t)$: Aggregate rate at link l from all the N sources, for $1 \le l \le L$

y_l: Steady-state value of $Y_i(t)$

$P_l(t)$: Congestion measure at link l, for $1 \le l \le L$. This is later identified as the buffer occupancy at the link.

p_l: Steady-state value of $P_l(t)$

$\tau_{li}^f(t)$: Propagation + Transmission + Queuing delay between the ith source and link l, in the forward direction

$\tau_{li}^b(t)$: Propagation + Transmission + Queuing delay between the ith source and link l, in the backward direction

$T_i(t) = \tau_{li}^f(t) + \tau_{li}^b(t)$ Total round trip delay

$Q_i(t)$: Aggregate of all congestion measures for source i, along its route for $1 \le i \le N$

q_i: Steady-state value of $Q_i(t)$

$b_l(t)$: Buffer occupancy at the link l

Note that

$$Y_l(t) = \sum_{i=1}^{N} X_{li} R_i(t - \tau_{li}^f(t)), \quad 1 \le l \le L, \quad \text{and} \tag{1}$$

$$Q_i(t) = \sum_{l=1}^{L} X_{li} P_l(t - \tau_{li}^b(t)), \quad 1 \le i \le N \tag{2}$$

In steady state,

$$y = Xr \quad \text{and} \quad q = X^T p. \tag{3}$$

Assume that the equilibrium data rate is given by

$$r_i = f_i(q_i), \quad 1 \le i \le N \tag{4}$$

where f_i is a positive, strictly monotone decreasing function. This is a natural assumption to make because if the congestion along a source's path increases, then it should lead to a decrease in its data rate.

Define

$$U_i(r_i) = \int_{r_i} f_i^{-1}(r_i) dr_i \quad \text{so that} \quad \frac{dU_i(r_i)}{dr_i} = f_i^{-1}(r_i) \text{ for } 1 \le i \le N \tag{5}$$

Because U_i has a positive increasing derivative, it follows that it is monotone increasing and strictly concave.

By construction, the equilibrium rate r_i is the solution to the maximization problem

$$\max_{r_i}[U_i(r_i) - r_i q_i].$$

(6)

This equation has the following interpretation: If $U_i(r_i)$ is the utility that the source attains as a result of transmitting at rate r_i, and q_i is price per unit data that it is charged by the network, then Equation 6 leads to a maximization of a source's profit.

Note that Equation 6 is an optimization carried out by each source independently of the others (i.e., the solution r_i is *individually optimal*). We wish to show that r_i is also the solution to the following *global optimality* problem:

$$\max_{r \geq 0} \sum_{i=1}^{N} U_i(r_i), \quad \text{subject to}$$

(7)

$$Xr \leq C.$$

(8)

Equations 7 and 8 constitute what is known as the primal problem. A unique maximizer, called the primal optimal solution, exists because the objective function is strictly concave, and the feasible solution set is compact. A fully distributed implementation to solve the optimality problem described by equations 7 and 8 is not possible because the sources are coupled to each other through the constraint equation 8).

There are two ways to approach this problem:

1. By modifying the objective function (equation 7) for the primal problem, by adding an extra term called the penalty or barrier function, or
2. By solving the problem that is dual to that described by equations 7 and 8.

In this chapter, we pursue the second option and solve the dual problem (we will briefly describe the solution based on the primal problem in Section 3.7). It can be shown that the solution to the primal problem leads to a direct feedback of buffer-related data without any averaging at the nodes, and the solution to the dual problem leads to processing at the nodes before feedback of more explicit information [1]. In general, we will show that the dual problem leads to congestion feedback that is proportional to the queue size at the congested node, and hence is more appropriate for modeling congestion control systems with AQM algorithms operating at the nodes.

The duality method is a way to solve equations 7 and 8 (Appendix 3.D), which naturally leads to a distributed implementation, as shown next. Let λ_i be the Lagrange multipliers and define the Lagrangian $L(r,\lambda)$ for equations 7 and 8 by

$$L(r, \lambda) = \sum_{i=1}^{N} U_i(r_i) - \sum_{l=1}^{L} \lambda_l(y_l - C_l)$$

$$= \sum_{i=1}^{N} U_i(r_i) - \sum_{l=1}^{L} \lambda_l \sum_{i=1}^{N} X_{li} r_i + \sum_{l=1}^{L} \lambda_l C_l$$

$$= \sum_{i=1}^{N} U_i(r_i) - \sum_{i=1}^{N} r_i \sum_{l=1}^{L} X_{li} \lambda_l + \sum_{l=1}^{L} \lambda_l C_l$$

(9)

$$= \sum_{i=1}^{N} [U_i(r_i) - \bar{q}_i r_i] + \sum_{l=1}^{L} \lambda_l C_l \quad \text{where}$$

$$\bar{q}_i = \sum_{l=1}^{L} X_{li} \lambda_l \quad 1 \leq i \leq N$$

The dual function is defined by

$$D(\lambda) = \max_{r_i \geq 0} L(r, \lambda)$$

$$= \sum_{i=1}^{N} \max_{r_i \geq 0} [U_i(r_i) - \bar{q}_i r_i] + \sum_{l=1}^{L} \lambda_l C_l \tag{10}$$

Note that the values

$$r_i^{\max} = U_i'^{-1}(\bar{q}_i) = U_i'^{-1}\left(\sum_{l=1}^{L} X_{li} \lambda_l\right), \quad 1 \leq i \leq N \tag{11}$$

that maximize $L(r, \lambda)$, can be computed separately by each source without the need to coordinate with the other sources, in N separate subproblems. However, as equation 11 shows, a source needs information from the network, in the form of $\bar{q}_i$, before it can compute its optimum rate. Hence, to complete the solution we need to solve the dual problem (i.e., find $\lambda_l, 1 \leq l \leq L$) such that

$$\min_{\lambda \geq 0} D(\lambda) \tag{12}$$

and substitute them into the equation 11 for $r_i^{\max}$. The convex duality theorem then states that the optimum $r_i^{\max}$ computed in equation 10 also maximize the original primal problem (equation 7).

The dual problem (equation 12) can be solved using the gradient projection method [8], such that

$$\lambda_l^{n+1} = \left[\lambda_l^n - \gamma \frac{\partial D(\lambda)}{\partial \lambda_l}\right]^+ \tag{13}$$

where $\gamma > 0$ is the step size and $[z]^+ = \max\{z, 0\}$. From equation 10, it follows that

$$\frac{\partial D(\lambda)}{\partial \lambda_l} = C_l - \sum_{i=1}^{N} X_{li} r_i^{\max} = C_l - y_l(r^{\max}), \quad 1 \leq l \leq L \tag{14}$$

Substituting equation 14 back into equation 13, we get

$$\lambda_l^{n+1} = [\lambda_l^n + \gamma(y_l(r_i^{\max}) - C_l)]^+ \tag{15}$$

Note that the Lagrange multipliers λ_l behave as a congestion measure at the link because this quantity increases when the aggregate traffic rate at the link $y_l(r^{\max})$ exceeds the capacity C_l of the link and conversely decreases when the aggregate traffic falls below the link capacity. Hence, it makes sense to identify the Lagrange multipliers λ_l with the link congestion measure p_l, so that $\lambda_l = p_l, 1 \leq l \leq L$, and

$$p_l^{n+1} = [p_l^n + \gamma(y_l(r_i^{\max}) - C_l)]^+ \tag{16a}$$

or in the fluid limit

$$\frac{dp_l}{dt} = \begin{cases} \gamma(y_l(t) - C_l) & \text{if} \quad p_l(t) > 0 \\ \gamma(y_l(t) - C_l)^+ & \text{if} \quad p_l(t) = 0 \end{cases} \tag{16b}$$

Equations 11 and 16 constitute the solutions to the dual problem. This solution can be implemented in a fully distributed way at the N sources and L links, in the following way:

At link l, $1 \leq l \leq L$

1. Link l obtains an estimate of the total rate of the traffic from all sources that pass through it, y_l.
2. It periodically computes the congestion measure p_l using equation 16a, and this quantity is communicated to all the sources whose route passes through link l. This communication can either explicit as in ECN schemes or implicit as in random packet drops with RED.

At source i, $1 \leq i \leq N$

1. Source i periodically computes the aggregate congestion measure for all the links which lie along its route given by

$$q_i^n = \sum_{l=1}^{L} X_{li}\, p_l^n \tag{17}$$

2. Source i periodically chooses its new rate using the formula

$$r_i^n = U_i'^{-1}(q_i^n) \tag{18}$$

From equations 17 and 18, we obtain the rate control equations for the congestion control problem, if the utility function U_i is known. This distributed procedure is strongly reminiscent of the way TCP congestion control operates, and hence it will not come as a surprise that it can be put into this framework. Hence, TCP congestion control can be interpreted as a solution to the problem of maximizing a global network utility function (equation 7) under the constraints (equation 8). In the next section, we obtain expressions for the utility function U for TCP Reno.

Note that for the case $\gamma = 1$, equation 16b is precisely the equation satisfied by the queue size process at the node; hence, the feedback variable $p_l(t)$ can be identified as the queue size at link l. AQM type schemes can also be put in this framework, as explained next.

The RED algorithm can be described as follows: Let b_l be the queue length at node l and let b_l^{av} be its average; then they satisfy the following equations:

$$b_l^{n+1} = [b_l^n + y_l^n - C_l]^+$$
$$b_l^{av,n+1} = (1 - \alpha_l) b_l^{av,n} + \alpha_l b_l^n \tag{19}$$

In the fluid limit, these become

$$\frac{db_l(t)}{dt} = \begin{cases} y_l(t) - C_l & \text{if } b_l(t) > 0 \\ [y_l(t) - C_l]^+ & \text{if } b_l(t) = 0 \end{cases} \tag{20}$$

and

$$\frac{db_l^{av}(t)}{dt} = -\alpha_l C_l(s_l(t) - b_l^{av}(t)) \tag{21}$$

for some constant $0 \leq \alpha \leq 1$. Then the dropping probability p_l is given by

$$p_l^n = \begin{cases} 0 & \text{if } b_l^{av,n} < B_{min} \\ K(b_l^{av,n} - B_{min}) & \text{if } B_{min} < b_l^{av,n} < B_{max} \\ 1 & \text{if } b_l^{av,n} > B_{max} \end{cases} \tag{22}$$

If we ignore the queue length averaging and let $B_{min} = 0$ and consider only the linear portion of equation 22, then the dropping probability becomes

$$p_l^n = Kb_l^n \tag{23}$$

This is referred to as a proportional controller and is discussed further in Section 3.4.1.2 of this chapter. Taking the fluid limit and using equation 20, we get

$$\frac{dp_l(t)}{dt} = K\frac{db_l(t)}{dt}$$

$$= \begin{cases} K(y_l(t) - C_l) & if \quad b_l(t) > 0 \\ K[y_l(t) - C_l]^+ & if \quad b_l(t) = 0 \end{cases} \tag{24}$$

But equation 24 is exactly in the form (equation 16b) that was derived from the gradient projection method for minimizing the dual problem. Hence, a proportional controller–type RED arises as a natural consequence of solving the dual problem at the network nodes.

3.2.1 UTILITY FUNCTION FOR TCP RENO

There are two ways in which the theoretical results from Section 3.2 can be used in practice:

- Given the system dynamics and the source rate function f (equation 4), compute the network utility function U (equation 5) that this rate function optimizes.
- Given a network utility function U, find the system dynamics and the source rate function that optimizes this utility function.

In this section, we use the first approach, in which a fluid model description for TCP Reno is used to derive the network utility function that it optimizes. We start by deriving an equation for the TCP Reno's window dynamics in the fluid limit.

Note that the total round trip delay is given by

$$T_i(t) = D_i + \sum_l X_{li}\frac{b_l(t)}{C_l} \tag{25}$$

where $D_i = T_{id} + T_{iu}$ is the total propagation delay and $b_l(t)$ is the ith queue length at time t. The source i rate $R_i(t)$ at time t is defined by

$$R_i(t) = \frac{W_i(t)}{T_i(t)} \tag{26}$$

Using the notation from Section 3.2.1, the aggregate congestion measure $Q_i(t)$ at a source can be written as

$$Q_i(t) = 1 - \prod_{l \in L_i}(1 - P_l(t - \tau_{li}^b(t))) \approx \sum_{l \in L_i} P_l(t - \tau_{li}^b(t)) \tag{27}$$

because it takes $\tau_{li}^b(t)$ seconds for the ACK feedback from link 1 to reach back to source i. Note that equation 27 is in the form required in equation 2. The aggregate flow rate at link 1 is given by

$$Y_l(t) = \sum_l X_{li}R_i(t - \tau_{li}^f(t)) \tag{28}$$

because it takes $\tau_{li}^f(t)$ seconds for the data rate at source i to reach link 1.

The rate of change in window size at source i for TCP Reno is then given by the following equation in the fluid limit:

$$\frac{dW_i(t)}{dt} = \frac{R_i(t - T_i(t))[1 - Q_i(t)]}{W_i(t)} - R_i(t - T_i(t))Q_i(t)\frac{1}{2}\frac{4W_i(t)}{3} \tag{29}$$

The first term on the Right Hand Side (RHS) of equation 29 captures the rate of increase in window size, which is the rate at which positive ACKs return to the source multiplied by the increase in window size caused by each such ACK during the congestion avoidance phase. The second term captures the rate of decrease of the window size when the source gets positive congestion indications from the network (the factor 4/3 is added to account for the small-scale fluctuation of $W_i(t)$; see Low [3]). Note that equation 29 ignores the change in window size caused by timeouts.

We now make the following approximations: We ignore the queuing delays in equation 25 so that the round trip delay is now fixed and approximated by

$$T_i = D_i + \sum_l \frac{X_{li}}{C_l} \tag{30}$$

The throughput is then approximated by

$$R_i(t) \approx \frac{W_i(t)}{T_i}. \tag{31}$$

It follows from (29) and (31) that

$$\frac{dR_i(t)}{dt} \approx \frac{R_i(t - T_i)[1 - Q_i(t)]}{R_i(t)T_i^2} - \frac{2R_i(t)R_i(t - T_i)Q_i(t)}{3} \tag{32}$$

We now assume that $R_i(t) \approx R_i(t - T_i)$, so that equation 32 reduces to

$$\frac{dR_i(t)}{dt} \approx \frac{[1 - Q_i(t)]}{T_i^2} - \frac{2R_i^2(t)Q_i(t)}{3} \tag{33}$$

Note that we ignored the propagation delays in the simplifications that led to equation 33. However, modeling these delays is critical in doing a stability analysis of the system, which we postpone to Section 3.4.

In steady state, it follows from equation 33 that

$$r_i = \frac{1}{T_i}\sqrt{\frac{3}{2}\frac{1 - q_i}{q_i}} \tag{34}$$

so that we again recovered the square-root formula. Its inverse is given by

$$q_i = \frac{\frac{1}{T_i^2}}{\frac{1}{T_i^2} + \frac{2}{3}r_i^2} = \frac{1}{1 + \frac{2}{3}r_i^2 T_i^2} \tag{35}$$

which is in the form postulated in equation 4. From equation 5, it follows that the utility function for TCP Reno is given by

$$U_i(r_i) = \int \frac{\frac{1}{T_i^2}}{(\frac{1}{T_i^2} + \frac{2}{3}r_i^2)}\,dr_i = \frac{\sqrt{3/2}}{T_i}\tan^{-1}\left(\sqrt{\frac{2}{3}}r_i T_i\right) \tag{36}$$

Note that for small values of q_i, equation 34 reduces to the expression that is familiar from Chapter 2

$$r_i = \frac{1}{T_i}\sqrt{\frac{3}{2q_i}} \tag{37}$$

If equation 37 is used in equation 5 instead of equation 34, then

$$q_i = \frac{3}{2r_i^2 T_i^2} \tag{38}$$

and the utility function assumes the simpler form

$$U_i(r_i) = -\frac{1.5}{T_i^2 r_i} \tag{38}$$

Equation 38 is of the form

$$U_i(r_i) = -\frac{w_i}{r_i} \quad \text{with} \quad w_i = \frac{1}{T_i^2} \tag{39}$$

Utility functions of the form equation 39 are known to lead to rates that minimize "potential delay fairness" in the network (Appendix 3.E), that is, they minimize the overall potential delay of transfers in progress.

If the utility function is of the form

$$U_i(r_i) = w_i \log r_i \tag{40}$$

then it maximizes the "proportional fairness" in the network. It can be shown that TCP Vegas's utility function is of the form (40)[9] hence it achieves proportional fairness.

A utility function of type

$$U_i(r_i) = \lim_{\alpha \to \infty} \frac{r_i^{1-\alpha}}{1-\alpha} \tag{41}$$

leads to a max-min fair allocation of rates [10]. Max-min fairness is in some sense the ideal way of allocating bandwidth in a network; however, in general, it is difficult to achieve max-min fairness using AIMD type algorithms. It can be achieved by using explicit calculations at the network nodes, as was done by the ATM ABR scheme.

The theory developed in the previous two sections forms a useful conceptual framework for designing congestion control algorithms. In Chapter 9, we discuss the recent application of these ideas to the design of congestion control algorithms, which also uses techniques from machine learning theory.

3.3 GENERALIZED TCP—FRIENDLY ALGORITHMS

In this section, we use the theory developed in Section 3.2 to analyze a generalized version of the TCP congestion control algorithm with nonlinear window increment—decrement rules, called GAIMD. We then derive conditions on the GAIMD parameters to ensure that if TCP GAIMD and

Reno pass through a bottleneck link, then they share the available bandwidth fairly. This line of investigation was originally pursued to design novel congestion control algorithms for traffic sources such as video, which may not do well with TCP Reno.

Define the following:

$\alpha_s(R_s(t))$: Rule for increasing the data rate in the absence of congestion
$\beta_s(R_s(t))$: Rule for decreasing the rate in the presence of congestion

Then the rate dynamics is governed by the following equation:

$$\frac{dR_s(t)}{dt} = (1 - Q_s(t))R_s(t - T_s)\alpha_s(R_s(t)) - Q_s(t)R_s(t - T_s)\beta_s(R_s(t)) \tag{42}$$

Comparing equation 42 with equation 32, it follows that for TCP Reno,

$$\alpha_s(R_s) = \frac{1}{R_sT_s^2} \quad \text{and} \quad \beta_s(R_s) = \frac{R_s}{2} \tag{43}$$

From equation 42, it follows that in equilibrium,

$$q_s = \frac{\alpha_s(r_s)}{\alpha_s(r_s) + \beta_s(r_s)} = f_s(r_s) \tag{44}$$

so that the utility function for GAIMD is given by

$$U_s(r_s) = \int \frac{\alpha_s(r_s)}{\alpha_s(r_s) + \beta_s(r_s)} dr_s \tag{45}$$

Define an algorithm to be TCP-friendly if its utility function coincides with that of TCP Reno. From equations 44 and 35, it follows that an algorithm with increase–decrease functions given by (α_s, β_s) is TCP friendly if and only if

$$\frac{\alpha_s(r_s)}{\alpha_s(r_s) + \beta_s(r_s)} = \frac{2}{2 + r_s^2T_s^2} \quad \text{i.e.} \quad \frac{\alpha_s(r_s)}{\beta_s(r_s)} = \frac{2}{r_s^2T_s^2} \tag{46}$$

Following Bansal and Balakrishnan [11], we now connect the rate increase–decrease rules to the rules used for incrementing and decrementing the window size.

Consider a nonlinear window increase–decrease function parameterized by integers (k,l) and constants (α, β) and of the following form (these rules are applied on a per RTT basis):

$$W \leftarrow W + \frac{\alpha}{W^k} \quad \text{On positive ACK} \tag{47a}$$

$$W \leftarrow W - \beta W^l \quad \text{On packet drop} \tag{47b}$$

Equations 47a and 47b are a generalization of the AIMD algorithm to nonlinear window increase and decrease and hence are known as GAIMD algorithms. For (k,l) = (0,1), we get AIMD; for (k,l) = (−1,1), we get multiplicative increase/multiplicative decrease (MIMD); for (k,l) = (−1,0), we get multiplicative increase/additive decrease (MIAD); and for (k,l) = (0,0), we get additive increase/additive decrease (AIAD).

Using the same arguments as for TCP Reno, the window dynamics for this algorithm are given by

$$\frac{dW_s(t)}{dt} = (1 - Q_s(t))R_s(t - T)\frac{\alpha}{W_s^{k+1}(t)} - Q_s(t)R_s(t - T_s)\beta W_s^l(t)$$

Substituting $W_s(t) = R_s(t)T_s$, it follows that

$$\frac{dR_s(t)}{dt} = (1 - Q_s(t))R_s(t - T_s)\frac{\alpha}{R_s^{k+1}(t)T_s^{k+2}} - Q_s(t)R(t - T_s)\beta R_s^l(t)T_s^{l-1} \tag{48}$$

Comparing this equation with equation 42, we obtain the following expressions for the rate increase−decrease functions for the GAIMD source that corresponds to equations 47a and 47b:

$$\alpha_s(r_s) = \frac{\alpha}{r_s^{k+1}T_s^{k+2}} \quad \text{and} \quad \beta_s(r_s) = \beta r_s^l T_s^{l-1} \tag{49}$$

Substituting equation 49 back into the TCP friendliness criterion from equation 46 yields

$$\frac{\alpha}{\beta}\frac{1}{(r_sT_s)^{k+l+1}} = \frac{2}{r_s^2T_s^2} \tag{50}$$

Hence, the algorithm is TCP friendly if and only if

$$k + l = 1 \quad \text{and} \quad \frac{\alpha}{\beta} = 2 \tag{51}$$

Note that if $l < 1$, then this implies that window is reduced less drastically compared with TCP on detection of network congestion. Using equation 51, it follows that in this case, $0 < k < 1$, so that the window increase is also more gradual as compared with TCP.

If equate $dR_s/dt = 0$ in equilibrium, then we obtain the following expression, which is the analog of the square-root formula for GAIMD algorithms:

$$r_s = \left(\frac{\alpha}{\beta}\right)^{1/k+l+1}\frac{1}{T_s}\left(\frac{1}{q_s^{1/k+l+1}} - 1\right) \approx \left(\frac{\alpha}{\beta}\right)^{1/k+l+1}\frac{1}{T_s}\frac{1}{q_s^{1/k+l+1}} \tag{52}$$

Note that the condition $k + l = 1$ also leads to the square root law for TCP throughput.

3.4 STABILITY ANALYSIS OF TCP WITH ACTIVE QUEUE MANAGEMENT

The stability of a congestion control system is defined in terms of the behavior of the bottleneck queue size b(t). If the bottleneck queue size fluctuates excessively and very frequently touches zero, thus leading to link under utilization, then the system is considered to be unstable. Also, if the bottleneck queue size grows and spends all its time completely full, which leads to excessive packet drops, then again the system is unstable. Hence, ideally, we would like to control the system so that the bottleneck queue size stays in the neighborhood of a target length, showing only small fluctuations.

It has been one of the achievements of fluid modeling of congestion control systems that it makes it possible to approach this problem by using the tools of classical control system theory. This program was first carried out by Vinnicombe [12] and Holot et al. [6,7] The latter group of researchers modeled TCP Reno, for which they analyzed the RED controller, and another controller that they introduced called the PI controller. Since then, the technique has been applied to many

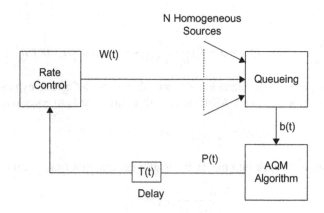

FIGURE 3.2

Block diagram of the control system.

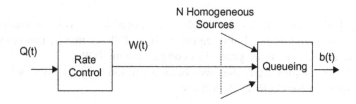

FIGURE 3.3

The open loop system.

other congestion control algorithms and constitutes one of the basic techniques in the toolset for analyzing congestion control.

To analyze the stability of the system, we will follow Holot and colleagues [6,7] and use a simplified model shown in Figure 3.2. In particular, we assume that there are N homogeneous TCP sources, all of which pass through single bottleneck node.

Initially, let's consider the open-loop system shown in Figure 3.3. Later in this and subsequent sections, we will connect the queue length process $b(t)$ with congestion indicator process $Q(t)$, using a variety of controllers. Using equation 29, its window control dynamics are given by

$$\frac{dW(t)}{dt} = \frac{R(t - T(t))[1 - Q(t)]}{W(t)} - R(t - T(t))W(t)\frac{Q(t)}{2} \tag{53}$$

and substitute $W(t) = R(t)T(t)$ in the first term on the RHS and make the approximations $R(t) \approx R(t - T(t))$, $1 - Q(t) \approx 1$, leading to the equation

$$\frac{dW(t)}{dt} = \frac{1}{T(t)} - \frac{W(t)W(t - T(t))}{2T(t - T(t))}Q(t) \tag{54}$$

where $T(t) = \frac{b(t)}{C} + D$.

The fluid approximation for the queue length process at the bottleneck can be written as

$$\frac{db(t)}{dt} = \frac{W(t)}{T(t)}N(t) - C \tag{55}$$

Equations 54 and 55 give the nonlinear dynamics for the rate control and queuing blocks, respectively, in Figure 3.3. To simplify the optimal control problem so that we can apply the techniques of optimal control theory, we now proceed to linearize these equations. With $(W(t), b(t))$, and $Q(t)$ as the input, the operating point (W_0, Q_0, P_0) is defined by $dW/dt = 0$ and $db/dt = 0$, which leads to

$$\frac{dW}{dt} = 0 \Rightarrow W_0^2 Q_0 = 2 \tag{56}$$

$$\frac{db}{dt} = 0 \Rightarrow W_0 = \frac{CT_0}{N} \tag{57}$$

where

$$T_0 = \frac{b_0}{C} + D \quad \text{as per Equation 25} \tag{58}$$

Assuming $N(t) = N$ and $T(t) = T_0$ as constants, equations 54 and 55 can be linearized around the operating points (W_0, b_0, Q_0) (Appendix 3.A), resulting in

$$\frac{dW_\delta(t)}{dt} = -\frac{2N}{CT_0^2}W_\delta(t) - \frac{C^2 T_0}{2N^2}Q_\delta(t) \tag{59}$$

$$\frac{db_\delta(t)}{dt} = \frac{N}{T_0}W_\delta(t) - \frac{1}{T_0}b_\delta(t) \tag{60}$$

where

$$W_\delta = W - W_0$$
$$b_\delta = b - b_0$$
$$Q_\delta = Q - Q_0$$

The Laplace transforms of equations 59 and 60 are given by

$$U_{tcp}(s) = \frac{W_\delta(s)}{Q_\delta(s)} = \frac{\frac{T_0 C^2}{2N^2}}{s + \frac{2N}{T_0^2 C}} \qquad U_{queue}(s) = \frac{b_\delta(s)}{W_\delta(s)} = \frac{\frac{N}{T_0}}{s + \frac{1}{T_0}} \tag{61}$$

so that the Laplace transform of the plant dynamics for the linearized TCP + queuing system is

$$U(s) = U_{tcp}(s)U_{queue}(s) = \frac{\frac{C^2}{2N}}{\left(s + \frac{2N}{T_0^2 C}\right)\left(s + \frac{1}{T_0}\right)} = \frac{\frac{(CT_0)^3}{(2N)^2}}{\left(\frac{s}{2N/CT_0^2} + 1\right)(sT_0 + 1)} \tag{62}$$

and it relates the change in the packet marking probability Q_δ to the change in queue size b_δ.

System stability can be studied with the help of various techniques from optimal control theory, including Nyquist plots, Bode plots, and root locus plots [13]. Of these, the Nyquist plot is the most amenable to analyzing systems with delay lags of the type seen in these systems and hence is

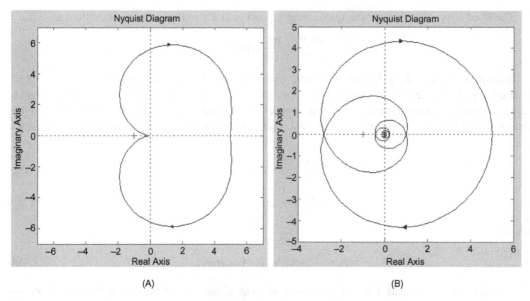

FIGURE 3.4

Example Nyquist plots without loop delay (**A**) and with loop delay (**B**).

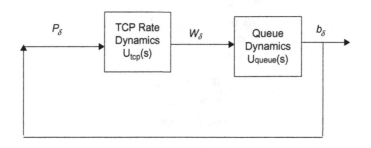

FIGURE 3.5

System without Active Queue Management (AQM) controller with propagation delay ignored.

used in this chapter. Appendix 3.B has a quick introduction to the topic of the Nyquist stability criterion that the reader may want to consult at this point.

Assuming initially that there is no controller present, so that there is no AQM stabilization and the queue size difference is fed back to the sender with no delay, then the system is as shown in Figure 3.5, so that $Q_\delta = P_\delta = b_\delta$:

From Equation 62, the open loop transfer function of this system is of the form

$$U(s) = \frac{K}{(as + 1)(bs + 1)}$$

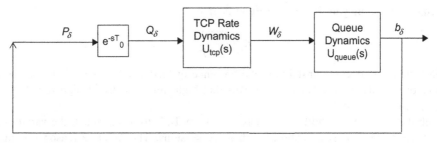

FIGURE 3.6

System without Active Queue Management (AQM) controller but with propagation delay included.

with a,b $>$ 0. The corresponding close loop transfer function W(s) is given by

$$W(s) = \frac{U(s)}{1 + U(s)} = \frac{K}{(as+1)(bs+1)+K}.$$

Using the Nyquist criterion, we can see that the locus of $U(j\omega)$ as ω varies from 0 to ∞, does not encircle the point $(-1, 0)$, even for large values of K; hence, the system is unconditionally stable (see Figure 3.4A).

Next let's introduce the propagation delay into the system, so that $Q_\delta(t) = P_\delta(t - T)$, as shown in Figure 3.6. In this case, equation 59 changes to

$$\frac{dW_\delta(t)}{dt} = -\frac{2N}{CT_0^2}W_\delta(t) - \frac{C^2T_0}{2N^2}P_\delta(t-T)$$

This introduction of the delay in the feedback loop can lead to system instability, as shown next. The open loop and closed loop transfer functions for this system are given by

$$U'(s) = U(s)e^{-sT_0} = \frac{Ke^{-sT_0}}{(as+1)(bs+1)}$$

$$W'(s) = \frac{Ke^{-sT_0}}{(as+1)(bs+1)+Ke^{-sT_0}}$$

From the Nyquist plot for $U'(j\omega)$ shown in Figure 3.4B, note the following:

- The addition of the delay component has led to a downward spiraling effect in the locus of $U'(j\omega)$. This is because $U'(j\omega) = |U'(j\omega)|e^{-j \, \arg(U'(j\omega))}$ where the point $(\omega, U'(j\omega))$ on the curve makes the following angle with the real axis:
  $\arg(U'(j\omega)) = \omega T_0 + \tan^{-1}a\omega + \tan^{-1}b\omega$
  Hence, as ω increases, the first term on the RHS increases linearly, and the other two terms are limited to at most $\frac{\pi}{2}$ each.
- The system is no longer unconditionally stable, and as the gain K increases, it may encircle the point $(-1,0)$ in the clockwise direction, thus rendering it unstable.

From equation 62, the gain K for TCP Reno is given by

$$K = \frac{(CT_0)^3}{(2N)^2}$$

so that the system can become unstable in the presence of feedback if either (1) C increases or (2) T_0 increases or if N decreases. Thus, this proves that high link capacity or high round trip latency can cause system instability.

Although the onset of instability with increasing C or T_0 is to be expected, the variation with N implies that the system gains in stability with more sessions. The intuitive reason for this is that more sessions average out the fluctuations because of the high variations in TCP window size (especially the decrease by half on detecting congestion). With only a few sessions, these variations affect the stability of the system because even a single packet drop causes a large drop in window size. On the other hand, with many connections, the decrease in window size of any one of them does not have as large an effect. Some of the high-speed variations of TCP that we will meet in Chapter 5 reduce their windows by less than half on detecting packet loss, thus reducing K and subsequently increasing their stability in the presence of large C and T_0.

3.4.1 THE ADDITION OF CONTROLLERS TO THE MIX

Because the system shown in Figure 3.6 can become unstable, we now explore the option of adding a controller into the loop, as shown in Figure 3.7, and then adjusting the controller parameters in order to stabilize the system. We will first analyze the RED controller, and then based on the learning from its analysis, introduce two other controllers, the Proportional and the PI controllers, that are shown to have better performance than the RED controller.

3.4.1.1 Random Early Detection (RED) Controllers

The RED controller is shown in Figure 3.8, and its Laplace transform is given by (see Appendix 3. C for a derivation)

$$V_{red}(s) = \frac{L_{red}}{\frac{s}{K} + 1} \quad \text{where} \tag{63}$$

$$L_{red} = \frac{max_p}{max_{th} - min_{th}} \quad \text{and} \quad K = -\frac{\log(1 - w_q)}{\delta} \tag{64}$$

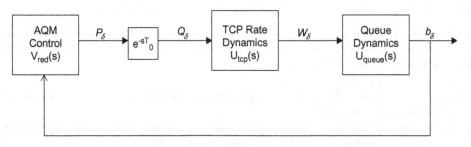

FIGURE 3.7

Congestion control system with a controller in the loop.

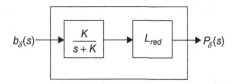

FIGURE 3.8

Random Early Detection (RED) controller.

where w_q is the weighing factor used to smoothen out the queue size estimate and δ is the queue size sampling frequency, which is set to $1/C$. The other RED parameters are defined in Section 1.4.2 in Chapter 1. As Figure 3.8 shows, the RED controller consists of a Low Pass Filter (LPF) followed by a constant gain.

The objective of the optimal control problem is to choose RED parameters L_{red} and K to stabilize the system shown in Figure 3.7. Note that the open loop transfer function for the system is given by

$$T(s) = U_{tcp}(s)U_{queue}(s)V_{red}(s)e^{-sT_0}$$

$$= \frac{\dfrac{L_{red}(CT_0)^3}{(2N)^2}e^{-sT_0}}{\left(\dfrac{s}{K}+1\right)\left(\dfrac{s}{2N/CT_0^2}+1\right)\left(\dfrac{s}{1/T_0}+1\right)} \tag{65}$$

To apply the Nyquist criterion, set $s = j\omega$, so that
$T(j\omega) = |T(j\omega)|e^{-j\,\arg(T(j\omega))}$ where

$$|T(j\omega)| = \frac{\dfrac{L_{red}(CT_0)^3}{(2N)^2}}{\sqrt{\left(\frac{\omega}{K}\right)^2+1}\sqrt{\left(\frac{\omega}{2N/CT_0^2}\right)^2+1}\sqrt{\left(\frac{\omega}{1/T_0}\right)^2+1}} \quad \text{and} \tag{66}$$

$$\arg(T(j\omega)) = \omega T_0 + \tan^{-1}\frac{\omega}{K} + \tan^{-1}\frac{\omega}{2N/CT_0^2} + \tan^{-1}\frac{\omega}{1/T_0} \tag{67}$$

Holot et al. [6] proved the following result:
Let L_{red} and K satisfy:

$$\frac{L_{red}(T^+C)^3}{(2N^-)^2} \leq \sqrt{\frac{\omega_c^2}{K^2}+1} \quad \text{where} \tag{68}$$

$$\omega_c = 0.1\min\left\{\frac{2N^-}{(T^+)^2C}, \frac{1}{T^+}\right\} \tag{69}$$

then the linear feedback control system in Figure 3.7 using a RED controller is stable for all $N \geq N^-$ and all $T_0 \leq T^+$.

To prove this, we start with the following observation: From equation 66, it follows that

$$|T(j\omega)| \leq \frac{\frac{L_{red}(CT_0)^3}{(2N)^2}}{\sqrt{\left(\frac{\omega}{K}\right)^2 + 1}} \tag{70}$$

Furthermore, if $\omega = \omega_c, N \geq N^-, T_0 \leq T^+$, then it follows from equations 68 and 70 that

$$|T(j\omega_c)| \leq 1 \tag{71}$$

From this, we conclude that the critical frequency ω_* at which $|T(j\omega_*)| = 1$, satisfies the relation $\omega_* \leq \omega_c$ (this is because $|T(j\omega)|$ is monotonically decreasing in ω). Hence, it follows from the Nyquist criterion that if we can show that the angle arg $T(j\omega_c)$ satisfies the condition

$$\arg T(j\omega_c) < \pi \text{ radians} \tag{72}$$

then the system has a positive phase margin (PM) given by

$$PM \geq \pi - \arg T(j\omega_c) > 0$$

and hence is stable. Note that the fact that PM > 0 implies that $T(j\bar{\omega}) < 1$, where $\bar{\omega}$ is the frequency at which $\arg(T(j\bar{\omega})) = \pi$, that is, the gain margin is also positive.

From Equation 67 it follows that

$$\arg(T(j\omega_c)) = \omega_c T^+ + \tan^{-1} \frac{\omega_c}{K} + \tan^{-1} \frac{\omega_c}{2N^-/C(T^+)^2} + \tan^{-1} \frac{\omega_c}{1/T^+} \tag{73}$$

Since

$$\omega_c = 0.1 \min\left\{\frac{2N^-}{(T^+)^2 C}, \frac{1}{T^+}\right\}$$

it follows that

$$\omega_c T^+ = 0.1 \min\left\{\frac{2N^-}{T^+ C}, 1\right\}$$

so that $\omega_c T \leq 0.1$ radians. Equation 69 also implies that

$$\frac{\omega_c}{2N^-/C(T^+)^2} \leq 0.1 \quad \text{and} \quad \frac{\omega_c}{1/T^+} \leq 0.1 \text{ so that}$$

$$\tan^{-1} \frac{\omega_c}{2N^-/C(T^+)^2} \leq 0.1 \quad \text{and} \quad \tan^{-1} \frac{\omega_c}{1/T^+} \leq 0.1. \text{ Lastly, because}$$

$$\tan^{-1} \frac{\omega_c}{K} \leq \frac{\pi}{2}, \text{ it follows that}$$

$$\arg(T(j\omega_c)) \leq 0.1 + \frac{\pi}{2} + 0.1 + 0.1 = 1.87 \text{ radians or } 107°,$$

which implies that the $PM \geq 72°$. This proves equation 72 and consequently the stability result.

The following example from Holot et al. [6] shows how equations 68 and 69 can be used to obtain appropriate RED parameters:

Consider the case: $C = 3750$ packets/sec, $N^- = 60$ and $T^+ = 0.246$ sec. From equation 69, it follows that

$$\omega_c = 0.1 \min(0.5259, 4.0541) = 0.053 \quad radians/sec$$

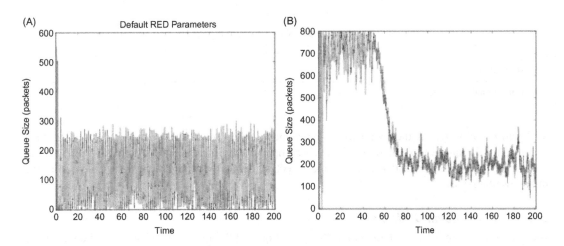

FIGURE 3.9

Variation of the queue size under Random Early Detection (RED).

Choosing K = 0.005, it follows from equation 68 that $L_{red} \leq 1.86(10)^{-4}$. Choosing $\max_p = 0.1$ and because $L_{red} = \max_p/(\max_{th} - \min_{th})$, it follows that $\max_{th} - \min_{th} \approx 540$ packets. The other RED parameters are calculated as $\delta = \frac{1}{C} = 2.66(10)^{-4}$, which yields $\alpha = 1.33(10)^{-6}$.

Figure 3.9A shows the case when the RED parameters are set without taking equation 68 into account, and we can observe the large buffer oscillations that result. When the parameters are set as per equation 68, then they result in a smoother buffer variation as shown in Figure 3.9B. Note the large amount of time that it takes for the queue to settle down in Figure 3.9B, which is a consequence of the small value of ω_c that was used to get a good phase margin.

As the link capacity C or the round trip latency increases or the number N of connections decreases, the RED parameters L_{red} and K have to be changed to maintain the inequality (equation 68). We can do the following:

- Adapt L_{red}: This can be done by changing the value of the marking probability $\max_p$ while keeping the queue thresholds the same. Note that reducing $\max_p$ has the effect of reducing the number of dropped or marked packets when the average queue size is between the threshold values. This causes the queue size to increase beyond $\max_{th}$, thus leading to increased packet drops because of buffer overflow. On the other hand, increasing $\max_p$ has the effect of increasing the number of RED drops and thus decreasing throughput. By using equation 68 as a guide, it is possible to adapt L_{red} more intelligently as a function of changing parameters. An alternative technique for adapting RED was given by Feng et al. [14], in which they used the behavior of the average queue size to adapt $\max_p$. Thus, if the queue size spent most of its time near $\max_{th}$, then $\max_p$ was increased, and if it spent most of its time at $\min_{th}$ or under, $\max_p$ was reduced.

- Adapt K: From equation 64, K can be reduced by decreasing the averaging constant w_q. However, note that decreasing w_q causes the smoothing function to become less responsive to queue length fluctuations, which again leads to poorer regulation of the queue size.

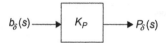

FIGURE 3.10

The proportional controller.

From equation 69, as the round trip latency increases, w_c decreases, which increases the time required for the queue to settle down. We can compensate by increasing the constant from 0.1, but the earlier analysis showed that this has the effect of decreasing the PM and thus increasing the queue oscillations.

3.4.1.2 Proportional Controllers

As shown in Figure 3.10, the RED controller from Figure 3.8 reduces to a proportional controller if K is chosen to be very large, which also corresponds to removing the low-pass filter entirely. This implies that the feedback from the bottleneck node is simply a scaled version of the (slightly delayed) queue length delta rather than the average queue length.

If we denote the proportionality factor by K_P, then from equation 65, it follows that the transfer function is given by

$$T_P(s) = U_{tcp}(s)U_{queue}(s)V_P(s)e^{-sT_0}$$

$$= \frac{\frac{K_P(CT_0)^3}{(2N)^2}e^{-sT_0}}{\left(\frac{s}{2N/CT_0^2}+1\right)\left(\frac{s}{1/T_0}+1\right)} \tag{74}$$

and in the frequency domain

$$T_P(j\omega) = |T_P(j\omega)|e^{-j \arg(T_P(j\omega))}$$

We now carry out a stability analysis for this system using the same procedure that was used for the RED controller. Hence, we will choose a critical frequency w_c such that with the appropriate choice of the controller parameters $|T_p(w_c)| \leq 1$, and then show that the PM at $\omega = w_c$ is positive, which is sufficient to prove stability.

If we choose w_c as the geometric mean of the roots $p_{TCP} = \frac{2N}{CT_0^2}$ and $p_{queue} = \frac{1}{T_0}$ so that

$$w_c = \sqrt{\frac{2N}{CT_0^3}} \tag{75}$$

then under the condition

$$K_P = \frac{\sqrt{\left(\frac{w_c}{2N/CT_0^2}\right)^2+1}\sqrt{\left(\frac{w_c}{1/T_0}\right)^2+1}}{\frac{(CT_0)^3}{(2N)^2}} \tag{76}$$

it follows from equation 74 that $|T_p(\omega_c)| = 1$. Note that this choice of K_p precisely cancels out the high loop gain caused by TCP's window dynamics. Also note that

$$\arg(T_P(j\omega_c)) = \omega_c T_0 + \tan^{-1}\frac{\omega_c}{2N/C(T_0)^2} + \tan^{-1}\frac{\omega_c}{1/T_0} \tag{77}$$

Because ω_c is the geometric mean of p_{TCP} and p_{queue}, it can be readily seen that

$$\tan^{-1}\frac{\omega_c}{2N/C(T_0)^2} + \tan^{-1}\frac{\omega_c}{1/T_0} = \frac{\pi}{2}. \tag{78}$$

Recall from equation 56 that $W_0 = \frac{T_0 C}{N}$. It is plausible that $W_0 > 2$, from which it follows that

$$\omega_c T_0 = \sqrt{\frac{2N}{CT_0}} < 1 \tag{79}$$

From equations 77 to 79, it follows that $\arg(T_P(j\omega_c)) < 1 + \frac{\pi}{2}$ radians $= 147°$; hence, the Phase Margin is given by PM $= 180° - 147° = 33°$, which proves stability of the proportional controller.

The cancellation of the loop gain using the Proportional controller constant K_p (using equation 76) is cleaner than the cancellation using L_{red} or K in RED controllers because the latter can lead to large queue length variations as we saw in the previous section. Recently proposed protocols such as DCTCP (see Chapter 7) use a proportional controller. However, a proportional controller by itself does not work well in certain situations; in particular, just like the RED controller, it may lead to a steady-state error between the steady state output and the reference value. In the next section, we discuss the PI controller, which corrects for this problem.

Figure 3.11 compares the performance of the RED and proportional controllers, and we can see that the latter has much faster response time and also lower queue size fluctuations in equilibrium.

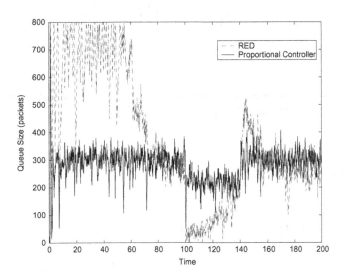

FIGURE 3.11

Comparison of the Random Early Detection (RED)and proportional controllers.

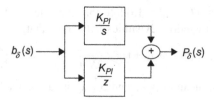

FIGURE 3.12

Block diagram of the proportional-integral (PI) controller.

3.4.1.3 Proportional-Integral (PI) Controllers

Integral controllers have the property that the steady-state buffer occupancy error is zero. It is possible to design an integral controller for AQM that can clamp the queue size to some reference value regardless of the load value. The simplest of such integral controllers is the PI controller, which is given by the transfer function (Figure 3.12):

$$V_{PI}(s) = K_{PI} \frac{\left(\frac{s}{z} + 1\right)}{s} \tag{80}$$

The transfer function for the system with the PI controller is given by

$$T_{PI}(s) = U_{tcp}(s)U_{queue}(s)V_{PI}(s)e^{-sT_0}$$

$$= \frac{\dfrac{K_{PI}(CT_0)^3}{(2N)^2}\left(\dfrac{s}{z} + 1\right)e^{-sT_0}}{s\left(\dfrac{s}{2N/CT_0^2} + 1\right)\left(\dfrac{s}{1/T_0} + 1\right)} \tag{81}$$

and in the frequency domain

$$T_{PI}(j\omega) = |T_{PI}(j\omega)|e^{-j \arg(T_{PI}(j\omega))}$$

The following choice of parameters guarantees stability of the PI controlled system:
Choose the zero z of the PI controller as

$$z = p_{tcp} = \frac{2N}{CT_0^2} \tag{82}$$

and choose the critical frequency ω_c as

$$\omega_c = \frac{\beta}{T_0} \tag{83}$$

where β is chosen to set the PM in a later step. If K_{PI} is chosen as

$$K_{PI} = \frac{\omega_c \sqrt{(\omega_c T_0)^2 + 1}}{\dfrac{(CT_0)^3}{(2N)^2}} \tag{84}$$

so that it cancels out the high loop gain caused by TCP's window dynamics, then it follows that $|T_{PI}(j\omega_c)| = 1$, and hence to show stability, it is sufficient to show that $\arg(T_{PI}(j\omega_c)) < \pi$ radians. Note that

$$\arg(T_{PI}(j\omega_c)) = \frac{\pi}{2} + \omega_c T_0 + \tan^{-1}\omega_c T_0$$

$$= \frac{\pi}{2} + \beta + \tan^{-1}\beta \qquad (85)$$

If β is chosen to be in the range $0 < \beta < 0.85$, then from equation 85, it follows that $\arg(T_{PI}(j\omega_c)) < \pi$ radians. For example, if $\beta = 0.5$, then the PM is given by $PM = 30°$.

Figure 3.13A [7] shows the result of a simulation with a bottleneck queue size of 800 packets, in which the reference b_0 of the PI controller was set to 200 packets and the traffic consisted of a mixture of http and ftp flows. It clearly shows the faster response time PI compared with the RED controller as well as the regulation of the buffer occupancy to the target size of 200 packets. Figure 3.13B shows the case when the number of flows has been increased to the point that the system is close to its capacity. Neither RED nor the proportional controllers are able to stabilize the queue because high packet drop rates have pushed the operating point beyond the size of the queue. The PI controller continues to exhibit acceptable performance, although its response time is a little slower.

The transfer function of the PI controller is described in the s domain in equation 80. For a digital implementation, this description needs to be converted into a z-transform. Using a standard bilinear transform and with the choice of a sampling frequency f_s that has to be 10 to 20 times the loop bandwidth, equation 80 can be transformed to the following

$$V_{PI}(z) = \frac{az - c}{z - 1} \qquad (86)$$

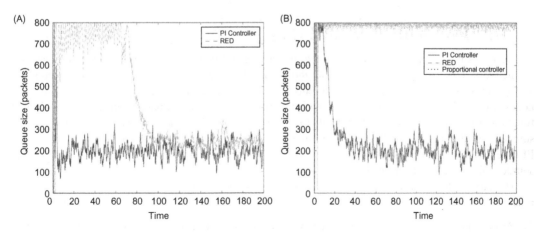

FIGURE 3.13

Comparison of the proportional-integral (PI) and Random Early Detection (RED) controllers.

The input into the controller is $b_\delta = b - b_0$, and the output is P_δ. Assuming $P_0 = 0$, it follows from (86) that

$$\frac{P(z)}{b_\delta(z)} = \frac{az - c}{z - 1} = \frac{a - cz^{-1}}{1 - z^{-1}} \tag{87}$$

This equation can be converted into a difference equation, so that at time $t = kS$, where $S = 1/f_s$

$$P(kS) = ab_\delta(kS) - cb_\delta((k-1)S) + P((k-1)S) \tag{88}$$

This equation can also be written as

$$P(kS) = (a - c)b_\delta(kS) + c(b_\delta(kS) - b_\delta((k-1)S) + P((k-1)S) \tag{89}$$

Hence, when the system converges (i.e., $P(kS)$ becomes approximately equals to $P((k-1)S)$) both $b_\delta(kS) = b(kS) - b_0(kS)$ and $b_\delta(kS) - b_\delta((k-1)S) = b(kS) - b((k-1)S)$ go to zero, which implies that the queue length has converged to the reference value b_0, and the derivative of the queue length has converged to zero. By equation 55, a zero derivative implies that that input rate of the flows to the bottleneck node exactly matches the link capacity so that there is no up or down fluctuation in the queue level.

The idea of providing difference + derivative AQM feedback has proven to be very influential and constitutes part of the standard toolkit for congestion control designers today. Recently designed algorithms such the IEEE Quantum Congestion Notification (QCN) protocol (see Chapter 8) and XCP/RCP (see Chapter 5), use this idea to stabilize their system.

Despite its superior stability properties, the implementation of PI controllers in TCP/IP networks faces the hurdle that the TCP packet header allows for only 1 bit of congestion feedback. The more recently designed IEEE QCN protocol has implemented a PI controller using 6 bits of congestion feedback in the packet header [15] and is described in Chapter 8.

3.5 THE AVERAGING PRINCIPLE (AP)

The discussion in Section 3.4 showed that to improve stability for the congestion control algorithm, the network needs to provide information about both the deviation from a target buffer occupancy and the derivative of the deviation. This puts the burden of additional complexity on the network nodes. In practice, this is more difficult to implement than when compared with adding additional functionality to the end systems instead. In this section, we will describe an ingenious way the source algorithm can be modified without touching the nodes, which has the same effect as using a PI-type AQM controller. This is done by applying the so-called Averaging Principle (AP) to the source congestion control rules [16].

The AP is illustrated in Figure 3.14. It shows a congestion control algorithm, in which the rate reacts to two factors:

1. Periodically once every τ seconds, the source changes the transmit rate R_C, either up or down, based on the feedback it is getting from the network.
2. At the midpoint between two network-induced rate changes, the source changes its rate according to the following rule: Let R_T be the value of the rate before the last feedback-induced

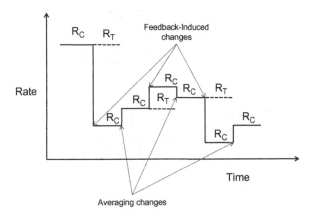

FIGURE 3.14

Averaging principle–based rate control.

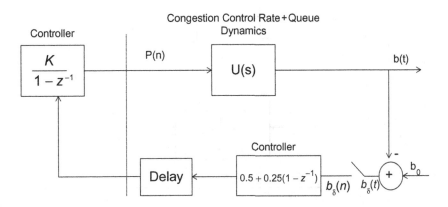

FIGURE 3.15

Equivalent Active Queue Management (AQM) control scheme to the averaging principle.

change. Then $\tau/2$ time units after every feedback induced change, the AP controller performs an "averaging change" when the rate R_C is changed as follows:

$$R_C \leftarrow \frac{R_C + R_T}{2}$$

It can be shown that there exists an AQM controller of the type that was derived in Section 3.4, given by (see Figure 3.15)

$$P(k) = 0.5Kb_\delta(k) + 0.25K(b_\delta(k) - b_\delta(k-1)) + P(k-1) \tag{90}$$

such that the AP controller is exactly equivalent to this controller.

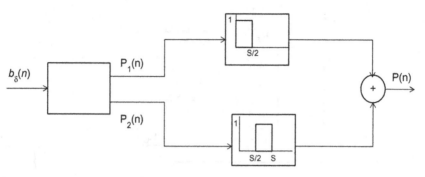

FIGURE 3.16

Controller 1.

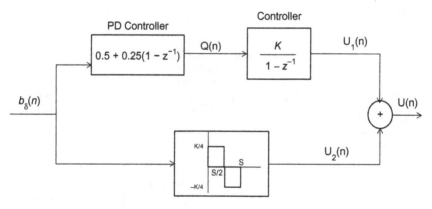

FIGURE 3.17

Controller 2.

To prove this, consider the following two controllers shown in Figures 3.16 and 3.17. Both controllers map a sequence of sampled queue error samples $b_\delta(n)$ to an input signal P(n) that drives the congestion control rate determination function. Controller 1 is an AP controller, and the upper branch of controller 2 is the AQM controller from Figure 3.17. In the following, we will show that $P(n) = U(n)$ and that the lower branch of controller 2 can be ignored, so that $P(n) \approx U_1(n)$.

The following equations describe the input-out relations for the two controllers.

Controller 1 (AP controller):

$$P_1(n) = P_2(n-1) + Kb_\delta(n) \tag{91}$$

$$P_2(n) = \frac{P_1(n) + P_2(n-1)}{2} \tag{92}$$

$$P(n) = \begin{cases} P_1(n) & if \quad nS \le t < nS + \dfrac{S}{2} \\[2ex] P_2(n) & if \quad nS + \dfrac{S}{2} \le t < nS + S \end{cases} \tag{93}$$

Controller 2 (approximate PD controller):

$$U_1(n) = U_1(n-1) + KQ(n) \tag{94}$$

$$Q(n) = 0.5b_\delta(n) + 0.25(b_\delta(n) - b_\delta(n-1)) \tag{95}$$

$$U_2(n) = \begin{cases} \dfrac{K}{4}b_\delta(n) & nS \le t < nS + \dfrac{S}{2} \\[2ex] -\dfrac{K}{4}b_\delta(n) & nS + \dfrac{S}{2} \le t < nS + S \end{cases} \tag{96}$$

$$U(n) = U_1(n) + U_2(n) \tag{97}$$

Define

$$P_m(n) = \frac{P_1(n) + P_2(n)}{2} \tag{98}$$

From equations 91 and 92, it follows that

$$\begin{aligned} P_m(n) &= \frac{P_2(n-1) + Kb_\delta(n)}{2} + \frac{P_1(n) + P_2(n-1)}{4} \\[1ex] &= \frac{P_2(n-1)}{2} + \frac{Kb_\delta(n)}{2} + \frac{P_2(n-1)}{4} + \frac{Kb_\delta(n)}{4} + \frac{P_2(n-1)}{4} \\[1ex] &= P_2(n-1) + \frac{3K}{4}b_\delta(n) \end{aligned} \tag{99}$$

We now show that

$$P_1(n) = P_m(n) + \frac{K}{4}b_\delta(n), \text{ and} \tag{100}$$

$$P_2(n) = P_m(n) - \frac{K}{4}b_\delta(n) \tag{101}$$

To prove equation 100, note that from equations 99 and 91, it follows that

$$P_m(n) = P_1(n) - Kb_\delta(n) + \frac{3K}{4}b_\delta(n) = P_1(n) - \frac{Kb_\delta(n)}{4}.$$

To prove equation 101, first note from equations 99 and 92 that

$$\begin{aligned} P_m(n) &= 2P_2(n) - P_1(n) + \frac{3K}{4}b_\delta(n) \\[1ex] &= 2P_2(n) - (2P_m(n) - P_2(n)) + \frac{3K}{4}b_\delta(n) \\[1ex] &= 3P_2(n) - 2P_m(n) + \frac{3K}{4}b_\delta(n) \end{aligned}$$

Comparing equations 100 and 101 with equations 96 and 97, it follows that if we can show $U_1(n) = P_m(n)$, then it follows that $U(n) = P(n)$, and the two controllers will be equivalent. This can be done by showing that $U_1(n)$ and $P_m(n)$ satisfy the same recursions.

From equations 99, 101, and 95, it follows that

$$P_m(n) \quad = P_m(n-1) - \frac{Kb_\delta(n-1)}{4} + \frac{3K}{4}b_\delta(n)$$

$$= P_m(n-1) + KQ(n) \tag{102}$$

Comparing equations 102 and 94, it follows that $P_m(n) = U_1(n)$ for all n, and as a consequence we get $P(n) = U(n)$ (i.e., the two controllers are equivalent). Because the contribution of $U_2(n)$ can be ignored [16], it follows that $P(n) \approx U_1(n)$, and the AQM and AP controllers are almost identical.

We will encounter congestion control protocols such a TCP BIC later in the book (see Chapter 5) that are able to operate in a stable manner in very high-speed networks even with traditional AQM schemes. These protocols may owe their stability to the fact that their rate control rules incorporate averaging of the type discussed here.

3.6 IMPLICATIONS FOR CONGESTION CONTROL ALGORITHMS

From the analysis in the previous few sections, a few broad themes emerge that have influenced the design of congestion control algorithms in recent years:

- AQM schemes that incorporate the first or higher derivatives of the buffer occupancy process lead to more stable and responsive systems. This was shown to be the case in the analysis of the PI controller. Also, because the first derivative of the buffer occupancy process can be written as

$$\frac{db(t)}{dt} = C - \sum_i R_i$$

  it also follows that knowing the derivative is equivalent to knowing how close the queue is to its saturation point C. Some protocols such as QCN (see Chapter 8) feed back the value of db/dt directly, and others such as XCP and RCP (see Chapter 5) feed back the rate difference in the RHS of the equation.
- If the network cannot accommodate sophisticated AQM algorithms (which is the case for TCP/IP networks), then an AP-based algorithm can have an equivalent effect on system stability and performance as the derivative-based feedback. Examples of algorithms that have taken this route include the BIC and CUBIC algorithms (see Chapter 5) and QCN (see Chapter 8).

3.7 FURTHER READING

Instead of taking the dual approach to solving equations 7 and 8 it is possible to solve the primal problem directly by eliminating the rate constraint condition (equation 8) and modifying the objective function as follows [9]:

$$U(r_1, \ldots, r_N) = \sum_{i=1}^{N} U_i(r_i) - \sum_{l=1}^{L} \int_0^{Y_l(t)} f_l(y)dy \tag{103}$$

where $U_i(r_i)$ are strictly concave functions and the increasing, continuous function f_l is interpreted as a congestion price function at link l and the convex function $\int_0^{Y_l(t)} f_l(y)dy$ is known as the barrier function. To impose the constraint that the sum of the data rates at a link should be less than the link capacity, the barrier function can be chosen in a way such that it increases to infinity when the arrival rate approaches the link capacity.

It follows that $U(r_1,\ldots,r_N)$ is a strictly concave function and it can be shown that the problem

$$\max_{r_i \geq 0} U(r_1, \ldots, r_N) \tag{104}$$

decomposes into N separate optimization subproblems that can be solved independently at each of the sources. The solution to the optimization problem at each source node is given by

$$U_i'(r_i) = \sum_{l:l \in A_i} f_l\left(\sum_{s:s \in B_l} r_s\right) \tag{105}$$

where A_i is the set of nodes that connection i passes through and B_l is the set of connections that pass through node l. This can be interpreted as a congestion feedback of $f_l(\sum_s r_s)$ back to the source from each of the nodes that the connection passes through, and is the equivalent of equation 11 for the dual problem.

Just as we used the gradient projection method to obtain an iterative solution to the dual problem (equation 13), we can also apply this technique to iteratively solve the primal problem, leading to the following expression for the optimal rates:

$$\frac{dr_i}{dt} = k_i(r_i)\left(U_i'(r_i) - \sum_{l:l \in A_i} f_l\left(\sum_{s:s \in B_l} r_s\right)\right) \tag{106}$$

where k_r is any nondecreasing continuous function such that $k_r(x) > 0$ for $x > 0$. If $k_r > 0$, then in equilibrium setting, $dr_i/dt = 0$ leads back to equation 105. Equation 106 is known as the primal algorithm for the congestion control problem. For example, equation 33 for TCP Reno for small values of Q_i can be put in the form

$$\frac{dR_i(t)}{dt} = \frac{2R_i^2(t)}{3}\left(\frac{3}{2T_i^2 R_i^2(t)} - Q_i\right)$$

which is in the form (106) with

$$k_i(r_i) = \frac{2r_i^2(t)}{3} \quad \text{and} \quad U_i'(r_i) = \frac{3}{2T_i^2 r_i^2(t)} \tag{107}$$

Equation 38 for the utility function can then be obtained using equation 107.

A very good description of the field of optimization and control theory applied to congestion control is given in Srikant's book [9]. It has a detailed discussion of the barrier function approach to system optimization, as well as several examples of the application of the Nyquist criterion to various types of congestion control algorithms.

For cases when the system equilibrium point falls on a point on nonlinearity, the linearization technique is no longer applicable. In this case, techniques such as Lyapunov's second theorem have been applied to study system stability.

APPENDIX 3.A LINEARIZATION OF THE FLUID FLOW MODEL

The right-hand sides of the fluid flow model for TCP congestion control that analyzed Section 3.4 are as follows:

$$f(W, W_R, b, p) = \frac{1}{T(t)} - \frac{W(t)W^R(t)}{2T(t)} p(t - T(t))$$

$$g(W, b) = \frac{W(t)}{T(t)} N(t) - C \tag{A1}$$

where $T(t) = \frac{b(t)}{C} + D$, $W_R(t) = W(t - T(t))$ and $T_R(t) = T(t - T(t))$.

We wish to linearize these equations about their equilibrium points

$$W_0^2 P_0 = 2 \quad \text{and} \quad W_0 = \frac{CT_0}{N}.$$

This can be done using the perturbation formula

$$f_\delta(t) = \frac{\partial f}{\partial W} W_\delta + \frac{\partial f}{\partial W^R} W_\delta^R + \frac{\partial f}{\partial b} b_\delta + \frac{\partial f}{\partial p} p_\delta \quad \text{and} \tag{A2}$$

$$g_\delta(t) = \frac{\partial g}{\partial b} b_\delta + \frac{\partial g}{\partial W} W_\delta. \tag{A3}$$

By using straightforward differentiation, it can be shown that

$$\frac{\partial f}{\partial W} = \frac{\partial f}{\partial W_R} = -\frac{N}{CT_0^2}$$

$$\frac{\partial f}{\partial b} = 0$$

$$\frac{\partial f}{\partial p} = \frac{C^2 T_0}{2N^2} \tag{A4}$$

$$\frac{\partial g}{\partial b} = -\frac{1}{T_0}$$

$$\frac{\partial g}{\partial W} = \frac{N}{T_0}$$

Substituting equation A4 back into equations A2 and A3 and then into the original differential equation, we obtain the linearized equations

$$\frac{dW_\delta(t)}{dt} = -\frac{2N}{CT_0^2} W_\delta(t) - \frac{C^2 T_0}{2N^2} P_\delta(t - T_0)$$

$$\frac{db_\delta(t)}{dt} = \frac{N}{T_0} W_\delta(t) - \frac{1}{T_0} b_\delta(t) \tag{A5}$$

APPENDIX 3.B **THE NYQUIST STABILITY CRITERION**

The Nyquist criterion is used to study the stability of systems that can modeled by linear differential equations in the presence of a feedback loop. In Figure 3.B1, G(s) is the Laplace transform of the system being controlled, and H(s) is the Laplace transform of the feedback function. It can be easily shown that the end-to-end transform for this system is given by

$$L(s) = \frac{Y(s)}{U(s)} = \frac{G(s)}{1 + G(s)H(s)} \tag{B1}$$

To ensure stability, all the roots of the equation $1 + G(s)H(s) = 0$, which in general are complex numbers, have to lie in the left half of the complex plane. The Nyquist criterion is a technique for verifying this condition that is often easier to apply than finding the roots, and it also provides additional insights into the problem.

Nyquist criterion: Let C be a close contour that encircles the right half of the complex plane, such that no poles or zeroes of H(s)G(s) lie on C. Let Z and P denote the number of poles and zeroes, respectively, of H(s)G(s) that lie inside C. Then the number of times M that $H(j\omega)G(j\omega)$ encircles the point $(-1,0)$ in the clockwise direction, as ω is varied from $-\infty$ to $+\infty$, is equal to Z − P.

Note that the contour C in the procedure described above is chosen so that it encompasses the right half of the complex plane. *As ω is varied from $-\infty$ to $+\infty$*, the function $H(j\omega)G(j\omega)$ maps these points to the target complex plane, where it describes a curve. For the system to be stable, we require that $Z = 0$, and because $M = Z - P$, it follows that:

- If $P = 0$, then stability requires that $M = 0$, that is, there should no clockwise encirclements of the point $(-1,0)$ by the locus of $H(j\omega)G(j\omega)$.
- If $P > 0$, then $M = -P$, i.e., the locus of $H(j\omega)G(j\omega)$ should encircle the point $(-1,0)$ P times in the counterclockwise direction.

Figure 3.B2 shows an example of the application of the Nyquist criterion to the function $G(j\omega)$ along with some important features. Note that curve for $G(j\omega)$ goes to $-\infty$ as $\omega \to 0$, and approaches 0 as $\omega \to 0$. We will use the notation $G(j\omega) = |G(j\omega)|e^{-j\,\arg(G(j\omega))}$, where $|G(j\omega)|$ is the

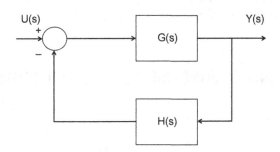

FIGURE 3.B1

Feedback control system.

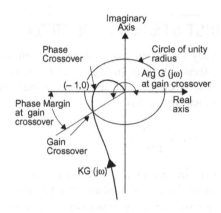

FIGURE 3.B2

An example of a Nyquist plot.

length of the line going from the origin to $G(j\omega)$ and $\arg(G(j\omega))$ is the angle that this line makes with the real axis. Note the following features in the graph:

- The point $(-a, 0)$ where the $G(j\omega)$ curve intersects with the real axis is called the phase crossover point because at this point $\arg(G(j\omega)) = \pi$. The gain margin (GM) of the system is defined by the distance between the phase crossover point and the $(-1, 0)$, i.e.,

$$GM = 1 - a \tag{B2}$$

- As the Gain Margin decreases, the system tends towards instability.
- The point where the $G(j\omega)$ curve intersects with the unit circle is called the gain crossover point because at this point $|G(j\omega)| = 1$. The phase margin (PM) of the system is defined by the angle between the crossover point and the negative real axis. Just as for the GM, a smaller PM means that the system is tending toward instability. Generally a PM of between 30 and 60 degrees is preferred.

In the applications of the Nyquist criterion in this book, we usually find a point ω_c such that $|G(j\omega_c)| \leq 1$. This implies that the gain crossover point ω_* is such that $0 \leq \omega_* \leq \omega_c$. Hence, if we can prove that $\arg(G(j\omega_c)) < \pi$, then the system will be stable.

APPENDIX 3.C TRANSFER FUNCTION FOR THE RED CONTROLLER

In this appendix, we derive the expression for the transfer function of the RED controller [17], which is diagrammed in Figure 3.C1 and is given by

$$V_{red}(s) = \frac{L_{red}}{\frac{s}{K} + 1} \quad \text{where}$$

$$L_{red} = \frac{\max_p}{\max_{th} - \min_{th}} \quad \text{and} \quad K = -\frac{\log(1 - w_q)}{\delta}$$

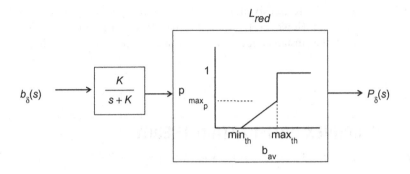

FIGURE 3.C1

Transfer function for the Random Early Detection (RED) controller.

We start with the following equation that describes the operation of the queue averaging process

$$x((k+1)\delta) = (1 - w_q)x(k\delta) + w_q b(k\delta) \qquad \text{(C1)}$$

where $b(k\delta)$ is instantaneous queue length at the sampling time $k\delta$ and $x(k\delta)$ is the average queue length at that time. Assume that this difference equation can be put in the form of the following differential equation

$$\frac{dx}{dt} = Kx(t) + Lb(t)$$

Then, in a sampled data system, $x(t_{k+1})$ can be written

$$x(t_{k+1}) = e^{K(t_{k+1} - t_k)}x(t_k) + \int_{t_k}^{t_{k+1}} e^{K(t_{k+1} - \tau)}Lb(t_k)d\tau$$

$$= e^{K\delta}x(t_k) - (1 - e^{K\delta})\frac{Lb(t_k)}{K} \qquad \text{(C2)}$$

Comparing (C1) with (C2), it follows that $L = -K$ and

$$1 - w_q = e^{K\delta} \text{ so that}$$

$$K = \frac{\log_e(1 - w_q)}{\delta}$$

Hence, the differential equation for the averaging process is given by $\frac{dx}{dt} = Kx(t) - Kb(t)$, which in the transform space translates into

$$\frac{X(s)}{b(s)} = \frac{K}{s + K}$$

This signal is further passed through the thresholding process as shown in Figure 3.B1 before yielding the final output that is fed back to the source.

Note that K determines the responsiveness of the filter so higher the value of K, the faster it will respond to sudden change. However, too high a value for K will result in the situation in which the filter starts tracking the instantaneous value of the buffer size, resulting in continuous oscillations.

APPENDIX 3.D **CONVEX OPTIMIZATION THEORY**

Definition 1: A set C is said to be convex if the following property holds:

$$ax + (1 - a)y \in C, \quad \forall x, y \in C, \alpha \in (0, 1] \tag{D1}$$

Definition 2: Define the function $f:C \rightarrow R^n$, where $C \in R^n$ is a convex set. The function is said to be convex if

$$f(ax + (1 - a)y) \leq af(x) + (1 - a)f(y) \quad \forall x, y \in C, \quad \forall a \in [0, 1]. \tag{D2a}$$

The function is said to be concave if

$$f(ax + (1 - a)y) \geq af(x) + (1 - a)f(y) \quad \forall x, y \in C, \quad \forall a \in [0, 1]. \tag{D2b}$$

The function is said to be strictly convex (concave) if the above inequalities are strict when $x \neq y$ *and* $a \in (0, 1]$.

Consider the following optimization problem:

$$\max_x f(x) \tag{D3a}$$

subject to

$$Px \leq b$$
$$Qx = 0 \tag{D3b}$$

where f(x) is a differentiable concave function and P and Q are matrices. The values of x that satisfy the constraints (D3b) form a convex set.

The Lagrangian function L for this problem is defined by

$$L(x, \lambda, \mu) = f(x) - \lambda^T(Px - c) - \mu^T Qx \tag{D4}$$

where $\lambda \geq 0, \mu$ are called the dual variables or the Lagrangian multipliers for this problem.

Karush-Kuhn-Tucker theorem: x is a solution to the optimization problem (D3a–b) if and only if it satisfies the following conditions:

$$\Delta f(x) - P^T \lambda - Q^T \mu = 0$$
$$\lambda^T(Px - b) = 0$$
$$Px \leq b \tag{D5}$$
$$Qx = 0$$
$$\lambda \geq 0$$

Definition 3: Define the dual function $D(\lambda, \mu)$ by

$$D(\lambda, \mu) = \max_{x \in C} L(x, \lambda, \mu) \qquad (D6)$$

where C is the set of all x that satisfy the constraints(D3b).

Strong Duality Theorem: Let $\hat{x}$ be the point that solves the constrained optimization problem (equations D3a and D3b). If the Slater constraint qualification conditions are satisfied, then

$$\inf_{\lambda \geq 0, \mu} D(\lambda, \mu) = f(\hat{x}) \qquad (D7)$$

APPENDIX 3.E **A GENERAL CLASS OF UTILITY FUNCTIONS**

Consider a network with K connections and define the following utility function for connection k [10], given by

$$U_k(r_k) = w_k \frac{r^{1-\alpha_k}}{1 - \alpha_k} \quad k = 1, \ldots, K \qquad (E1)$$

for some $\alpha_k > 0$, where r is the steady state throughput for connection k. Note that the parameters α_k controls the trade-off between fairness and efficiency. Consider the following special cases for $1 \leq k \leq K$:

$$\alpha_k = 0: \quad U_k(r_k) = w_k r_k \qquad (E2)$$

This utility function assigns no value to fairness and simply measures total throughput.

$$\alpha_k = 1: \quad U_k(r_k) = \lim_{\alpha_k \to 1} w_k \frac{r^{1-\alpha_k}}{1 - \alpha_k} = w_k \log r_k \qquad (E3)$$

This network resource allocation that minimizes this utility function is known as weighted proportionally fair. The logarithmic factor means that an algorithm that minimizes this function will cut down one user's allocation by half as long as it can increase another user's allocation by more than half. The TCP Vegas algorithm has been shown to minimize this utility function.

$$\alpha_k = 2: U_k(r_k) = \frac{w_k}{r_k} \qquad (E4)$$

The network resource allocation corresponding to this utility function is called weighted minimal potential delay fair, and as shown in this chapter, this is function TCP Reno minimizes. This metric seeks to minimize the total time of fixed-length file transfers.

$$\alpha_k = \alpha, w_k = 1 \quad \forall k: U_k(r_k) = \lim_{\alpha \to \infty} \frac{r_k^{1-\alpha}}{1 - \alpha} \qquad (E5)$$

Minimizing this metric is equivalent to achieving max-min fairness in the network [9].

REFERENCES

[1] Kelly FP. Fairness and stability of end-to-end congestion control. Eur J Control 2003;9:149−65.
[2] Kelly FP, Maulloo AK. Tan DKH. Rate control for communication networks: shadow pricing, proportional fairness and stability. J Oper Res Soc 1998;49(3):237−52.
[3] Low SH. A duality model of TCP and queue management algorithms. IEEE/ACM Trans Netw 2003;11 (4):525−36.
[4] Low SH, Lapsley DE. Optimization flow control I: basic algorithm and convergence. IEEE/ACM Trans Netw 1999;7(6):861−74.
[5] Kunniyur S, Srikant R. End-to-end congestion control schemes: utility functions, random losses and ECN marks. UIUC CSL 2000;3:1323−32.
[6] Holot CV, Misra V, Towsley D, Gong W-B. A control theoretic analysis of RED. IEEE INFOCOM 2001;3:1510−19.
[7] Holot CV, Misra V, Towsley D, Gong W-B. On designing improved controllers for AQM routers supporting TCP flows. IEEE INFOCOM 2001;3:1726−34.
[8] Low SH, Paganini F, Doyle JC. Internet congestion control. IEEE Control Syst 2002;22(1):28−43.
[9] Srikant R. The Mathematics of Internet Congestion Control. Reinach: Birkhauser; 2004.
[10] Mo J, Walrand J. Fair end-to-end window based congestion control. IEEE/ACM Trans Netw 2000;8 (5):556−67.
[11] Bansal D, Balakrishnan H. Binomial congestion control algorithms. IEEE INFOCOM 2001;2:631−40.
[12] Vinnicombe G. On the stability of networks operating TCP-like congestion control. Proc IFAC World Congress, Barcelona, 2002.
[13] Ogata K. Modern control engineering. 5th ed. Boston, MA: Prentice-Hall; 2009.
[14] Feng W, Kandlur D, Saha D, et al. A self-configuring RED gateway. IEEE INFOCOM 1999;3:1320−8.
[15] Alizadeh M, Atikoglu B, Kabbani A, et al. Data center transport mechanisms: congestion control theory and IEEE standardization. 46th annual allerton conference, 2008. p. 1270−1277.
[16] Alizadeh M, Kabbani A, Atigoglu B, Prabhakar B. Stability analysis of QCN: the averaging principle. ACM SIGMETRICS, 2011. p. 49−60.
[17] Misra V, Gong W, Towsley D. Fluid based analysis of a network of AQM routers supporting TCP flows with an application to RED. ACM SIGCOMM 2000;30(4):151−60.

SUGGESTED READING

Le Boudec JY. Rate adaptation, congestion control and fairness: a tutorial. Ecole Lausanne: Polytechnique Fédérale de Lausanne; 2012.
Gibbens RJ, Kelly FP. Resource pricing and the evolution of congestion control. Automatica 1999;35 (12):1969−85.
Low SH, Paganini F, Wang J, Doyle JC. Linear stability of TCP/RED and a scalable control. Comput Netw 2003;43(5):633−47.
Massoulie L, Roberts J. Bandwidth sharing: objectives and algorithms. IEEE/ACM Trans Netw 2002;10 (3):320−8.

APPLICATIONS

2

CONGESTION CONTROL IN BROADBAND WIRELESS NETWORKS

4.1 INTRODUCTION

When users access the Internet using cable, DSL, or wireless mediums, they are doing so over access networks. Over the course of the past 20 years, these networks have been deployed worldwide and today constitute the most common way to access the Internet for consumers. These networks are characterized by transmission mediums such as air, cable, or copper lines, which presented formidable barriers to the reliable transmission of digital data. These problems have been gradually overcome with advances in networking algorithms and physical media modulation technology so that reliable high-speed communication over access networks is a reality today.

In this chapter, the objective is to discuss congestion control over broadband wireless networks. Common examples of broadband wireless networks deployed today include WiFi networks that operate in the unlicensed frequency bands and broadband cellular networks such as 2G, 3G, and LTE that operate in service provider—owned licensed bands. When TCP is used as the transport protocol over these networks, it runs into a number of problems that are not commonly found in wireline networks; some of these are enumerated in Section 4.2. As a result, a lot of effort over the past 10 to 15 years has gone into finding ways in which the wireless medium can be made more data friendly. A lot of this work has gone into improving the wireless physical layer with more robust modulation and more powerful error correction schemes, but equally important have been the advances in the Medium Access Control (MAC) and Transport Layers. Some of this effort has gone into modifying the congestion control algorithm to overcome wireless-related link impairments, and this is the work that described in this chapter.

The fundamental problem that hobbles TCP over wireless links is the fact that it cannot differentiate between congestion and link-error related packet drops. As a result, it reacts to link errors by reducing its transmit window, but the more appropriate reaction would be to retransmit the lost packet. By using the expression for the average TCP throughput that was derived in Chapter 2,

$$R_{avg} = \frac{1}{T}\sqrt{\frac{3}{2p}}$$

this problem can be solved in several ways:

- By making the wireless link more robust by using channel coding: This leads to a reduction in the wireless link error rate p.
- By retransmitting the lost packets quickly at lower layers of the stack (called Automatic Retransmissions [ARQ]), so that TCP does not see the drops. This also leads to a reduction in p at the cost of an increase in T because of retransmissions.
- By introducing special algorithms at the TCP source that are able to differentiate between congestion drops and link-error related drops. We will discuss one such algorithm called TCP Westwood, which we will show has the same effect on the throughput as a reduction in the link error rate p.
- By splitting the end-to-end TCP connection into two parts, such that the wireless link falls into a part whose congestion control has been specially designed for wireless environments. This technique works because by splitting the connection, we reduce the latency T for each of the resulting two connections. Furthermore, the use of one of the three techniques mentioned above can reduce p.

Modern broadband wireless systems such as LTE have largely solved the link error caused packet drop problem through a combination of strong channel coding and retransmissions. In fact, recent studies of wireless link performance show very few packet losses. However, link errors have been replaced by a new problem in these networks, namely, a large amount of variability in the link latency, leading to a problem that has been christened "bufferbloat."

The rest of this chapter is organized as follows. In Section 4.2, we introduce the broadband wireless architecture and enumerate the problems that wireless networks present for TCP. In Sections 4.3 and 4.4, we describe several techniques that are used to improve TCP performance in wireless networks, including Split Connections, Bandwidth Estimators, Loss Discrimination Algorithms, and Zero Receive Window (ZRW) ACKs. We illustrate these ideas with a description and analysis of TCP Westwood, which was specifically designed for wireless environments. In Section 4.5, we use the analytical tools developed in Chapter 2 to do performance modeling of TCP running over wireless links that implement techniques such Forward Error Correction (FEC) and Automatic Retransmissions (ARQ) to improve robustness. In Section 4.6, we analyze the bufferbloat issue, its causes, and some of the solutions that have been suggested. Section 4.7 has some useful rules that can be used to test whether link errors are indeed causing packet drops and the effectiveness of various techniques to combat it.

An initial reading of this chapter can be done in the sequence $4.1 \rightarrow 4.2 \rightarrow 4.3 \rightarrow 4.4 \rightarrow 4.7$ (for those interested in techniques to overcome wireless related link errors) or in the sequence $4.1 \rightarrow 4.2 \rightarrow 4.6 \rightarrow 4.7$ (for those interested in the bufferbloat problem and its solutions). Section 4.5 has more advanced material on the analysis of FEC and ARQ algorithms.

4.2 WIRELESS ACCESS ARCHITECTURE AND ISSUES

Figure 4.1 is a simplified picture of typical cellular network architecture. Mobile users are connected to a base station unit over a shared wireless connection, and their traffic is backhauled to a wireless gateway, which serves as the demarcation point between the cellular network and the rest of the Internet. The cellular base station is responsible for transforming the digital signal into an analogue waveform for

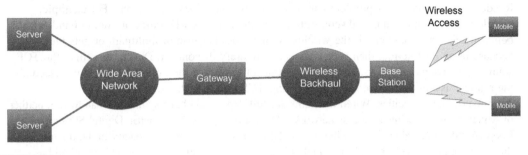

FIGURE 4.1

Cellular wireless architecture.

over-the-air transmission, as well as for efficiently sharing the shared wireless medium among multiple users. Modulation techniques have improved over the years, and today both WiFi and LTE networks use an algorithm called OFDMA (orthogonal frequency-division multiplexing). OFDMA is extremely robust against multipath fading, which is the main cause of signal distortion in cellular wireless. All traffic going to the mobiles is constrained to pass through the gateway, which is responsible for higher level functions such as enabling user mobility between base stations and user authentication, sleep mode control, and so on. This gateway is called a packet gateway (PGW) in LTE networks, and Gateway GPRS Support Node (GGSN) or Packet Data Serving Node (PDSN) in 3G networks.

Some of the issues that cause performance problems for TCP in wireless networks are the following:

- Higher link error rates: This has traditionally been the biggest problem with wireless networks and is caused by difficult propagation conditions in the air, leading to high link attenuations and multipath creating reflections from surrounding objects. With the improvement in modulation and network coding techniques over the past 20 years, the error rates have decreased significantly, but they are still much higher compared with wired transmission mediums.
- High link latency: Higher link latency in access networks is partially caused by the physical layer technology used to overcome wireless medium—related transmission problems. A good example of this coding technology is FEC, which helps to make the medium more reliable but leads to higher latency. Also, the MAC layer algorithm operating on top of the physical layer, which is used to share the access medium more efficiently and provide quality of service (QoS) guarantees, introduces latencies of its own. This problem was particularly onerous in the first generation cellular data networks, namely GPRS, which had link latencies of the order of 1 second or more. The latency decreased to about 100 ms in 3G networks and is about 50 ms in LTE. This is still a fairly large number considering that coast-to-coast latency across the continental United States is about 23 ms.
- Large delay variations: This is common in wireless cellular networks and is caused by the base station adapting its physical layer transmission parameters such as modulation and coding, as a function of link conditions, on a user by user basis. This causes the effective channel capacity to fluctuate over a wide range, leading to a phenomenon called bufferbloat. This is caused by the fact the TCP window can never be perfectly matched with the varying link capacity, and at times when the capacity is low and the window is much bigger, the buffer occupancy increases, as shown in Chapter 2.

- Random disconnects: This problem can be caused by one of several reasons. For example, mobile users are momentarily disconnected from the network when they are doing hand-offs between cells. Alternatively, if the wireless signal fades because of multipath or gets blocked because of an obstruction, then it can cause a temporary disconnect. During this time, the TCP source stops receiving ACKs, and if the disconnect time is of the order of 100s of milliseconds, the retransmission timer expires, thus affecting TCP throughput.
- Asymmetric link capacities: Wired mediums are full duplex and have symmetric bandwidth, neither of which is true for wireless access networks. Networks such as Asymmetric Digital Subscriber Loop (ADSL) and Cable Hybrid Fiber Coax (HFC) posses much more capacity in the downlink direction compared with the uplink, and this is also true for cellular wireless. This problem has lessened with the introduction of newer technologies, but it still cannot be ignored. When the uplink has much lower bandwidth compared with the downlink, then the inter-ACK time interval is no longer a good estimate of the bandwidth of the downlink bottleneck capacity; hence, TCP's self-clocking mechanism breaks down. The analysis in Chapter 2 has been extended to asymmetric links by Lakshman and Madhow [1] and Varma [2].

4.3 SPLIT-CONNECTION TCP

This section describes and analyzes Split-Connection TCP. This is not a new congestion control algorithm but a way to change the structure of the congestion control system so that the problematic part of the network can be isolated. This is done by abandoning the end-to-end nature of the TCP transport layer in favor of multiple TCP-controlled segments in series (Figure 4.2).

As shown, the end-to-end connection traverses two segments in series, the wide area network (WAN) network and the wireless network, with the gateway node that was introduced in Section 4.2 at the boundary between the two. The TCP connection from a server in the WAN to a mobile client is split into two parts, with the first TCP connection (called TCP1) extending from the server to the gateway, and the second TCP connection (called TCP2) extending from the gateway to the client node. The system operates as follows:

- When the server initiates a TCP connection with a client, the connection set-up message is intercepted by the gateway, which then proceeds to do the following: (1) reply to the connection set-up back to the server, as if it were the client, thus establishing the TCP1 connection, and (2) establish the TCP2 connection with the client, with itself as the end point.

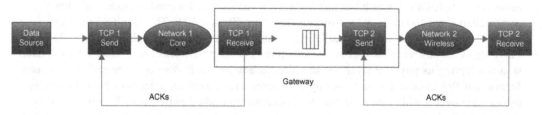

FIGURE 4.2

Split TCP connection.

- During the data transfer phase of the connection, the gateway intercepts all packets coming from the server over TCP1 and immediately ACKs them back. At the same time, it forwards the packet on TCP2 to the client and discards it after it receives the corresponding ACK from the client.
- If the TCP2 is operating at a slower speed than TCP1, then the data buffers in the gateway start to fill up, and the gateway then proceed to backpressure the server by reducing the size of the receive window in TCP1's ACK packets.

The design described differs from the one in the original paper on split TCP [3] in the following way: Bakre and Badrinath assumed that the TCP connection would be split at the wireless base station rather than at the gateway. Doing so introduces some additional complications into the design because if the mobile client moves from one base station to another, then the entire state information about the connection and the buffered packets have to be transferred to the new base station. In the design shown in Figure 4.2, on the other hand, this situation is avoided because the split happens at the gateway node, which remains the same even as the client changes base stations.

The benefits of a split-connection TCP design are the following:

- The TCP congestion control algorithms operating on each segment of the network can be tailored to the specific characteristics of the network. The core network is typically constructed from highly reliable optical connections and hence has very low link error rates. The access network, on the other hand, may present several transmission-related problems that were described earlier. As a result, the congestion control algorithm over the wireless network can be specially tailored to overcome these link problems. Note that this can be done without making any changes to TCP1, which is typically running on some server in the Internet and hence cannot be modified easily
- Because of the way that TCP throughput varies as a function of the round trip latency and link error rates, the split-connection design can result in a significant boost to the throughput even in the case in which legacy TCP is used on both connections. This claim is proven below.

Define the following:

R_{ns}: Throughput of the end-to-end non-split TCP connection
R_{sp}: End-to-end throughput for the split-TCP connection
R_1: Throughput of TCP1 in the split-connection case
R_2: Throughput of TCP2 in the split-connection case
T: Round trip latency for the non-split connection
T_2: Round trip latency for TCP2 in the split-connection case
q_2: Error rate for the bottleneck link in the wireless network

For the non-split case, we will assume that the bottleneck link is located in the wireless network.

Using the formula for TCP throughput developed in Chapter 2, it follows that the TCP throughput for the non-split case is given by

$$R_{ns} = \frac{1}{T}\sqrt{\frac{3}{2q_2}} \qquad (1)$$

For the split-TCP connection, the end-to-end throughput is given by

$$R_{sp} = \min(R_1, R_2) \tag{2}$$

Because the end-to-end bottleneck for the non-split connection exists in the wireless network, it follows that even for the split case, this node will cause the throughput of TCP2 to be lower than that of TCP1, so that

$$R_{sp} = R_2 \tag{3}$$

Note that the throughput over the access network in the split-connection network is given approximately by

$$R_2 \approx \frac{1}{T_2}\sqrt{\frac{3}{2q_2}} \tag{4}$$

This formula is not exact because it was derived in Chapter 2 under the assumption of a persistent data source that never runs short of packets to transmit. In the split-connection case, the data source for TCP2 is the packets being delivered to it by TCP1, which may run dry from time to time. However, for the case when $R_2 < R_1$, the higher speed core network will feed packets faster than the wireless network can handle it, thus leading to a backlog in the receive buffers in the gateway node. Hence, equation 4 serves as good approximation to the actual throughput.

It follows that

$$\frac{R_{sp}}{R_{ns}} \approx \frac{T}{T_2} > 1 \tag{5}$$

which implies that simply splitting the TCP connection causes the end-to-end throughput to increase. The intuitive reason for this result is the following. By splitting the connection, we reduced the round trip latency of each of the resulting split connections compared with the original, thus boosting their throughput.

If the connection over the wireless network is completely lost over extended periods of time, as is common in cellular networks, and then TCP2 stops transmitting, and the gateway ultimately runs out of buffers and shuts down the TCP1 by reducing its receive window size to zero. This shows that TCP1 is not completely immune to problems in the wireless network even under the split-connection design. Hence, it is necessary to introduce additional mechanisms to boost TCP2's performance over and above what TCP Reno can deliver. Techniques to do this are described in the remainder of this chapter.

From equation 5, it is clear that when T and T_2 are approximately equal (as in satellite access networks), then R_{ns} is approximately equal to R_{sp}, that is, there are no performance benefits to splitting the connection. However, equation 5 assumes that plain TCP Reno is being used for TCP2. If instead we modify TCP2 so that it is more suited to the access network, then we may still see a performance benefit by splitting the connection. For example, in satellite networks, if we modify the window increment rule for TCP2 and use a much larger window size than the one allowed for by TCP Reno, then there will be a boost in the split network performance.

The main issues with the split TCP design are the following:

- Additional complexity: Split TCP requires that the gateway maintain per-connection state. In the original design, the splitting was done at the base station, where processing power could be an issue; however, the gateway-based implementation makes this less of an issue because most gateways are based on high-end routers. Migrating the state from one base station to another on client handoff was another complication in the original design that is avoided in the proposed design.

- The end-to-end throughput for split TCP may not show much improvement if the connection over the wireless network is performing badly. Hence split TCP has to go hand in hand with additional mechanisms to boost the performance of TCP2.
- Split TCP violates the end-to-end semantics for TCP because the sending host may receive an ACK for a packet over TCP1 before it has been delivered to the client.

4.4 ALGORITHMS TO IMPROVE PERFORMANCE OVER LOSSY LINKS

The analysis in Section 4.3 showed that by simply splitting the TCP connection, we got an improvement in TCP throughput because the round trip delay over the wireless network is lower than the end-to-end latency for the non-split connection. For the case when link conditions in the wireless network are so bad that performance boost caused by the lower latency in the access is overwhelmed by the performance impact of link losses, we need to modify TCP2 to combat the link-specific problems that exist there. Note that these enhancements can also be implemented for the non-split TCP connection, which will also result in improvement in its performance. In practice, though, it may be easier to deploy these changes locally for TCP2 at the gateway node because this is under the operator's control.

The suggestions that have been made to improve TCP performance in the presence of wireless link impairments fall into the following areas:

1. Using available bandwidth estimates (ABEs) to estimate transmit rates: The TCP sender does not keep an estimate of the bottleneck link bandwidth; as a result, when it encounters congestion, it simply cuts down its window size by half. However, if the sender were able to keep an accurate estimate of the bottleneck link bandwidth (or ABE), then it can reduce its window size in a more intelligent fashion. This not only helps to reduce convergence time for the algorithm to the correct link rate, but also if the packet loss occurs because of link errors (rather than congestion), then the ABE rate is not reduced, which is reflected in the fact that the resulting sending rate remains high. As a result, these types of algorithms exhibit better performance in the presence of wireless link losses.

2. Loss Discrimination Algorithm (LDA): On detection of packet loss, if the TCP sender were given the additional information by an LDA about whether the loss was caused by congestion or link errors, then it can improve the congestion control algorithm by reducing its window size only if the loss was caused by congestion and simply retransmitting the missing packet if the loss was caused by link errors.

3. ZRW ACKs: In case the wireless link gets disconnected over extended periods of time, the TCP sender can undergo multiple time-outs, which will prevent transmission from restarting even after the link comes back up. To prevent this from occurring, the TCP receiver (or some other node along the path) can shut down the sender by sending a TCP ACK with a zero size receive window, which is known as a ZRW ACK.

4.4.1 AVAILABLE BANDWIDTH ESTIMATION AND TCP WESTWOOD

A number of TCP algorithms that use ABE to set their window sizes have appeared in the literature. The original one was proposed by Casetti et al. [4], and the resulting TCP congestion algorithm was named TCP Westwood. This still remains one of the more popular algorithms in this category and is currently deployed in about 3% of servers worldwide (see Yalu [5]).

The TCP Westwood source attempts to measure the rate at which its traffic is being received, and thus the bottleneck rate, by filtering the stream of returning ACKs. This algorithm does not use out-of-band probing packets to measure throughput because they have been shown to significantly bias the resulting measurement. It was later shown that the original Westwood proposal overestimates the connection bandwidth because of the phenomenon of ACK compression [6]. In this section, we will present a slightly modified version called TCP Westwood +, which corrects for this problem.

The rate_control procedure for the original TCP Westwood is as follows:

```
rate_control( )

{
        if (n DUPACKS are received)
                ssthresh = (ABE * RTT_min)/seg_size
                if (cwin > ssthresh)
                            cwin = ssthresh
                endif
        endif
        if (coarse timeout expires)
                    ssthresh = (ABE * RTT_min)/seg_size
                    if ssthresh < 2
                        ssthresh = 2
                    endif
        cwnd = 1
        endif

}
```

In the above pseudocode, ABE is the estimated connection bandwidth at the source, RTT_min is the estimated value of the minimum round trip delay, and seg_size is the TCP packet size. The key idea in this algorithm is to set the window size after a congestion event equal to an estimate of the bottleneck rate for the connection rather than reducing the window size by half as Reno does. Hence, if the packet loss is attributable to link errors rather than congestion, then the window size remains unaffected because the ABE value does not change significantly as a result of packet drops.

Note that from the discussion in Chapter 2, ABE*RTT is an estimate of the ideal window size that the connection should use, given estimated bandwidth ABE and round trip latency RTT. However, by using RTT_{min} instead of RTT, Westwood sets the window size to a smaller value, thus helping to clear out the backlog at the bottleneck link and creating space for other flows.

The key innovation in Westwood was to estimate the ABE using the flow of returning ACKs, as follows:

Define the following:

t_k: Arrival time of the kth ACK at the sender
d_k: Amount of data being acknowledged by the kth ACK
$\Delta_k = t_k - t_{k-1}$ Time interval between the kth and $(k-1)^{rst}$ ACKs
$R_k = \frac{d_k}{\Delta_k}$, Instantaneous value of the connection bandwidth at the time of arrival of the kth ACK
$\hat{R}_k$: Low-pass filtered (LPF) estimate of the connection bandwidth
τ: Cut-off frequency of the LPF

The LPF estimate of the bandwidth is then given by

$$\hat{R}_k = \frac{2\tau - \Delta_k}{2\tau + \Delta_k} \hat{R}_{k-1} + \frac{\Delta_k}{2\tau + \Delta_k}(R_k + R_{k-1}) \tag{6}$$

As pointed out by Mascolo et al. [7], low-pass filtering is necessary because congestion is caused by the low-frequency components and because of the delayed ACK option. The filter coefficients are time varying to counteract the fact that the sampling intervals Δ_k are not constant.

It was subsequently shown [6,7] that the filter (equation 6) overestimates the available bandwidth in the presence of ACK compression. ACK compression is the process in which the ACKs arrive back at the source with smaller interarrival times that do not reflect the bottleneck bandwidth of the connection. To correct this problem, Mascolo et al. [7] made the following change to the filtering algorithm to come up with Westwood +: Instead of computing the bandwidth R_k after every ACK is received, compute it once every RTT seconds. Hence, if D_k bytes are acknowledged during the last RTT interval Δ_k, then

$$R_k = \frac{D_k}{\Delta_k} \tag{7}$$

By doing this, Westwood+ evenly spreads the bandwidth samples over the RTT interval and hence is able to filter out the high-frequency components caused by ACK compression.

Note that the window size after a packet loss is given by

$$W \leftarrow \hat{R} \times T \quad where \quad \hat{R}(t) = \frac{W(t)}{T_s}$$

where T is the minimum round trip latency and T_s is the current smoothed estimate of the round trip latency. This can also be written as

$$W \leftarrow W \frac{T}{T_s}$$

Hence, the change in window size is given by $W(T_s - T)/T_s$. This equation shows that Westwood uses a multiplicative decrease policy, where the amount of decrease is proportional to the queuing delay in the network. It follows that TCP Westwood falls in the class of additive increase/multiplicative decrease (AIMD) algorithms; however, the amount of decrease may be more or less than that of TCP Reno, depending on the congestion state of the network. Hence, it is important to investigate its fairness when competing with other Westwood connections and with

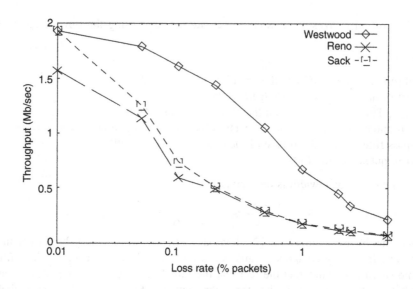

FIGURE 4.3

Throughput versus link error rate performance for Westwood versus Reno.

Reno connections. Casetti et al. [4] carried out one such simulation study in which they showed that when competing with Reno connections, Westwood gets 16% more bandwidth than its fair share, which they deemed to be acceptable. Figure 4.3 shows the throughput of Westwood and Reno as a function of link error rate for a link of capacity 2 mbps. As can be seen, there is a big improvement in Westwood throughput over that of Reno when the loss rates are around 0.1%.

Other schemes to estimate the connection bandwidth include the work by Capone et al. [8] as part of their TCP TIBET algorithm, in which they use a modified version of the filter used in the Core Stateless Fair Queuing Estimation algorithm [9] and obtained good results. Another filter was proposed by Xu et al. [10] as part of their TCP Jersey design. This filter was derived from the Time Sliding Window (TSW) estimator that was proposed by Clarke and Fang [11].

4.4.1.1 TCP Westwood Throughput Analysis

It has been shown by Greico and Mascolo [12] that the expected throughput of TCP Westwood in the presence of link error rate p is given by

$$R_{avg} \propto \frac{1}{\sqrt{pT_s(T_s - T)}} \tag{8}$$

Equation 8 can be derived used the machinery developed in Section 3.2.1 of Chapter 3, and we proceed to so next using the same notation that was used there. Recall that in the fluid limit, the window size for TCP Reno obeyed the following equation (equation 29 in Chapter 3):

$$\frac{dW(t)}{dt} = \frac{R(t - T(t))[1 - Q(t)]}{W(t)} - \frac{R(t - T(t))Q(t)W(t)}{2} \tag{9}$$

For TCP Westwood, the first term on the RHS remains the same because this governs the window size increase during the congestion avoidance phase. The second term changes because the window decrease rule is different, and the resulting equation is given by

$$\frac{dW(t)}{dt} = \frac{R(t - T(t))[1 - Q(t)]}{W(t)} + R(t - T(t))Q(t)(\hat{R}(t)T - W(t)) \tag{10}$$

In equation 10 we replaced $\frac{W(t)}{2}$, which is window decrease rule for Reno by $\hat{R}(t)T - W(t)$, which the window change under Westwood. Next using the approximation that $R(t) \approx \frac{W(t)}{T_s}$ and $\hat{R}(t) \approx R(t)$, we obtain

$$\frac{dR(t)}{dt} = \frac{1 - Q(t)}{T_s^2} + Q(t)R^2(t)\frac{T}{T_s} - Q(t)R^2(t) \tag{11}$$

Setting $\frac{dR(t)}{dt} = 0$ and Q(t) = P(t-T) = p, in equilibrium, we obtain

$$R_{avg} = \frac{1}{\sqrt{T_s(T_s - T)}} \sqrt{\frac{1 - p}{p}} \approx \frac{1}{\sqrt{pT_s(T_s - T)}} \tag{12}$$

where R_{avg} and p are the steady state values of R(t) and P(t), respectively.

Assuming that the queuing delay $(T_s - T)$ can be written as a fraction k of the average round trip latency,

$$T_s - T = kT_s \text{ such that } 0 \le k \le 1.$$

Then equation 12 can be written as

$$R_{avg} = \frac{1}{T_s}\sqrt{\frac{1}{kp}}$$

On comparing this equation with that for TCP Reno, it follows that TCP Westwood has the effect of a net reduction in link error rate by the fraction k. This reduction is greatest when the queuing delay is small compared with the end-to-end latency. From this, it follows that Westwood is most effective over long-distance links and least effective in local area network (LAN) environments with a lot of buffering.

4.4.2 LOSS DISCRIMINATION ALGORITHM (LDA)

Loss Discrimination Algorithms are useful tools that can be used to differentiate between packet losses caused by congestion versus those caused by link errors. This information can be used at sender to appropriately react on receiving duplicate ACKs by not reducing the window size if link errors are the cause of the packet drop.

We will describe an LDA that was proposed by Fu and Liew as part of their TCP Veno algorithm [13]. This mechanism was inspired by the rules used by TCP Vegas to detect an increase in queue size along the connection's path.

Readers may recall from the description of TCP Vegas from Chapter 1 that this algorithm uses the difference between expected throughput and the actual throughput values to gauge the amount of congestion in the network. Defining $R_E(t)$ to be the expected value of the throughput and D(t) the difference between the throughputs, we have

$$D(t) = R_E(t) - R(t) = \frac{W(t)}{T} - \frac{W(t)}{T_s} = R(t)[T_s - T] \qquad (13)$$

In equation 13, T_s is a smoothed value of the measured round trip time. By Little's law, $D(t)$ equals the queue backlog along the path.

The congestion indicator in the LDA is set to 0 if $D(t)$ is less than 3 and is set to 1 otherwise. Fu and Liew [13] used this rule in conjunction with Reno's regular multiplicative decrease rule and a slightly modified additive increase rule and observed a big increase in TCP performance in the presence of random errors.

Another LDA was proposed by Xu et al. [10] and works as follows: Unlike the LDA described earlier, this LDA requires that the network nodes pass on congestion information back to the source by appropriately marking the ACK packets traveling in the reverse direction if they observe that their average queue length has exceeded some threshold. The average queue length is computed using a low-pass filter in exactly the same way as for marking packets in the RED algorithm. The only difference is that a much more aggressive value for the smoothing parameter is used. Xu et al. [10] suggest a value of 0.2 for the smoothing parameter as opposed to 0.002, which is used for RED. Using this LDA, they showed that their algorithm, TCP Jersey, outperformed TCP Westwood for the case when the link error rate equaled or exceeded 1%, and they attributed this improvement to the additional boost provided by the LDA.

4.4.3 ZERO RECEIVE WINDOW (ZRW) ACKs

A problem that is unique to wireless is that the link may get disconnected for extended periods, for a number of different reasons. When this happens, the TCP source will time out, perhaps more than once, resulting in a very large total time-out interval. As a result, even after the link comes back up, the source may still be in its time-out interval.

The situation described can be avoided by putting the TCP source into a state where it freezes all retransmit timers, does not cut down its congestion window size, and enters a persist mode. This is done by sending it an ACK in which the receive window size is set to zero. In this mode, the source starts sending periodic packets called Zero Window Probes (ZWPs). It continues to send these packets until the receiver responds to a ZWP with a nonzero window size, which restarts the transmission.

There have been two proposals in the literature that use ZRW ACKs to combat link disconnects:

- The Mobile TCP or M-TCP protocol by Brown and Singh [14]: M-TCP falls within the category of split-TCP designs, with the connection from the fixed host terminated at the gateway and a second TCP connection between the gateway and the client. However, unlike I-TCP, the gateway does not ACK a packet from the fixed host immediately on reception but waits until the packet has been ACK'd by the client, so that the system maintains end-to-end TCP semantics. In this design, the gateway node is responsible for detecting whether the mobile client is in the disconnect state by monitoring the ACKs flowing back from it on the second TCP connection. When the ACKs stop coming, the gateway node sends a zero window ACK back to the source node, which puts it in the persist mode. When the client gets connected again, the gateway sends it a regular ACK with a nonzero receive window in response to a ZWP to get the packets flowing again. To avoid the case in which the source transmits a window full of packets, all of which get lost over the second connection, so that there is no ACK stream coming back that can be used for the zero window ACK, Brown and Singh suggested that the gateway modify the ACKs being sent to the fixed host, so that the last byte is left un-ACKed. Hence, when the client disconnect does happen, the gateway can then send an ACK back to the fixed host with zero window indication.

- The Freeze TCP protocol by Goff et al. [15]: In this design, the zero window ACK is sent by the mobile client rather than the gateway. The authors made this choice for a couple of reasons, including (1) the mobile client has the best information about the start of a network disconnect (e.g., by detecting the start of a hand-off) and hence is a natural candidate to send the zero window ACK, and (2) they wanted to avoid any design impact on any node in the interior of the network so that Freeze TCP would work on an end-to-end basis. They also borrowed a feature from an earlier design by Cacares and Iftode [16] by which when the disconnect period ends, the client sends three Duplicate ACKs for the last data segment it received before the disconnection for the source to retransmit that packet and get the data flowing again. Note that Freeze TCP can be implemented in the context of the split-TCP architecture, such that the zero window ACKs can be sent by the mobile client to the gateway node to freeze the second TCP connection over the access network.

In general, client disconnect times have been steadily reducing as the mobile hand-off protocols improve from GPRS onward to LTE today. Hence, the author is not aware of any significant deployment of these types of protocols. They may be more relevant to wireless local area networks (WLANs) or ad-hoc networks in which obstructions could be the cause of link disconnects.

4.4.4 TCP WITH AVAILABLE BANDWIDTH ESTIMATES AND LOSS DISCRIMINATION ALGORITHMS

The following pseudocode, adapted from Xu et al. [10], describes the modified congestion control algorithm in the presence of both the ABE and LDA algorithms. Note that the variable LDA is set to 1 if the sender decides that the packet loss is attributable to congestion and set to 0 if it is attributable to link errors. Also, SS, CA, fast_recovery, and explicit_retransmit are the usual TCP Reno Slow Start, Congestion Avoidance, Fast Recovery, and packet retransmission procedures as described in Chapter 1. An example of a rate_control procedure is the one given for TCP Westwood in Section 4.4.1.

```
recv( )                                              1

{

        ABE( )                                       2
        If ACK and LDA = 0                           3
                SS( ) or CA( )                       4
        end if                                       5
        if ACK and LDA = 1                           6
                rate_control( )                      7
                SS( ) or CA( )                       8
        end if                                       9
```

```
        if nDUPACK and LDA = 1                          10
                rate control( )                         11
                explicit_retransmit( )                  12
                fast_recovery( )                        13
        end if                                          14
        if nDUPACK and LDA = 0                          15
                explicit_retransmit( )                  16
                fast_recovery( )                        17
        end if                                          18
    }
```

Note that if packet loss is detected (nDUPACK = true) but LDA = 0 (i.e., there is no congestion detected), then the source simply retransmits the missing packet (line 16) without invoking the rate_control procedure. On the other hand, even if there is no packet loss but congestion is detected, then the source invokes rate_control without doing any retransmits (lines 6–9).

4.5 LINK-LEVEL ERROR CORRECTION AND RECOVERY

A more direct way of solving the problem of link layer reliability is by reducing the effective error rate that is experienced by TCP. There are several ways this can be done:

- The problem can be attacked at the physical layer by using more powerful error-correcting codes. For example, LTE uses a sophisticated error correction scheme called Turbo Coding to accomplish this. Other error correction schemes in use include Reed-Solomon and convolutional coding [17].
- Link layer retransmissions or ARQ: As the name implies, the system tries to hide packet loss at the link layer by retransmitting them locally. This is a very popular (and effective) method, widely used in modern protocols such as LTE and WiMAX.
- Hybrid schemes: Both physical layer error correction and link layer retransmissions can be combined together in an algorithm known as Hybrid ARQ (HARQ). In these systems, when a packet arrives in error at the receiver, instead of discarding it, the receiver combines its signal with that of the subsequent retransmission, thereby obtaining a stronger signal at the physical layer. Modern wireless systems such as LTE and WiMAX have deployed HARQ.

From theoretical studies as well as practical experience from deployed wireless networks, link layer techniques have proven very effective in combating link errors. As a result, all deployed cellular data networks, including 3G, LTE, and WiMAX, include powerful ARQ and FEC components at the wireless link layer.

4.5.1 PERFORMANCE OF TCP WITH LINK-LEVEL FORWARD ERROR CORRECTION (FEC)

Link-level FEC techniques include algorithms such as convolutional coding, turbo coding, and Reed-Solomon coding, and all modern cellular protocols, including 3G and LTE, incorporate them as part of the physical layer. FEC algorithms were discovered in the 1950s, but until 1980 or so, their use was confined to space and military communications because of the large processing power they required. With

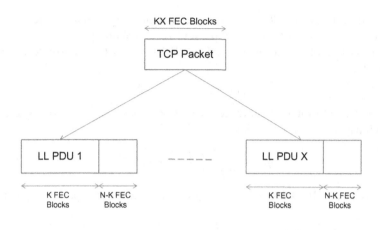

FIGURE 4.4

Relation between TCP packets and link-level Packet Data Units (PDUs) with Forward Error Correction (FEC).

the advances in semiconductor technology, link-level FEC is now incorporated in every wireless communication protocol today and has started to move up the stack to the transport and even application layers. The algorithms have also become better with time; for example, turbo coding, which was discovered in the 1990s, is a very powerful algorithm that takes the system close to the theoretical Shannon bound. When compared with ARQ, FEC has some advantages; ARQ results in additional variable latency because of retransmissions that can throw off the TCP retransmit timer, but this is not an issue for FEC. This is especially problematic for long satellite links, for which ARQ may be an inappropriate solution.

Following Barakat and Altman [18], we present an analysis of the TCP throughput over a link that is using a link-level block FEC scheme such as Reed-Solomon coding.

Define the following (Figure 4.4):

X: Number of link-level transmission units (called LL PDUs) formed from a single TCP packet
T: Minimum round trip latency for TCP
q: Probability that a LL PDU is received in error in the absence of FEC
q_T: Probability that a LL PDU is received in error in the presence of FEC
(N,K): Parameters of the FEC scheme, which uses a block code [17]. This consists of K FEC units of data, to which the codec adds (N-K) FEC units of redundant coding data, such that each LL PDU consists of N units in total.
$p_{FEC}(N,K)$: Probability that a TCP packet is lost in the presence of FEC with parameters (N,K)
C: Capacity of the link in units of FEC units per second

We now use the square-root formula (see Chapter 2) to derive an expression for the TCP throughput as a function of the link and FEC parameters.

Because there are KX FEC data units that make up a TCP packet, it follows that the average TCP throughput in the presence of FEC with parameters (N,K) is given by

$$R_{avg}(N,K) = \min\left(\frac{KX}{T} \sqrt{\frac{3}{2p_{FEC}(N,K)}}, \frac{K}{N}C \right) \qquad (14)$$

Also, as a result of the block FEC, the link capacity reduces by a factor of (K/N).

We now derive an expression for the TCP packet loss probability p(N,K).

A TCP packet is lost when one or more of the X LL PDUs that constitute it arrive in error. Hence, it follows that

$$p_{FEC}(N,K) = 1 - (1 - q_T)^X \tag{15}$$

An LL PDU is lost when more than (N-K) of its FEC block units are lost because of transmission errors, which happens with probability

$$q_T = \sum_{i=N-K+1}^{N} \binom{N}{i} q^i (1-q)^{N-i} \tag{16}$$

From equations 15 and 16, it follows that the probability that a TCP packet is lost is given by

$$p_{FEC}(N,K) = 1 - \left[1 - \left(\sum_{i=N-K+1}^{N} \binom{N}{i} q^i (1-q)^{N-i}\right)\right]^X \tag{17}$$

From equation 16, it is clear that the addition of FEC reduces the loss probability of LL PDUs (and as a result that of TCP packets), which results in an increase in TCP throughput as long as the first term in the minimum in equation 14 is less than the second term. As we increase N, we reach a point where the two terms become equal, and at this point, the FEC entirely eliminates all link errors. Any increase in FEC beyond this point results in the deterioration of TCP throughput (i.e., there is more FEC than needed to clean up the link). This implies that the optimal amount of FEC is the one that causes the two terms in equation 14 to be equal, that is,

$$\frac{NX}{T} \sqrt{\frac{3}{2p_{FEC}(N,K)}} = C \tag{18}$$

Figure 4.5 plots the TCP throughput as a function of the ratio N/K, for K = 10, 20, and 30. Increasing N/K while keeping K fixed leads to more FEC blocks per LL PDU, which increases the resulting throughput. Figure 4.5 also plots (K/N)C and the intersection of this curve with the throughput curve is the point that is predicted by equation 18 with the optimal amount of FEC.

The analysis presented assumed that the LL PDU loss probabilities form an iid process. A more realistic model is to assume the Gilbert loss model, in which errors occur in bursts. This reflects the physics of an actual wireless channel in which burst errors are common because of link fading conditions. However, this complicates the analysis considerably, and a closed form simple expression is no longer achievable. Interested readers are referred to Barakat and Altman [18] for details of the analysis of this more complex model.

4.5.2 PERFORMANCE OF TCP WITH LINK-LEVEL AUTOMATIC RETRANSMISSIONS AND FORWARD ERROR CORRECTION

Link-level ARQ or retransmission is an extremely effective way of reducing the link error rate. Figures 4.6A and 4.6B are plotted from measurements made from a functioning broadband wireless

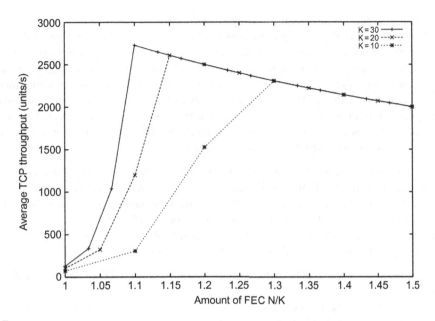

FIGURE 4.5

TCP throughput versus N/K for different values of K.

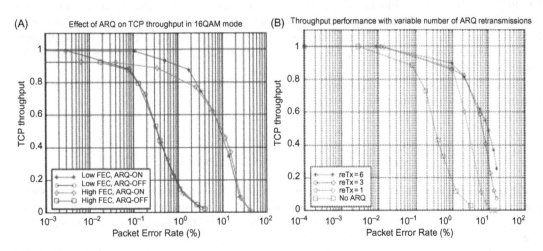

FIGURE 4.6

(A) TCP throughput in the presence of Forward Error Correction (FEC) and Automatic Retransmission (ARQ).

(B) Variation of TCP throughput with number of ARQ retransmissions.

system [19] that has been commercially deployed. As shown in Figure 4.6A, even with an error rate as high as 10%, the TCP throughput remains at 40% of the maximum. Figure 4.6B shows that the throughput performance improves as the number of ARQ retransmissions is increased, but after six or so retransmissions, there is no further improvement. This is because at high error rates, the number of retransmissions required to recover a packet grows so large that the resulting increase in end-to-end latency causes the TCP retransmit timer to expire, thus resulting in a time-out. This observation also points to an important issue when using ARQ at the link layer. Because of its interaction with TCP's retransmissions, ARQ can in fact make the overall performance worse if not used carefully. Hence, some guidelines for its use include:

- The maximum number of ARQ retransmissions should be capable of being configured to a finite number, and if the LL-PDU is still received in error, then it should be discarded (and let TCP recover the packet). The max number of retransmissions should be set such the total time to do so is significantly less than the TCP retransmit time-out (RTO) interval.
- ARQ should be configurable on a per connection basis, so that connections that do not need the extra reliability can either turn it off or reduce the number of retransmissions.

Modern implementations of ARQ in wireless protocols such as LTE or WiMAX follow these rules in their design.

In this section, following Barakat and Fawal [20], we extend the analysis in Section 4.5.1 to analyze the performance of TCP over a link implementing a Selective Repeat ARQ scheme (in addition to FEC) and in-order delivery of packets to the IP layer at the receiver. We will reuse the definitions used in Section 4.5.1, so that a TCP packet of size KX FEC blocks is split into X LL PDUs, each of which is made up of K FEC blocks (see Figure 4.4). To each of these K FEC blocks we add (N-K) redundant FEC blocks to obtain a Reed Solomon−encoded LL PDU of size N FEC blocks. If the FEC does not succeed in decoding an LL PDU, the SR-ARQ scheme is invoked to recover it by doing retransmissions. The retransmissions will be done a maximum number of times, denoted by M. If the LL PDU fails to get through even after M retransmissions, the ARQ-SR assumes that it cannot be recovered and leaves its recovery to TCP.

Recall from equation 52 in Chapter 2 that the expression for average TCP throughput in the presence of random loss and time-outs is given by

$$R_{avg} = \min\left(\frac{KX}{E(T_{ARQ})\sqrt{\frac{2p_{ARQ}}{3}} + RTO \cdot p_{ARQ}(1 + 32p_{ARQ}^2)\min\left(1, 3\sqrt{\frac{3p_{ARQ}}{8}}\right)}, \alpha C\right) \quad (19)$$

where the throughput is in units of FEC units per second and α is the fraction of the link bandwidth lost because of the FEC and LL PDU retransmissions, p_{ARQ} is the probability that a TCP packet is lost despite ARQ, $E(T_{ARQ})$ is the average round trip latency, C is the capacity of the link, and RTO is the TCP timeout value.

Note that in equation 19, we have replaced T, which is the nonqueuing part of the round trip latency in equation 52 of Chapter 2, by the average value $E(T_{ARQ})$. The reason for this is that in the presence of ARQ, the nonqueuing part of the round trip latency is no longer fixed but varies randomly depending on the number of link retransmissions.

As in the previous section, we will assume that q is the probability that an LL PDU transmission fails because of link errors in the absence of FEC and ARQ. Note that to find R_{avg}, we need to find expressions for $E(T_{ARQ})$, p_{ARQ}, and α as functions of the link, ARQ, and FEC parameters q, N, K, M, and X.

The ARQ-SR receiver acknowledges each LL PDU either with an ACK or a NACK. The LL PDUs that are correctly received are resequenced before being passed on to the IP layer. A TCP packet is lost if one or more of its constituent LL PDUs is lost. Under the assumption that LL PDUs are lost independently of each other with loss rate q_F, we obtain the probability of a TCP packet loss as

$$p_{ARQ} = 1 - (1 - q_F)^X \tag{20}$$

We now obtain an expression for q_F. Note that an LL PDU is lost if all M retransmissions fail, in addition to the loss of the original transmission, for a total of (M + 1) tries. The probability that a single LL PDU transmission fails in the absence of ARQ but with FEC included is given by

$$q_T = \sum_{i=N-K+1}^{N} \binom{N}{i} q^i (1-q)^{N-i} \tag{21}$$

so that the probability that an LL PDU is lost after the M ARQ retransmissions is given by

$$q_F = q_T^{M+1} \tag{22}$$

By substituting equation 22 in equation 20, we obtain the following expression for the TCP packet loss probability p_{ARQ} in the presence of both FEC and ARQ:

$$p_{ARQ} = 1 - \left[1 - \left(\sum_{i=N-K+1}^{N} \binom{N}{i} q^i (1-q)^{N-i} \right)^{M+1} \right]^X \tag{23}$$

To obtain an expression for α, which is the amount of link bandwidth left over after the FEC and ARQ overheads are accounted for, note the following:

- A fraction (K/N) of the link bandwidth is lost because of the FEC overhead.
- A fraction $(1 - q_T)$ of the link bandwidth is lost because of dropping of LL PDUs that arrive in error.
- A fraction $(1 - q_F)^{X-1}$ of the link bandwidth is lost because of LL PDUs that arrive intact but are dropped anyway because one or more of the other (X − 1) LL PDUs that are part of the same TCP packet do not arrive intact, despite the M retransmissions.

Hence, the fraction of the link bandwidth that is available for TCP packet transmission is given by

$$\alpha = (1 - q_F)^{X-1} (1 - q_T) \frac{K}{N} \tag{24}$$

We next turn to the task of finding the average round trip latency $E(T_{ARQ})$ for the TCP packets. Define the following:

τ: The time interval from the start of transmission of an LL PDU and the receipt of its acknowledgement

D: One-way propagation delay across the link

M_i: Number of retransmissions for the i_{th} packet, $1 \le i \le X$, until it is delivered error free. Note that $M_i \le M$.

T_0: Average round trip latency for the TCP packet, excluding the delay across the bottleneck link

t, t_0: Random variables whose average equals T and T_0, respectively

Then τ is given by

$$\tau = 2D + \frac{N}{C} \tag{25}$$

Assume that all the X LL PDUs that make up a TCP packet are transmitted back to back across the link. Then the ith LL PDU starts transmission at time $\frac{(i-1)N}{C}$, and it takes $\frac{N}{C} + 2D + M_i\tau$ seconds to finish its transmission and receive a positive acknowledgement. Hence, it follows that

$$t = t_0 + 2D + \max_{1 \le i \le X}\left(\frac{iN}{C} + M_i\tau\right) \tag{26}$$

We will now compute the expected value of t under the condition that the TCP packet whose delay is being computed has been able to finish its transmission.

Define Z as

$$Z = \max_{1 \le i \le X}\left(\frac{iN}{C} + M_i\tau\right) \tag{27}$$

It follows that

$$E(T_{ARQ}) = T_0 + 2D + E^0(Z) \tag{28}$$

where

$$E^0(Z) = \int_0^{\frac{XN}{C}+M\tau} P^0(Z > z)dz \tag{29}$$

Note that the upper limit of integration is given by $\frac{XN}{C} + M\tau$ because this is the maximum value of Z. Note that

$$P^0(Z > z) = 1 - P^0(Z \le z) = 1 - \prod_{i=1}^{X} P^0\left(\frac{iN}{C} + M_i\tau \le z\right) \tag{30}$$

so that

$$E^0(Z) = \frac{XN}{C} + M\tau - \int_0^{\frac{XN}{C}+M\tau} \prod_{i=1}^{X} P^0\left\{M_i \le \left\lfloor \frac{z - \frac{iN}{C}}{\tau}\right\rfloor\right\}dz \tag{31}$$

Next we derive a formula for the probability distribution for M_i.

Note that the probability that all X LL PDUs that make up the packet are received successfully (after ARQ) is given by $(1 - q_T^{M+1})^X$ because the q_T^{M+1} is the probability that an LL PDU is received in error even after M retransmissions. It follows that

$$P^0(M_i = k) = \frac{q_T^k(1 - q_T)}{1 - q_T^{M+1}} \quad and \quad P^0(M_i \le k) = \frac{\sum_{j=0}^{k} q_T^k(1 - q_T)}{1 - q_T^{M+1}} = \frac{1 - q_T^{k+1}}{1 - q_T^{M+1}} \tag{32}$$

Equations 23 and 32 can then be used to evaluate $E^0(Z)$ in equation 31. This allows us to evaluate T in equation 28 and subsequently the average TCP throughput by using equation 19.

4.6 THE BUFFERBLOAT PROBLEM IN CELLULAR WIRELESS SYSTEMS

Until this point in this chapter, we have focused on the random packet errors as the main cause of performance degradation in wireless links. With advances in channel coding and smart antenna technology, as well as powerful ARQ techniques such as HARQ, this problem has been largely solved in recently designed protocols such as LTE. However, packet losses have been replaced by another link related problem, which is the large variability in wireless link latency. This can also lead to a significant degradation in system performance as explained below.

Recall from Chapter 2 that for the case when there are enough buffers to accommodate the maximum window size W_{max}, the steady-state maximum buffer occupancy at the bottleneck link is given by:

$$b_{max} = W_{max} - CT \tag{33}$$

From this we concluded that if the maximum window size is kept near CT, then the steady state buffer occupancy will be close to zero, which is the ideal operating case. In reaching this conclusion, we made the critical assumption that C is fixed, which is not the case for the wireless link. If C varies with time, then one of the following will happen:

- If $C > W_{max}/T$, then $b_{max} = 0$, i that is, there is no queue build at the bottleneck, and in fact the link is underused
- If $C << W_{max}/T$, then a large steady-state queue backlog will develop at the bottleneck, which will result in an increase in the round trip latency if the buffer size B is large. This phenomenon is known as bufferbloat.

Note that buffer size B at the wireless base station is usually kept large to account for the time needed to do ARQ and to keep a reservoir of bits ready in case the capacity of the link suddenly increases. Because C is constantly varying, the buffer will switch from the empty to the full state frequently, and when it is in the full state, it will cause a degradation in the performance of all the interactive applications that are using that link. Queuing delays of the order of several seconds have been measured on cellular links because of this, which is unacceptable for applications such as Skype, Google Hangouts, and so on. Also, the presence of a large steady-state queue size means that transient packet bursts, such as those generated in the slow-start phase of a TCP session, will not find enough buffers, which will result in multiple packet drops, leading to throughput degradation.

There are two main causes for the variation in link capacity:

- ARQ related retransmissions: If the ARQ parameters are not set properly, then the retransmissions can cause the link latency to go up and the capacity to go down.

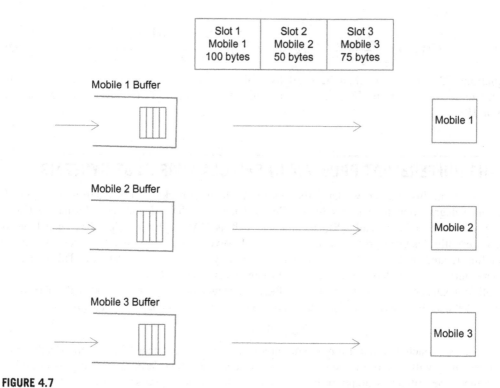

FIGURE 4.7

Downlink scheduling at a wireless base station.

• Link capacity variations caused by wireless link adaptation: This is the more important cause of capacity changes and is unique to wireless links. To maintain the robustness of transmissions, the wireless base station constantly monitors the quality of the link to each mobile separately, and if it detects problems, then it tries to make the link more robust by changing the modulation, coding or both. For instance, in LTE, the modulation can vary from a high of 256-QAM to a low of QPSK, and in the latter case, the link capacity is less than 25% of the former. This link adaptation is done on a user-by-user basis so that any point in time different mobiles get different performance depending on their link condition. The base station implements this system, by giving each mobile its own buffer space and a fixed time slot for transmission, and it serves the mobiles on a round robin basis. Depending on the current modulation and coding, different mobiles transmit different amounts of data in their slot, which results in the varying link capacity (Figure 4.7). In Figure 4.7 mobile 1 has the best link, so it uses the best modulation, which enables it to fit 100 bytes in its slot; mobile 2 has the worst link and the lowest modulation, so it can fit only 50 bytes in its slot.

From the description of the link scheduling that was given earlier, it follows that the traffic belonging to different mobiles does not get multiplexed together at the base station (i.e., as shown in Figure 4.7, a buffer only contains traffic going to single mobile). Hence, the congestion that a connection experiences is "self-inflicted" and not attributable to the congestive state of other connections.

Note that the rule of thumb that is used in wireline links to size up the buffer size (i.e., $B = CT$) does not work any longer because the optimal size is constantly varying with the link capacity. The bufferbloat problem also cannot be solved by simply reducing the size of the buffer because this will cause problems with the other functions that a base station has to carry out, such as reserving buffer space for retransmissions or deep packet inspections.

Solving for bufferbloat is a very active research topic, and the networking community has not settled on a solution yet, but the two areas that are being actively investigated are Active Queue Management (AQM) algorithms (see Section 4.6.1) and the use of congestion control protocols that are controlled by end-to-end delay (see Section 4.6.2).

4.6.1 ACTIVE QUEUE MANAGEMENT (AQM) TECHNIQUES TO COMBAT BUFFERBLOAT

AQM techniques such as Random Early Detection (RED) were designed in the mid 1990s but have not seen widespread deployment because of the difficulty in configuring them with the appropriate parameters. Also, the steadily increasing link speeds in wireline networks kept the network queues under control, so operators did not feel the need for AQM. However, the bufferbloat problem in cellular networks confronted them with a situation in which the size of the bottleneck queue became a serious hindrance to the system performance; hence, several researchers have revisited the use of traditional RED in controlling the queue size; this work is covered in Section 4.6.1.1.

Nichols and Jacobsen [21] have recently come up with a new AQM scheme called Controlled Delay (CoDel) that does not involve any parameter tuning and hence is easier to deploy. It is based on using delay in the bottleneck buffer, rather than its queue size, as the indicator for link congestion. This work is covered in Section 4.6.1.2.

4.6.1.1 Adaptive Random Early Detection

Recall from the description of RED in Chapter 1, that the algorithm requires that the operators choose the following parameters: the queue thresholds min_{th} and max_{th}, the maximum dropping probability max_p and the averaging parameter w_q. If the parameters are not set properly, then the analysis in Chapter 3 showed that it can lead to queue length oscillations, low link utilizations, or buffer saturation, resulting in excessive packet loss. Using the formulae in Chapter 3, it is possible to choose the appropriate parameters for a given value of the link capacity C, the number of connections N, and the round trip latency T. However, if any of these parameters is varying, as C is in the wireless case, then the optimal parameters will also have to change to keep up with it (i.e., they have to become adaptive).

Adaptive RED (ARED) was designed to solve the problem of automatically setting RED's parameters [22]. It uses the "gentle" version of RED, as shown in Figure 4.8. The operator has to set a single parameter, which is the target queue size, and all the other parameters are automatically set and adjusted over time, as a function of this. The main idea behind the adaptation in ARED is the following: With reference to Figure 4.8, assuming that averaging parameter w_q and the thresholds min_{th} and max_{th} are fixed, the packet drop probability increases if the parameter max_p is increased and conversely decreases when max_p is reduced. Hence, ARED can keep the buffer

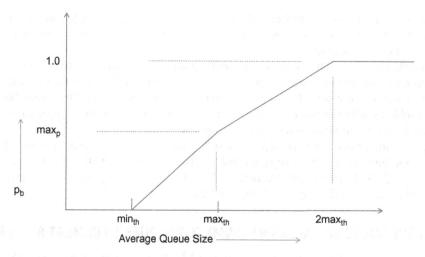

FIGURE 4.8

Random Early Detection (RED) packet drop/marking probability for "gentle" RED.

occupancy around a target level by increasing max_p if the buffer size is more than the target and decreasing max_p if the buffer size falls below the target. This idea was originally proposed by Feng et al. [23] and later improved upon by Floyd et al. [22], who used an AIMD approach to varying max_p, as opposed to multiplicative increase/multiplicative decrease (MIMD) algorithm used by Feng et al. [23]

The ARED algorithm is as follows:

```
ared( )
Every interval seconds:
          If (avg> target and maxp < = 0.5)
                  Increase maxp:
                  maxp ← maxp + a
          elseif (avg<target and maxp > = 0.01)
                  Decrease maxp:
                  maxp ← maxp * b                          1
```

The parameters in this algorithm are set as follows:

Avg: The smoothed average of the queue size computes as

$$avg \leftarrow (1 - w_q)avg + w_q q$$

w_q: This is set to

$$w_q = 1 - e^{-\frac{1}{C}} \tag{34}$$

interval: The algorithm is run periodically every interval seconds, where interval = 0.5 sec
a: The additive increment factor is set to a = min(0.01, max_p/4).

b: The multiplicative decrement factor is set to 0.9.

target: The target for the average queue size is set to the interval

$$target = [min_{th} + 0.4(max_{th} - min_{th}), min_{th} + 0.6(max_{th} - min_{th})]$$

max_{th}: Is set to $3*min_{th}$

min_{th}: This is the only parameter that needs to be manually set by the operator.

ARED was originally designed for wireline links, in which the capacity C is fixed and the variability is attributable to the changing load on the link (i.e., the number of TCP connections N). The algorithm needs to be adapted for the wireless case, in particular the use of equation 34 to choose w_q needs to be clarified because C is now varying. If w_q is chosen to be too large relative to the link speed, then it causes queue oscillations because the average tends to follow the instantaneous variations in queue size. Hence, one option is to choose the maximum possible value for the link capacity in equation 34, which would correspond to the mobile occupying the entire channel at the maximum modulation.

Also, the value of interval needs to be revisited because the time intervals during which the capacity changes are likely to be different than the time intervals during which the load on the link changes. Floyd et al. [22] showed through simulations that with interval = 0.5 sec, it takes about 10 sec for ARED to react to an increase in load and bring the queue size back to the target level. This is likely too long for a wireless channel, so a smaller value of interval is more appropriate.

4.6.1.2 Controlled Delay (CoDel) Active Queue Management

The CoDel algorithm is based on the following observations about bufferbloat, which were made by Nichols and Jacobsen [21]:

- Networks buffers exist to absorb transient packet bursts, such as those that are generated during the slow-start phase of TCP Reno. The queues generated by these bursts typically disperse after a time period equal to the round trip latency of the system. They called this the "good" queue. In a wireless system, queue spikes can also be caused to temporary decreases in the link capacity.
- Queues that are generated because of a mismatch between the window size and the delay bandwidth product, as given by equation 33, are "bad" queues because they are persistent or long term in nature and add to the delay without increasing the throughput. These queues are the main source of bufferbloat, and a solution is needed for them.

Based on these observations, they gave their CoDel algorithm the following properties:

- Similar to the ARED algorithm, it is parameter-less
- It treats the "good" queue and "bad" queues, differently, that is, it allows transient bursts to pass through while keeping the nontransient queue under control.
- Unlike RED, it is insensitive to round trip latency, link rates, and traffic loads.
- It adapts to changing link rates while keeping utilization high.

The main innovation in CoDel is to use the packet sojourn time as the congestion indicator rather than the queue size. This comes with the following benefits: Unlike the queue length, the sojourn time scales naturally with the link capacity. Hence, whereas a larger queue size is acceptable if the link rate is high, it can become a problem when the link rate decreases. This change is captured by the sojourn time. Hence, the sojourn time reflects the actual congestion experienced by a packet, independent of the link capacity.

CoDel tracks the minimum sojourn time experienced by a packet, rather than the average sojourn time, because the average can be high even for the "good" queue case (e.g., if a maximum queue size of N disperses after one round trip time, the average is still N/2). On the other hand, if there is even one packet that has zero sojourn time, then it indicates the absence of a persistent queue. The minimum sojourn time is tracked over an interval equal to the maximum round trip latency over all connections using the link. Moreover, because the sojourn time can only decrease when a packet is dequeued, CoDel only needs to be invoked at packet dequeue time.

To compute an appropriate value for the target minimum sojourn time, consider the following equation for the average throughput that was derived in Section 2.2.2 of Chapter 2:

$$R_{avg} = \frac{0.75}{\left[1 - \frac{\beta}{(1+\beta)^2}\right]} C \quad where \quad \beta = \frac{B}{CT} \tag{35}$$

Even at $\beta = 0.05$, equation 37 gives $R_{avg} = 0.78C$. Because β can be also interpreted as $\beta = $ (Persistent sojourn time)/T, it follows that the above choice can also be interpreted as: The persistent sojourn time threshold should be set to 5% of the round trip latency, and this is what Nichols and Jacobsen recommend. The sojourn time is measured by time stamping every packet that arrives into the queue and then noting the time when it leaves the queue.

When the minimum sojourn time exceeds the target value for at least one round trip interval, a packet is dropped from the tail of the queue. The next dropping interval is decreased in inverse proportion to the square root to the number of drops since the dropping state was entered. As per the analysis in Chapter 2, this leads to a gradual linear decrease in the TCP throughput, as can be seen as follows: Let N(n) and T(n) be the number of packets transmitted in n^{th} drop interval and the duration of the nth drop interval, respectively. Then the TCP throughput R(n) during the nth drop interval is given by

$$R(n) = \frac{N(n)}{T(n)} n = 1, 2, \ldots \tag{36}$$

Note that $T(n) = \frac{T(1)}{\sqrt{n}}$, while N(n) is given by the formula (see Section 2.3, Chapter 2)

$$N(n) = \frac{3}{8} W_m^2(n) \tag{37}$$

where $W_m(n)$ is the maximum window size achieved during the nth drop interval. Because the increase in window size during each drop interval is proportional to the size of the interval, it follows that $W_m(n) \propto \frac{1}{\sqrt{n}}$, from which it follows from equation 37 that $N(n) \propto \frac{1}{n}$. Plugging these into equation 36, we finally obtain that $R(n) \propto \frac{1}{\sqrt{n}}$.

The throughput decreases with n until the minimum sojourn time falls below the threshold at which time the controller leaves the dropping state. In addition, no drops are carried out if the queue contains less than one packet worth of bytes.

One way of understanding the way CoDel works is with the help of a performance measure called Power, defined by

$$Power = \frac{Throughput}{Delay} = \frac{R_{av}}{T_s}$$

Algorithms such as Reno and CUBIC try to maximize the throughput without paying any attention to the delay component. As a result, we see that in variable capacity links, the delay blows up because of the large queues that result. AQM algorithms such as RED (and its variants such as ARED) and CoDel, on the other hand, can be used to maximize the Power instead by trading off some of the throughput for a lower delay. On an LTE link, simulations have shown that Reno achieves almost two times the throughput when CoDel is not used; hence, the tradeoff is quite evident here. The reasons for the lower throughputs with CoDel are the following:

- As shown using equation 35, even without a variable link capacity, the delay threshold in CoDel is chosen such that the resulting average throughput is about 78% of the link capacity.
- In a variable capacity link, when the capacity increases, it is better to have a large backlog (i.e., bufferbloat) because the system can keep the link fully utilized. With a scheme such as CoDel, on the other hand, the buffer soon empties in this scenario, and as a result, some of the throughput is lost.

Hence, CoDel is most effective when the application needs both high throughput as well as low latency (e.g., video conferencing) or when lower speed interactive applications such as web surfing are mixed with bulk file transfers in the same buffer. In the latter case, CoDel considerably improves the latency of the interactive application at the cost of a decrease in the throughput of the bulk transfer application. If Fair Queuing is combined with CoDel, so that each application is given its own buffer, then this mixing of traffic does not happen, in which CoDel can solely be used to improve the performance of applications of the video conferencing type.

The analysis presented above also points to the fact that the most appropriate buffer management scheme to use is a function of the application. This idea is explored more fully in Chapter 9.

4.6.2 END-TO-END APPROACHES AGAINST BUFFERLOAT

AQM techniques against bufferbloat can be deployed only if the designer has access to the wireless base station whose buffer management policy is amenable to being changed. If this is not the case, then one can use congestion control schemes that work on an end-to-end basis but are also capable of controlling delay along their path. If it is not feasible to change the congestion algorithm in the remote-end server, then the split-TCP architecture from Section 4.3 can be used (see Figure 4.2). In this case, the new algorithm can be deployed on the gateway (or some other box along the path) while the legacy TCP stack continues to run from the server to the gateway.

In this section, we will describe a congestion control algorithms called Low Extra Delay Background Transport (LEDBAT) that is able to regulate the connections' end-to-end latency to some target value. We have already come across another algorithm that belongs to this category (i.e., TCP Vegas; see Chapter 1).

In general, protocols that use queuing delay (or queue size) as their congestion indicator, have an intrinsic disadvantage when competing with protocols such as Reno that use packet drops as the congestion indicator. The former tends to back off as soon as the queues start to build up, allowing the latter to occupy the all the bandwidth. However, if the system is designed in the split-connection approach, then the operator has the option of excluding the Reno-type algorithm entirely from the wireless subnetwork, so the unfairness issue will not arise in practice.

4.6.2.1 TCP LEDBAT

LEDBAT has been Bit Torrent's default transport protocol since 2010 [24] and as a result now accounts for a significant share of the total traffic on the Internet. LEDBAT belongs to the class of Less than Best Effort (LBE) protocols, which are designed for transporting background data. The design objective of these protocols is to grab as much of the unused bandwidth on a link as possible, and if the link starts to get congested, then quickly back off.

Even though LEDBAT was designed to be a LBE protocol, its properties make it suitable to be used in wireless networks suffering from bufferbloat. This is because LEDBAT constantly monitors its one-way link latency, and if it exceeds a configurable threshold, then it backs off its congestion window. As a result, if the wireless link capacity suddenly decreases, then LEDBAT will quickly detect the resulting increase in latency caused by the backlog that is created and decrease its sending rate. Note that if the split-TCP design is used, then only LEDBAT flow will be present at the base station (and furthermore, they will be isolated from each other), so that LEDBAT's reduction in rate in the presence of regular TCP will never be invoked.

LEDBAT requires that that each packet carry a timestamp from the sender, which the receiver uses to compute the one-way delay from the sender, and sends this computed value back to the sender in the ACK packet. The use of the one-way delay avoids the complications that arise in other delay-based protocols such as TCP Vegas that use the round trip latency as the congestion signal, and as a result delays experienced by ACK packets in the reverse link introduce errors in the forward delay estimates.

Define the following:

$\theta(t)$: Measured one-way delay between the sender and receiver
τ: The maximum queuing delay that LEDBAT may itself introduce into the network, which is set to 100 ms or less
T: Minimum measured one-way downlink delay
γ: The gain value for the algorithm, which is set to one or less.

The window increase−decrease rules for LEDBAT are as follows (per RTT):

$$W \leftarrow W + \gamma\left[1 - \frac{\theta(t) - T}{\tau}\right] \tag{38}$$

if no loss and

$$W \leftarrow \frac{W}{2} \tag{39}$$

on packet loss.

LEDBAT tries to maintain a fixed packet delay of τ seconds at the bottleneck. If the current queuing delay given by $\theta(t) - T$, exceeds the target τ, then the window is reduced in proportion to their ratio. When the measured queuing delay less that the target τ, then LEDBAT increases its window, but the amount of increase per RTT can never exceed 1.

There are some interesting contrasts between LEDBAT and Westwood even though their designs are similar:

- Whereas Westwood uses a smoothed estimate of the round trip latency to measure congestion, LEDBAT uses the latest unfiltered 1-way latency.
- LEDBAT is less aggressive in its window increase rule because Westwood follows Reno in increasing its window by 1 every RTT, but LEDBAT uses a window increase that is less than 1.
- The rule that LEDBAT uses to decrease its window size in congestion is similar to the one that Westwood uses on encountering a packet loss, as seen below:

$$\text{LEDBAT: } \Delta W = \gamma \left[\frac{\theta - T}{\tau} - 1 \right]$$

$$\text{Westwood: } \Delta W = W \left(\frac{T_s - T}{T_s} \right)$$

Hence, in both cases, the decrease is proportional to the amount of congestion delay, but in LEDBAT, the decrease is additive, but in Westwood, it is multiplicative.

Note that even though two different clocks are used to measure the one-way delays in LEDBAT because only the difference $\theta(t) - T$ appears in equation 38, any errors attributable to a lack of synchronization get cancelled out.

LEDBAT has been shown to have intraprotocol fairness issue if multiple LEDBAT connections are competing for bandwidth at a single node. If the bottleneck is at the wireless base station, then interaction between LEDBAT flows from different mobiles should not be an issue, since the per mobile queues are segregated from each other.

4.7 SOME DESIGN RULES

The following rules, which are based on the material in this chapter, can be used for designing congestion control systems that traverse wireless links:

- Compute the quantity $p(CT)^2$ for the system where p is the packet drop rate. If this number is around 8/3, then most of the packet drops are to buffer overflows rather than link errors, so no extra steps are needed to bring down the link error rate (refer to the discussion in Section 2.3.2 of Chapter 2 for the justification for this rule).
- If $p(CT)^2 \gg 8/3$, then the packet drops are being caused predominantly because of link errors. Furthermore, the link error rate is too high, and additional steps need to be taken to bring it down.
  - If the wireless link supports Reed-Solomon FEC, then use equation 20 to compute p_{FEC}, which is the link error rate in the presence of FEC. If $p_{FEC}(CT)^2 \sim 8/3$, then FEC is sufficient for good performance.
  - If $p_{FEC}(CT)^2 \gg 8/3$, then FEC is not sufficient. If the wireless link supports ARQ, then use equation 25 to compute p_{ARQ}, which is the link error rate with both ARQ

and FEC. If $p_{ARQ}(CT)^2 \sim 8/3$ for a certain number of retransmissions M, then link-level ARQ + FEC is sufficient for good performance.
- If FEC or ARQ are not available on the wireless link or if they do not result in a sufficient reduction in the error rate, then use the Transport layer techniques from Sections 4.3 and 4.4.
  - If the TCP stack at the source is under the designer's control, then techniques such TCP Westwood with ABE, LDA, or ZRW can be implemented.
  - If the TCP stack at the source is not under the designer's control, then use a split-level TCP design, with the splitting point implemented at a gateway-type device. In this case, techniques such as Westwood, ABE, or LDA can be implemented on the TCP2 connection.

If the link error rate is zero but the link shows large capacity variations, then bufferbloat may occur, and the following steps should be taken to limit it:

- If the base station software can be modified, then AQM schemes such ARED or CoDel should be used.
- If AQM is not an option, then the delay-based TCP protocols such as LEDBAT or Vegas should be used. This should be done in conjunction with a split-connection TCP architecture so that regular TCP continues to be used in the core packet network.

4.8 FURTHER READING

The techniques discussed in this chapter to mitigate packet losses work at either the transport layer (e.g., Westwood) or at the link layer (e.g., FEC or ARQ). However, some algorithms work cross-layer; the most well known among these is an algorithm called Snoop [25,26]. Snoop can be implemented at an intermediate point along the session path, either at the gateway or the base station. It works as follows: Downlink packets from the source are intercepted by Snoop and stored until it detects an ACK for that packet from the client. If a packet is lost, then Snoop intercepts the duplicate ACKs and suppresses them. It then retransmits the missing packet from its local cache, so that the source does not become aware of the loss. Hence, in some sense, Snoop operates like a TCP-aware link-level ARQ protocol.

Wireless links sometimes exhibit a large increase in their end-to-end latency because of link-level ARQ retransmissions or because of the extra latency during handoffs. This causes the TCP retransmit timer to time out even though no packets were lost. When the ACK for the retransmitted packet arrives, the source is not able to tell whether this ACK was for the original transmission or for the retransmission (this is called the ACK ambiguity problem) and assumes the latter. This leads to the retransmission of the entire window of packets. To correct this problem, Ludwig and Katz [27] designed an algorithm called TCP Eifel, which solves the ACK ambiguity problem by time stamping every TCP data packet and then having the receiver time stamp returning ACKs with the time stamp of the packet being ACK'd.

REFERENCES

[1] Lakshman TV, Madhow U. Window based error recovery and flow control with a slow acknowledgement channel: a study of TCP/IP performance. IEEE INFOCOM 1997;3:1199−209.

[2] Varma S. Performance and buffering requirements for TCP applications in asymmetric networks. IEEE INFOCOM 1999;3:1548−55.

[3] Bakre A, Badrinath BR. I-TCP: indirect TCP for mobile hosts. Proceedings of the fifteenth international conference on distributed computing systems, 1995. p. 136−143.

[4] Casetti C, Gerla M, Mascolo S, et al. TCP Westwood: end-to-end congestion control for wired/wireless networks. Wireless Netw 2002;8(5):467−79.

[5] Yang P, Luo W, Xu L, Deogun J, Lu Y. TCP congestion avoidance algorithm identification. International Conference on Distributed Computing Systems, 2011.

[6] Greico LA, Mascolo S. End-to-end bandwidth estimation for congestion control in packet networks. Presented at the second international workshop on QoS-IP, 2003.

[7] Mascolo S, Grieco LA, Ferorelli R, et al. Performance evaluation of Westwood+ TCP congestion control. Perform Eval 2004;55:93−111.

[8] Capone A, Fratta L, Martignon F. Bandwidth estimation schemes for TCP over wireless networks. IEEE Trans Mobile Comput 2004;3(2):129−43.

[9] Stoica I, Shenker S, Zhang H. Core-stateless fair queueing: achieving approximately fair bandwidth allocation in high speed networks. SIGCOMM 1998:118−30.

[10] Xu K, Tian Y, Ansari N. TCP-Jersey for wireless communications. IEEE JSAC 2004;22(4):747−56.

[11] Clark DD, Fang W. Explicit allocation of best effort packet delivery service. IEEE/ACM ToN 1998;6(4):362−73.

[12] Grieco LA, Mascolo S. Mathematical analysis of Westwood+ TCP congestion control. IEE Proc Control Theory Appl. 2005:35−42.

[13] Fu CP, Liew SC. TCP Veno: TCP enhancement for transmission over wireless access networks. IEEE JSAC 2003;21(2):216−28.

[14] Brown K, Singh S. M-TCP: TCP for mobile cellular networks. ACM SIGCOMM Comput Commun Rev 1997;27(5):19−43.

[15] Goff T, Phatak DS, Gupta V. Freeze TCP: A true end-to-end TCP enhancement mechanism for mobile environments. IEEE INFOCOM 2000;3:1537−45.

[16] Cacares R, Iftode L. Improving the performance of reliable transport protocols in mobile computing environments. IEEE JSAC 1994;13(5):850−7.

[17] Lee EA, Messerschmitt DG. Digital communication. Dordrecht: Kluwer Academic; 1994.

[18] Barakat C, Altman E. Bandwidth tradeoff between TCP and link-level FEC. Comput Netw 2002;39:133−50.

[19] Varma S, Michail T. Early results from next generation wireless broadband systems. Aperto Netw Tech Rep 2002.

[20] Barakat C, Fawal A. Analysis of link-level hybrid FEC/ARQ for wireless links and long lived TCP traffic. INRIA Res Rep 2004;57(4):453−76.

[21] Nichols K, Jacobsen V. Controlled delay active queue management. IETF Draft 2014.

[22] Floyd S., Gummadi R., Shenker S. Adaptive RED: An algorithm for increasing the robustness of RED's Active Queue Management, Technical Report. 2001.

[23] Feng W, Kandlur D, Saha D, Shin K. A self configuring RED gateway. IEEE INFOCOM 1999;3:1320−8.

[24] Shalunov S, Hazel G, Iyengar J, Kuehlewind M. Low extra delay background transport (LEDBAT). IETF RFC 2012:6817.

[25] Balakrishnan H., Amir E., Katz R.H. Improving TCP/IP performance over wireless networks. ACM conference on mobile computing and networking, 1995. p. 2−11.

[26] Balakrishnan H, Seshan S, Katz R. Improving reliable transport and handoff performance in cellular wireless networks. ACM Wireless Netw 1995;1:469−81.

[27] Ludwig R, Katz R. The Eifel algorithm: making TCP robust against spurious retransmissions. ACM SIGCOMM 2000;30(1):30−6.

SUGGESTED READING

Baker F, Fairhurst G. IETF recommendations regarding active queue management. IETF Draft 2015, in press.

Balakrishnan H, Padmanabhan VN, Seshan S, Katz RH. A comparison of mechanisms for improving TCP performance over wireless links. IEEE Trans Netw 1997;5(6):756−69.

Chan MC, Ramjee R. Improving TCP/IP performance over third generation wireless networks. IEEE INFOCOM 2004;3:1893−904.

Chaskar HM, Lakshman TV, Madhow U. TCP over wireless with link level error control: Analysis and design methodology. IEEE/ACM Trans Netw 1999;7(5):605−15.

De Cicco L, Carlucci G, Mascolo S. Experimental investigation of the Google congestion control for real-time flows. ACM FhMN Workshop 2013:21−6.

Gong Y, Ross D, Testa C, et al. Fighting the bufferbloat: on the coexistence of AQM and low priority congestion control. Comput Netw 2013:411−16.

Jiang H, Wang Y, Lee K, Rhee I. Tackling bufferbloat in 3G/4G networks. ACM IMC Conference, 2012. p. 329−42.

Khademi N, Ros D, Welzl M. The new AQM kids on the block: much ado about nothing? University of Oslo Research Report, 2014.

Kuhn N, Lochin E, Mehani O. Revisiting old friends: is CoDel really achieving what RED cannot? OATAO 2014:3−8.

Sundararaj S, Duchamp D. Analytical characterization of the throughput of a split TCP connection. MS Thesis, Dept. of Computer Science, Stevens Institute of Technology, 2002.

Wei W, Zhang C, Zang H, et al. Inference and evaluation of split connection approaches in cellular data networks. PAM, 2006:21−30.

Winstein K, Sivaraman A, Balakrishnan H. Stochastic forecasts achieve high throughput and low delay over cellular networks. Usenix NSDI 2013.

CONGESTION CONTROL IN HIGH-SPEED NETWORKS

5.1 INTRODUCTION

Link speeds have exploded in the past 2 decades from tens of megabits to multiple gigabits per second for both local as well as long-distance networks. The original congestion control algorithms for TCP, such as Reno and Tahoe, worked very well as long as the link speeds were lower but did not scale very well to the higher speeds and longer propagation delays for several reasons:

- In Chapter 3, Section 3.4, by using a control theory framework, it was shown that TCP Reno becomes unstable if either the link capacity, the propagation delay, or both become large. This results in severe oscillations of the transmission rates and buffer occupancies, which has been observed in practice in high-speed networks.
- Consider the following scenario: The link capacity is 10 Gbps, and the Round Trip Latency (RTT) is 100 ms, so the delay bandwidth product is about 100,000 packets (for a packet size of 1250 bytes). For TCP to grow its window from the midpoint (after a multiplicative decrease) to full window size during the congestion avoidance phase, it will require 50,000 RTTs, which is about 5000 seconds (1.4 hours). If a connection finishes before then, the link will be severely underutilized. Hence, when we encounter a combination of high capacity and large end-to-end delay, the multiplicative decrease policy on packet loss is too drastic, and the linear increase is not quick enough.
- The square-root formula for TCP throughput (see Chapter 2) shows that for a round trip latency of T, the packet drop rate has to be less than $\frac{1.5}{(RT)^2}$ to sustain an average throughput of R. Hence, using the same link and TCP parameters as above, the packet drop rate has to be less than 10^{-10} to sustain a throughput of 10 Gbps. This is much smaller than the drop rate that can be supported by most links.

A number of alternate congestion control algorithms for high-speed networks were suggested subsequently to solve this problem, including Binary Increase Congestion control (BIC) [1], CUBIC [2], High-Speed TCP (HSTCP) [3], ILLINOIS [4], Compound TCP (CTCP) [5], YEAH [6], and FAST TCP [7]. The Linux family of operating systems offers users a choice of one of these algorithms to use (in place of TCP Reno) while using TCP CUBIC as the default algorithm. The Windows family, on the other hand, offers a choice between Reno and CTCP. As a result of the wide usage of Linux on web servers, it has recently been estimated [8] that about 45% of the servers on the Internet use either BIC or CUBIC, about 30% still use TCP Reno, and another 20% use CTCP.

In this chapter, we provide a description and analysis of the most popular high-speed congestion control algorithms, namely HSTCP, BIC, CUBIC, and CTCP. Each of these algorithms modifies the TCP window increase and decrease rules in a way such that the system is able to make better utilization of high-speed and long-distance links. We also discuss two other protocols, namely eXpress Control Protocol (XCP) and Rate Control Protocol (RCP). These need multi-bit network feedback, which has prevented their deployment in Internet Protocol (IP) networks. However, several interesting aspects of their design have influenced subsequent protocol design. Whereas XCP and RCP approach the high-speed congestion control problem by using an advanced Active Queue Management (AQM) scheme, the other algorithms mentioned are server based and designed to work with regular tail-drop or Random Early Detection (RED) routers.

The rest of this chapter is organized as follows: Section 5.2 introduces the concept of the Response Function and its utility in designing and analyzing congestion control algorithms, Sections 5.3 to 5.8 discuss the design and analysis of a number of high-speed congestion control algorithms, including HSTCP (Section 5.3), TCP BIC (Section 5.4.1), TCP CUBIC (Section 5.4.2), Compound TCP (Section 5.5), FAST TCP (Section 5.6), XCP (Section 5.7), and RCP (Section 5.8). Section 5.9 contains some observations on the stability of these algorithms.

An initial reading of this chapter can be done in the sequence $5.1 \rightarrow 5.2 \rightarrow 5.3$ followed by either 5.4 or 5.5 or 5.6 or 5.7 or 5.8 (depending on the particular algorithm the reader is interested in) $\rightarrow 5.9$.

5.2 DESIGN ISSUES FOR HIGH-SPEED PROTOCOLS

In networks with large link capacities and propagation delays, the congestion control protocol needs to satisfy the following requirements:

1. It should be able to make efficient use of the high-speed link without requiring unrealistically low packet loss rates. As pointed out in the introduction, this is not the case for TCP Reno, because of its conservative window increase and aggressive window decrease rules.
2. In case of very high-speed links, the requirement of intraprotocol fairness between the high speed TCP protocol and regular TCP is relaxed because regular TCP is not able to make full use of the available bandwidth. Hence, in this situation, it is acceptable for the high speed TCP variants to perform more aggressively than standard TCP.
3. If connections with different round trip latencies share a link, then they should exhibit good intraprotocol fairness.

Define the Response Function w of a congestion control algorithm as $w = R_{avg}.T$ packets per round trip time (ppr), where R_{avg} is the average throughput and T is the minimum round trip latency. This is sometimes also referred to as the average window because it is the average number of packets transmitted per round trip time. A basic tool used to evaluate high-speed designs is the log-log plot of the Response Function versus p (Figure 5.1). Note that the ability of a protocol to use the high amount of bandwidth available in high-speed networks is determined by whether it can sustain high sending rates under low loss rates. From Figure 5.1, it follows that a protocol becomes more scalable if its sending rate is higher under lower loss rates.

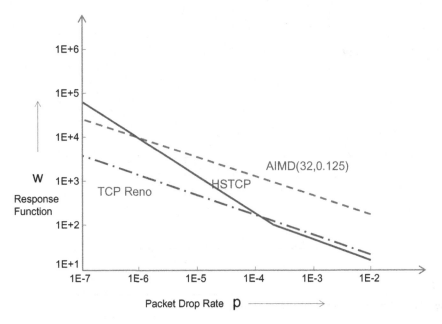

FIGURE 5.1

Comparison of TCP Reno with additive increase/multiplicative decrease (AIMD) (32,0.125) and High-Speed TCP (HSTCP).

From Chapter 2, the Response Function for TCP Reno is given by

$$w = \sqrt{\frac{3}{2p}} \quad or \quad \log w = 0.09 - 0.5 \log p \tag{1}$$

This plot is shown in Figure 5.1, along with the plot for the Response Function of some high-speed algorithms.

- Additive increase/multiplicative decrease AIMD(32, 0.125) corresponds to an AIMD algorithm (introduced in Section 2.3.1 of Chapter 2) with an additive increase of 32 packets and a multiplicative decrease factor of 0.125. From equation 72 in Chapter 2, the response function for AIMD(32, 0.125) is given by

$$\log w = 1.19 - 0.5 \log p \tag{2}$$

Hence AIMD(32, 0.125) has the same slope as Reno on the log-log plot but is able to achieve a higher window size for both high- and lower link speeds.
- The HSTCP response function is derived in Section 2.3 (equation 8), and is given by

$$\log w = \begin{cases} -0.82 - 0.82 \log p & \text{if} \quad p < 0.0015 \\ 0.09 - 0.5 \log p & \text{otherwise} \end{cases} \tag{3}$$

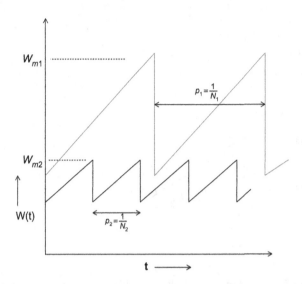

FIGURE 5.2

Illustrating relation between packet drop rate and link speed.

This response function coincides with that of Reno for larger values of the packet drop rate, but for smaller values, it exhibits a steeper slope, which explains its better performance in high-speed links.

Even though Figure 5.1 plots the response function versus the packet drop rate, it also implies a relationship between the response function and the link capacity as we show next. We will consider the case when all packet drops are due to buffer overflows, so from equation 53 in Chapter 2, it follows that the number of packets N transmitted during a single cycle for TCP Reno is given by

$$N = \frac{3W_m^2}{8}$$

where W_m is the maximum window size. But $W_m \approx CT$ if we ignore the contribution caused by the buffer occupancy. Hence, it follows that the packet drop probability p is given by

$$p = \frac{1}{N} \approx \frac{8}{3W_m^2} = \frac{8}{3(CT)^2}$$

which implies that the packet drop probability is inversely proportional to the square of the link speed. This is also illustrated in Figure 5.2, which shows the frequency of packet drops decreasing as the window size increases for two connections that pass through links with different capacities but with the same round trip latency. Hence, it follows that small values of p correspond to a large link capacity and vice versa.

Note the following features for the graph in Figure 5.1:

1. At small values of p (or equivalently for very high-speed links), it is desirable that the Response Function for the high-speed protocol be much larger than for TCP Reno because this

implies that for a given interval between packet drops (which is the inverse of the packet loss rate), the congestion window can grow to a much larger value compared with Reno. Note that this implies that if Reno and the high-speed protocol compete for bandwidth in a high-speed link, the latter will end up with a much larger portion of the bandwidth (i.e., the system will not be fair). However, this is deemed to be tolerable because the high-speed protocol is taking up link bandwidth that cannot be used by TCP Reno anyway.

2. At larger values of p (or equivalently lower speed links), it is desirable for TCP friendliness that the point at which the two curves cross over lie as much to the left as possible. The reason for this is that for lower speed links, the congestion control algorithm should be able to sustain smaller window sizes, which is better suited to coexisting with TCP Reno without taking away bandwidth from it. To do this, the Response Function for the high-speed algorithm should be equal to or lower than that for TCP Reno after the two curves cross over.

3. To investigate the third requirement regarding intraprotocol RTT fairness, we can make use of the following the result that was derived in Chapter 2:

    Assume that the throughput of a loss based congestion control protocol with constants A, e, d is given by

$$R = \frac{A}{T^e p^d} \quad \text{packets/s}$$

Then the throughput ratio between two flows with round trip latencies T1 and T2, whose packet losses are synchronized, is given by

$$\frac{R_1}{R_2} = \left(\frac{T_2}{T_1}\right)^{\frac{e}{1-d}} \tag{4}$$

Note that as d increases, the slope of the response function and RTT unfairness both increase (i.e., the slope of the response function on the log-log plot determines its RTT unfairness).

Thus, by examining the Response Function graph, one can verify whether the high-speed protocol satisfies all the three requirements mentioned.

To satisfy the first requirement, many high-speed algorithms use a more aggressive version of the Reno additive increase rule. Hence, instead of increasing the window size by one packet per round trip time, they increase it by multiple packets, and the increment size may also be a function of other factors such as the current window size or network congestion. However, to satisfy the second requirement of TCP friendliness, they modify the packet increase rule in one of several ways. For example:

- HSTCP [3] reverts to the TCP Reno packet increment rule when the window size is less than some threshold.
- Compound TCP [5] and TCP Africa [9] keep track of the connections' queue backlog in the network and switch to a less aggressive packet increment rule when the backlog exceeds a threshold.

There is also a tradeoff between requirements 2 and 3 as follows: Even though it is possible to design a more TCP-friendly protocol by moving the point of intersection with the TCP curve to a lower packet drop rate (i.e., to the left in Figure 5.1), this leads to an increase in the slope of the Response Function line, thus hurting RTT fairness.

5.3 HIGH SPEED TCP (HSTCP) PROTOCOL

HSTCP by Floyd et al. [3,10] was one of the first TCP variants designed specifically for high-capacity links with significant propagation delays. The design for HSTCP was based on the plot of the Response Function versus Packet Drop Rate introduced in the previous section and proceeds as follows: The ideal response function for a high-speed congestion control algorithm should have the following properties:

- The HSTCP Response Function should coincide with that of TCP Reno when the packet drop rate exceeds some threshold P (or equivalently when the congestion window is equal to or less than W packets). As a default HSTCP chooses $P_0 = 0.0015$ and $W_0 = 38$ packets.
- We next choose a large ppr, say, $W_1 = 83,000$ packets (which corresponds to a link capacity of 10 Gbps for packet size of 1500 bytes and round trip time $T = 100$ ms) and a corresponding packet loss rate of $P_1 = 10^{-7}$. For packet loss rates less than P_0, we specify that the HSTCP Response Function should pass through the points (P_0, W_0) and (P_1, W_1) and should also be linear on a log-log scale (Figure 5.3).

As a result, the Response Function for HSTCP is given by

$$\log w = S(\log p - \log P_0) + \log W_0 \tag{5}$$

where

$$S = \frac{\log W_1 - \log W_0}{\log P_1 - \log P_0} \tag{6}$$

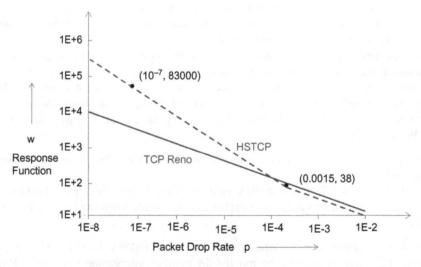

FIGURE 5.3

Comparison of response functions for TCP Reno versus High-Speed TCP (HSTCP).

Equation 5 can be rewritten as

$$w = W_0 \left(\frac{p}{p_0}\right)^S \text{ packets} \tag{7}$$

If we substitute the values of (P_0, W_0) and (P_1, W_1) in equation 6, then we obtain $S = -0.82$, so that the HSTCP Response Function is given by

$$w = \frac{0.15}{p^{0.82}} \quad \text{packets for } p \leq P_0. \tag{8}$$

We now derive an expression for the AIMD increase−decrease parameters for HSTCP. The window size W in HSTCP uses the following AIMD rules with increase−decrease functions $a(w)$ and $b(w)$ that are functions of the window size (these are implemented on a per-ACK basis):

$$ACK : W \leftarrow W + \frac{a(W)}{W}$$
$$Drop : W \leftarrow W - b(W)W \tag{9}$$

For the case $W \leq W_0$, HSTCP defaults to TCP Reno so that

$$a(W) = 1 \quad and \quad b(W) = 0.5 \quad for \quad W \leq W_0. \tag{10}$$

For $W > W_0$, we assume that $b(W)$ varies linearly with respect to $\log(W)$ for $W \in [W_0, W_1]$ With $b(W_0) = 0.5$ and $b(W_1) = B$, where B is the target minimum value for $B(w)$ for $W = W_1$, (Floyd et al. [3] recommend a value of $B = 0.1$ at $W = W_1$), we obtain

$$b(W) = (B - 0.5)\frac{\log W - \log W_0}{\log W_1 - \log W_0} + 0.5 \tag{11}$$

To obtain the corresponding $a(W)$, we use the following formula for the response function of AIMD congestion control (this was derived in Section 2.3.1 in Chapter 2). We choose a point $W \in [W_0, W_1]$ and compute the corresponding probability $P(W)$ by using equation 5. Substitute $(P(W), W)$ into the following equation

$$W = \sqrt{\frac{a(W)(2 - b(W))}{2P(W)b(W)}} \tag{12}$$

so that

$$a(W) = P(W)W^2 \frac{2b(W)}{2 - b(W)} \tag{13}$$

Note that there are a couple of heuristics in the use of equation 12: (1) equation 12 is a formula for the response time function, not the window size, and (2) equation 12 was derived for the case when a and b are constants, which is not the case here.

Table 5.1 gives the values of $a(W)$ and $b(W)$ using equations 11 and 13 for some representative values of W between 38 and 84,035.

Even though HSTCP is not widely used today, it was one of the first high-speed algorithms and served as a benchmark for follow-on designs that were done with the objective of addressing some of its shortcomings. A significant issue with HSTCP is the fact that the window increment function $a(w)$ increases as w increases and exceeds more 70 for large values of w, as shown in Table 5.1.

Table 5.1 Computation of a(W) and b(W)

W	a(W)	b(W)
38	1	0.5
1058	8	0.33
10661	30	0.21
21013	42	0.17
30975	50	0.15
40808	56	0.14
51258	61	0.13
71617	68	0.11
84035	71	0.1

a(W), defined in equation (13); b(W), defined in equation (11); W, HSTCP Window Size.

This implies that at the time when the link buffer approaches capacity, it is subject to a burst of more than 70 packets, all of which can then be dropped. Almost all follow-on high-speed designs reduce the window increase size as the link approaches saturation. HSTCP is more stable than TCP Reno at high speeds because it is less aggressive in reducing its window after a packet loss which reduces the queue size oscillations at the bottleneck node.

If we apply equation 4 to HSTCP, then substituting e = 1, d = 0.82, we obtain

$$\frac{R_1}{R_2} = \left(\frac{T_2}{T_1}\right)^{\frac{1}{1-d}} = \left(\frac{T_2}{T_1}\right)^{5.55} \tag{14}$$

Hence, because of the aggressive window increment policy of HSTCP, combined with small values of the decrement multiplier, connections with a larger round trip latency are at a severe throughput disadvantage. There is a positive feedback loop which causes the connection with the large latency to loose throughput, which operates as follows: Even if the two connections start with the same window size, the connection with smaller latency will gain a small advantage after a few round trip delays because it is able to increase its window faster. However this causes its window size to increase, which further accelerates this trend. Conversely the window size of the large latency connection goes into a downward spiral as reductions in its throughput causes a further reduction in its window size.

5.4 TCP BIC AND CUBIC

Both TCP BIC and CUBIC came from the High-Speed Networks Research Group at North Carolina State University [1,11]. TCP BIC was invented first and introduced the idea of binary search in congestion control algorithms, and TCP CUBIC was later designed to simplify the design of BIC and improve on some of its weaknesses. Both these protocols have been very successful, and currently TCP CUBIC serves as the default congestion control choice on the Linux operating system. It has been estimated [8] that TCP BIC is used by about 15% of the servers in the Internet, and CUBIC is used by about 30% of the servers.

The main idea behind TCP BIC and CUBIC, is to grow the TCP window quickly when the current window size is far from the link saturation point (at which the previous loss happened), and if it is close to the saturation point then the rate of increase is slowed down (see Figure 5.5 for BIC and Figure 5.8 for CUBIC). This results in a concave increase function, which decrements the rate of increase as the window size increases. The small increments result in a smaller number of packet losses if the window size exceeds the capacity. This makes BIC and CUBIC very stable and also very scalable. If the available link capacity has increased since the last loss, then both BIC and CUBIC increase the window size exponentially using a convex function. Since this function shows sub-linear increase initially, this also adds to the stability of the algorithm for cases in which the new link capacity did not increase significantly.

5.4.1 TCP BIC

The objective of BIC's design is to satisfy the three criteria of RTT fairness, TCP friendliness, and scalability. The algorithm results in a concave response time function for BIC as shown in Figure 5.4, from which we can observe the following:

- Because the BIC response time graph intersects with that of Reno around the same point as that of HSTCP, it follows BIC is also TCP friendly at lower link speeds.
- The slope of BIC's response time at first rises steeply and then flattens out to that of TCP Reno for larger link speeds. This implies that for high-speed links, BIC exhibits the RTT fairness property.
- Because of the fast initial rise in its response time, BIC scales well with link speeds.

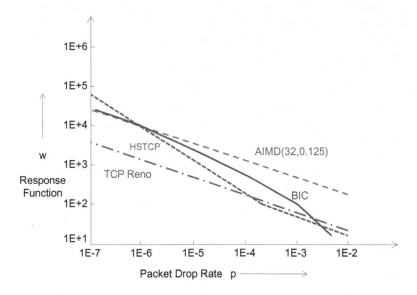

FIGURE 5.4

The concavity of the TCP Binary Increase Congestion control (BIC) response function.

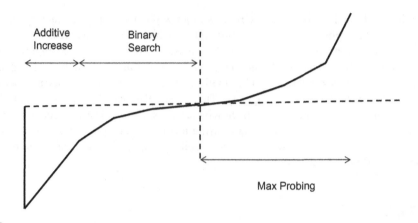

FIGURE 5.5

Window growth function of TCP BIC.

The evolution of BIC's congestion window proceeds in three stages (Figure 5.5): additive increase, binary search increase, and max probing.

5.4.1.1 Binary Search Increase

The Binary Search window increase rule in BIC was inspired by the binary search algorithm and operates as follows:

- If W_{max} is the maximum window size that was reached just before the last packet loss, and W_{min} is the window size just after the packet loss, then after 1 RTT, the algorithm computes W_{mid}, the midpoint between W_{max} and W_{min}, and sets the current window size to W_{mid}.
- After the resulting packet transmissions:
  - If there are no packet losses, then W_{min} is set to W_{mid}, or
  - If there are packet losses then W_{max} is set to W_{mid}.

For the case of no packet losses the process repeats for every RTT until the difference between W_{max} and W_{min} falls below a preset threshold S_{min}. Note that as a result of this algorithm, the window size increases logarithmically.

Just as for binary search, this process allows the bandwidth probing to be more aggressive when the difference between the current window and the target window is large and gradually becomes less aggressive as the current window gets closer to the target. This results in a reduction in the number of lost packets as the saturation point is reached. This behavior contrasts with HSTCP, which increases its rate near the link saturation point, resulting in excessive packet loss.

5.4.1.2 Additive Increase

When the distance to W_{mid} from the current W_{min} is too large, then increasing the window to that midpoint leads to a large burst of packets transmitted into the network, which can result in losses. In this situation, the window size is increased by a configured maximum step value S_{max}. This continues until the distance between W_{min} and W_{mid} falls below S_{max}, at which the W_{min} is set directly to W_{mid}. After a large window size reduction, the additive increase rule leads to an initial linear increase in window size followed by a logarithmic increase for the last few RTTs.

For large window sizes or equivalently for higher speed links, the BIC algorithm performs more as a pure additive increase algorithm because it spends most of its time in this mode. This implies that for high-speed links, its performance should be close to that of the AIMD algorithm, which is indeed the case from Figure 5.4.

5.4.1.3 Max Probing

When the current window size grows past W_{max}, the BIC algorithm switches to probing for the new maximum window, which is not known. It does so in a slow-start fashion by increasing its window size in the following sequence for each RTT: $W_{max} + S_{min}$, $W_{max} + 2S_{min}$, $W_{max} + 4S_{min}, \ldots, W_{max} + S_{max}$. The reasoning behind this policy is that it is likely that the new saturation point is close to the old point; hence, it makes sense to initially gently probe for available bandwidth before going at full blast. After the max probing phase, BIC switches to additive increase using the parameter S_{max}.

BIC also has a feature called **Fast Convergence** that is designed to facilitate faster convergence between a flow holding a large amount of bandwidth and a second flow that is starting from scratch. It operates as follows: If the new W_{max} for a flow is smaller than its previous value, then this is a sign of a downward trend. To facilitate the reduction of the flow's bandwidth, the new W_{max} is set to $(W_{max} + W_{min})/2$, which has the effect of reducing the increase rate of the larger window and thus allows the smaller window to catch up.

We now provide an approximate analysis of BIC using the sample path−based fluid approximation technique introduced in Section 2.3 of Chapter 2. This analysis explains the concave behavior of the BIC response time function as illustrated in Figure 5.4. We consider a typical cycle of window increase (see Figure 5.6), that is terminated when a packet is dropped at the end of the cycle.

Define the following:

W_{max}: Maximum window size
W_{min}: Minimum window size
N_1: Number of RTT rounds in the additive increase phase
N_2: Number of RTT rounds in the logarithmic increase phase
Y_1: Number of packets transmitted during the additive increase phase
Y_2: Number of packets transmitted during the logarithmic increase phase

As per the deterministic approximation technique, we make the assumption that the number of packets sent in each cycle of the congestion window is fixed (and equal to $1/p$, where p is the packet drop rate). The average throughput R_{avg} is then given by

$$R_{avg} = \frac{Y_1 + Y_2}{T(N_1 + N_2)} = \frac{1/p}{T(N_1 + N_2)} \tag{15}$$

We now proceed to compute the quantities Y_1, Y_2, N_1 and N_2.

Note that β is multiplicative decrease factor after a packet loss, so that

$$W_{min} = (1 - \beta)W_{max} \tag{16}$$

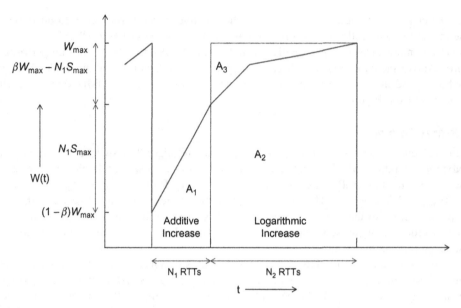

FIGURE 5.6

Evolution of TCP Binary Increase Congestion control (BIC) window size.

BIC switches to the logarithmic increase phase when the distance from the current window size to W_{max} is less than $2S_{max}$; hence, if this distance less than this, there is no additive increase. Because $W_{max} - W_{min} = \beta W_{max}$, it follows that N_1 is given by

$$N_1 = \max\left(\left\lceil \frac{\beta W_{max}}{S_{max}} \right\rceil - 2, 0\right) \tag{17}$$

and the total increase in window size during the logarithmic increase phase is given by $\beta W_{max} - N_1 S_{max}$, which we denote by X. Note that

$$\frac{X}{2} + \frac{X}{2^2} + \cdots + \frac{X}{2^{N_2}} = X - S_{min} \tag{18}$$

This equation follows from the fact that the X is reduced by half in each RTT of the logarithmic increase phase until the distance to W_{max} becomes less than S_{min}. From equation 18, it follows that

$$X\left(1 - \frac{1}{2^{N_2}}\right) = X - S_{min}, \text{ so that}$$

$$N_2 = \log\left(\frac{\beta W_{max} - N_1 S_{max}}{S_{min}}\right) + 2 \tag{19}$$

Note that 2 has been added in equation 19 to account for the first and last round trip latencies of the binary search increase.

We now compute Y_1 and Y_2. Y_1 is given by the formula

$$Y_1 = \frac{1}{T} \int_0^{N_1 T} W(T)dt \tag{20}$$

The integral is given by the area A_1 under the W(t) curve for the additive increase phase (Figure 5.6), which is given by

$$A_1 = (1 - \beta)W_{max}N_1 T + \frac{1}{2}(N_1 - 1)S_{max}N_1 T, \text{ so that}$$

$$Y_1 = (1 - \beta)W_{max}N_1 + \frac{1}{2}(N_1 - 1)S_{max}N_1 \tag{21}$$

Similarly, to compute Y_2, we need to find the area A_2 under the W(t) curve for the logarithmic increase phase. Note that from Figure 5.6, $A_3 = W_{max}N_2 - A_2$; hence, it is sufficient to find the area A_3. Define $Z = \beta W_{max} - N_1 S_{max}$, then A_3 is given by

$$A_3 = \left[\left(Z + \frac{Z}{2} \right) + \left(\frac{Z}{2} + \frac{Z}{2^2} \right) + \cdots + \left(\frac{Z}{2^m} + \frac{Z}{2^{m+1}} \right) + \cdots \right] - S_{min}$$

$$= 2Z - S_{min}$$

It follows that

$$Y_2 = W_{max}N_2 - 2(\beta W_{max} - N_1 S_{max}) + S_{min} \tag{22}$$

Because the total number of packets transmitted during a period is also given by 1/p, it follows that

$$\frac{1}{p} = Y_1 + Y_2 \tag{23}$$

Equation 23 can be used to express W_{max} as a function of p. Unfortunately, a closed-form expression for W_{max} does not exist in general, but it can computed for the following special cases:

1. $\beta W_{max} \gg 2S_{max}$

    This condition implies that the window function is dominated by the linear increase part, so that $N_1 >> N_2$ and from equations 17, 21, and 23, it can be shown that the average throughput is given by

$$R_{avg} \approx \frac{1}{T} \sqrt{\frac{S_{max}}{2} \frac{2 - \beta}{\beta} \frac{1}{p}} \tag{24}$$

    which is same as the throughput for a general AIMD congestion control algorithm that was derived in Chapter 2.

2. $\beta W_{max} > 2S_{max}$ and βW_{max} is divisible by S_{max}.

    From equations 21 to 23, it follows that

$$W_{max} = \frac{-b + \sqrt{b^2 + 4a\left(c + \frac{1}{p}\right)}}{2a} \tag{25}$$

where

$$a = \frac{\beta(2-\beta)}{2S_{max}} \quad b = \log\frac{S_{max}}{S_{min}} + \frac{2-\beta}{\beta} \quad c = S_{max} - S_{min}$$

and the throughput is given by

$$R_{avg} = \frac{1}{T}\frac{2-\beta}{p}\frac{1}{\sqrt{b^2 + 4a\left(c+\frac{1}{p}\right) + (1-\beta)b + \frac{\beta(2-\beta)}{2}}} \tag{26}$$

3. $\beta W_{max} \leq 2S_{max}$

This condition implies that $N_1 = 0$, and assuming $\frac{1}{p} \gg S_{min}$, W_{max} is approximately given by

$$W_{max} \approx \frac{1}{p}\frac{1}{\log\left(\frac{\beta W_{max}}{S_{min}}\right) + 2(1-\beta)} \tag{27}$$

This equation can be solved for W_{max} in terms of the LambertW(y) function (which is the only real solution to $xe^x = y$) to get

$$W_{max} = \frac{1}{p}\frac{\ln 2}{LambertW\left(\frac{4\beta e^{-2\beta \ln^2 \ln 2}}{pS_{min}}\right)} \tag{28}$$

so that

$$R_{avg} \approx \frac{Y_2}{TN_2} = \frac{W_{max}N_2 - 2\beta W_{max}}{TN_2} = \frac{W_{max}}{T}\left[1 - \frac{2\beta}{\log\left(\frac{\beta W_{max}}{S_{min}}\right) + 2}\right] \tag{29}$$

From these equations, we can draw the following conclusions:

- Because large values of W_{max} also correspond to large link capacities (because $W_{max} = CT$), it follows by a comparison of equations 24 and equation 72 in Chapter 2 that for high-capacity links, BIC operates similar to an AIMD protocol with increase parameter $a = S_{max}$, decrease parameter of $b = \beta$, and the exponent $d = 0.5$. This follows from the fact that for high-capacity links, the BIC window spends most of its time in the linear increase portion.
- For moderate values of C, we can get some insight into BIC's behavior by computing the constants in part 2. As recommended by Xu et al. [1], we choose the following values for BIC's parameters: $\beta = 0.125, S_{max} = 32, S_{min} = 0.01$. It follows that $a = 0.0036$, $b = 18.5$, and $c = 31.99$, and from equation 26, it follows that

$$R_{avg} = \frac{1.875}{T}\sqrt{\frac{1}{359.02p^2 + 0.014p}}$$

This formula implies that if $359p^2 >> 0.014p$, i.e., $p >> 3.9E(-5)$, then it follows that

$$R_{avg} = \frac{0.1}{Tp}$$

Hence, it follows that for larger packet drop rates (i.e., smaller values of C), the exponent $d = 1$.

Because $d = 0.5$ for large link capacities and $d = 1$ for smaller link capacities, it follows that for intermediate value of capacity $0.5 < d < 1$, which explains the concave shape of the BIC response function Figure 5.4.

Figure 5.7 from Xu et al. [1] shows the variation of the BIC response function as a function of S_{max} and S_{min}. Figure 5.7A shows that for a fixed value of S_{min}, increasing S_{max} leads to an increase in throughput for large link capacities. Figure 5.7B shows that for a fixed value of S_{max}, as S_{min} increases the throughput decreases for lower link capacities.

5.4.2 TCP CUBIC

TCP CUBIC is a follow-on design from the same research group that had earlier come up with TCP BIC [11]. Their main motivation in coming up with CUBIC was to improve on BIC in the following areas: (1) BIC's window increase function is too aggressive for Reno, especially under short RTT or low-speed networks, and (2) reduce the complexity of BIC's window increment–decrement rules to make the algorithm more analytically tractable and easier to implement.

Recall that BIC implemented the concave and convex functions that govern the window increase by using a binary search technique. To reduce the resulting complexity of the algorithm, CUBIC replaced the binary search by a cubic function, which contains both concave and convex portions. Another significant innovation in CUBIC is that the window growth depends only on the real time between consecutive congestion events, unlike TCP BIC or Reno in which the growth depends at the rate at which ACKs are returning back to the source. This makes the window growth independent of the round trip latency, so that if multiple TCP CUBIC flows are competing for bandwidth, then their windows are approximately equal. This results in a big improvement in the RTT fairness for CUBIC as shown later in this section.

Define the following:

$W(t)$: Window size at time t, given that the last packet loss occurred at $t = 0$
W_m: Window size at which the last packet loss occurred
τ: Average length of a cycle
α, K: Parameters of the window increase function
β: Multiplicative factor by which the window size is decreased after a packet loss, so that the new window is given by $(1 - \beta)W_m$

The window size increase function for TCP CUBIC is given by

$$W(t) = \alpha(t - K)^3 + W_m \tag{30}$$

Note that at $t = 0^+$, the window size is given by $W(0^+) = (1 - \beta)W_m$, so that

$$(1 - \beta)W_m = \alpha(-K)^3 + W_m, \text{ i.e.,}$$

$$K = \sqrt[3]{\frac{\beta W_m}{\alpha}} \tag{31}$$

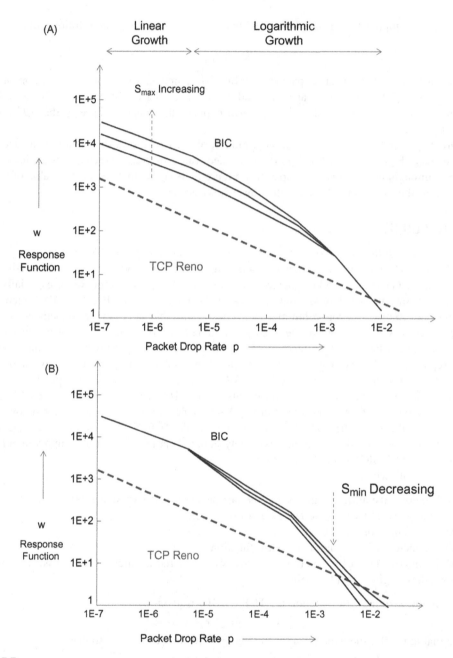

FIGURE 5.7

(A) TCP Binary Increase Congestion control (BIC) response function with varying S_{max}. (B) TCP BIC response function with varying S_{min}.

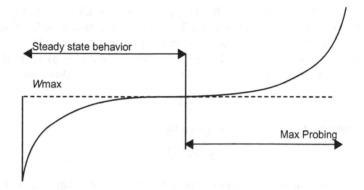

FIGURE 5.8

Window growth function for TCP CUBIC.

CUBIC runs in one of the following three different modes depending on the value of W(t):

1. CUBIC is in the TCP Mode if W(t) is less than the window size that TCP Reno would reach at time t.

   In short RTT networks, TCP Reno can grow faster than CUBIC because its window increases by one every RTT, but CUBIC's window increase rate is independent of the RTT. To keep CUBIC's growth rate the same as that of Reno in the situation, CUBIC emulates Reno's window adjustment algorithm after a packet loss event using an equivalent AIMD(α, β) algorithm as follows: Recall that the throughput for TCP Reno is given by

$$R = \frac{1}{T}\sqrt{\frac{3}{2p}}$$

and that for an AIMD(α, β) algorithm is given by

$$R = \frac{1}{T}\sqrt{\frac{\alpha(2-\beta)}{2\beta}\frac{1}{p}}$$

Hence, given β, a choice of

$$\alpha = \frac{3\beta}{2-\beta}$$

will ensure that the AIMD algorithm has the same average throughput as TCP Reno. Because the window size increases by α in every round trip and there are t/T round trips in time t, it follows that the emulated CUBIC window size after t seconds is given by

$$W_{AIMD}(t) = (1-\beta)W_m + \frac{3\beta}{(2-\beta)}\frac{t}{T}$$

   If W_{AIMD} is larger than W_{CUBIC} from equation 30, then W_{CUBIC} is set equal to W_{AIMD}. Otherwise, W_{CUBIC} is used as the current congestion window size.
2. If W(t) is greater than the corresponding TCP Reno window but less than W_m, then CUBIC is in the concave region.
3. If W(t) is larger than W_m, then CUBIC is in the convex region.

We now proceed to do an analysis of the throughput for TCP CUBIC. Again using the deterministic approximation technique from Section 2.3, we consider a typical cycle of window increase (Figure 5.9) that is terminated when a packet is dropped at the end of the cycle.

During the course of this cycle, the TCP window increases from $(1 - \beta)W_m$ to W_m, and we will assume that this takes on the average τ seconds. From equation 15, it follows that

$$\tau = \sqrt[3]{\frac{\beta W_m}{\alpha}} \tag{32}$$

Note that the throughput R(t) at time t, is given by

$$R(t) = \frac{W(t)}{T} \tag{33}$$

Again, using the deterministic assumption from Section 2.3 of Chapter 2, it follows that the average throughput is given by

$$R_{avg} = \frac{N}{\tau} \quad where \quad N = \frac{1}{p} \tag{34}$$

is the number of packets transmitted during a cycle. N is also given by

$$N = \int_0^\tau \frac{W(t)}{T} dt \tag{35}$$

Following the usual recipe, we equate N to 1/p, where p is the packet drop rate. Hence,

$$\frac{1}{p} = \int_0^\tau \frac{W(t)}{T} dt \tag{36}$$

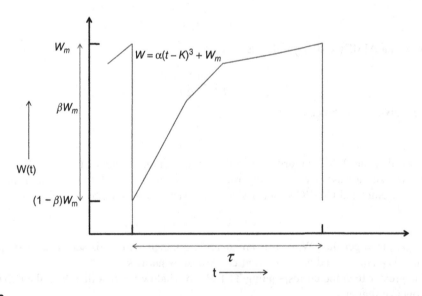

FIGURE 5.9

TCP CUBIC congestion window size over time.

Note that

$$\int_0^\tau W(t)dt = \int_0^\tau [\alpha(t-\tau)^3 + W_m]dt$$

$$= \tau W_m + \alpha \int_0^\tau (t-\tau)^3 dt \qquad (37)$$

$$= \tau W_m - \frac{\alpha\tau^4}{4}$$

Substituting equations 32 and 37 into equation 35, it follows that

$$\frac{T}{p} = W_m \left[\frac{\beta W_m}{\alpha}\right]^{1/3} - \frac{\alpha}{4}\left[\frac{\beta W_m}{\alpha}\right]^{4/3}$$

$$= W_m^{4/3} \frac{(4-\beta)}{4} \left(\frac{\beta}{\alpha}\right)^{1/3} \qquad (38)$$

This implies that

$$W_m = \sqrt[4]{\left(\frac{T}{p}\right)^3 \frac{\alpha}{\beta} \left(\frac{4}{4-\beta}\right)^3} \qquad (39)$$

and

$$\tau = \sqrt[3]{\left(\frac{\beta W_m}{\alpha}\right)} = \sqrt[4]{\frac{T}{p}\left(\frac{4}{4-\beta}\right)\left(\frac{\beta}{\alpha}\right)} \qquad (40)$$

The average throughput is then given by

$$R_{avg} = \frac{N}{\tau} = \frac{1/p}{\tau} = \sqrt[4]{\frac{\alpha(4-\beta)}{4p^3 T\beta}} \qquad (41)$$

From this equation, it follows that the response function for CUBIC is given by

$$\log w = \log R_{avg}T = 0.25 \log\frac{\alpha(4-\beta)}{4\beta} + 0.75 \log T - 0.75 \log p$$

Because CUBIC is forced to follow **TCP Reno** for smaller window sizes, its response function becomes

$$\log w = \begin{cases} 0.25 \log\dfrac{\alpha(4-\beta)}{4\beta} + 0.75 \log T - 0.75 \log p & if \quad p < \bar{p} \\ 0.09 - 0.5 \log p & if \quad p \geq \bar{p} \end{cases}$$

where

$$\log \bar{p} = \log\frac{\alpha(4-\beta)}{4\beta} + 3 \log T - 0.36.$$

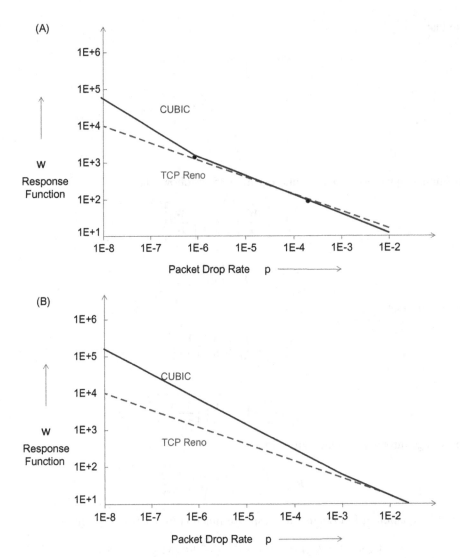

FIGURE 5.10

(A) Response function for TCP Reno and CUBIC for T = 10 ms. (B) Response function for TCP Reno and CUBIC for T = 100 ms.

Figure 5.10 clearly shows this piecewise linearity of the CUBIC response function for T = 10 ms and T = 100 ms, respectively.

Based on these equations, the response function for CUBIC can be regarded as a family of response functions parameterized by the round trip latency T. As shown in Figure 10A, for smaller values of T, the response functions of CUBIC and Reno mostly coincide, but for large values of T (see Figure 5.10B), the CUBIC response function grows faster and looks more like that of HSTCP.

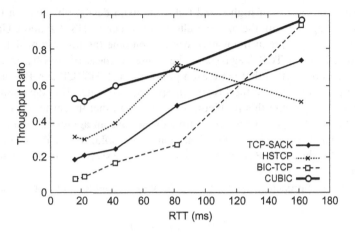

FIGURE 5.11

Intraprotocol fairness as a function of the round trip latency.

This is an interesting contrast with the behavior of HSTCP, in which the switch between HSTCP and TCP Reno happens as a function of the window size W alone, irrespective of the round trip latency T.

The dependency of the Reno–CUBIC cross-over point on T is a very attractive feature because most traffic, especially in enterprise environments, passes over networks with low latency, for whom regular TCP Reno works fine. If a high-speed algorithm is used over these networks, we would like it to coexist with Reno without overwhelming it, and CUBIC satisfies this requirement very well. Over high-speed long-distance networks with a large latency, on the other hand, TCP Reno is not able to make full use of the available bandwidth, but CUBIC naturally scales up its performance to do so.

Figure 5.11 shows the ratio between the throughputs of two flows of CUBIC, BIC, HSTCP, and TCP SACK, for a bottleneck link capacity of 400 mbps, and with one of the flows with a fixed RTT of 162 ms; the RTT of the other flow is varied between 16 ms and 162 ms. This clearly shows that CUBIC has better inter-RTT fairness than the other protocols. This can also be inferred from equation 4 because if we substitute e = 0.25 and d = 0.75, it follows that

$$\frac{R_1}{R_2} = \left(\frac{T_2}{T_1}\right)^{\frac{0.25}{1-0.75}} = \left(\frac{T_2}{T_1}\right).$$

Hence, TCP CUBIC has better intraprotocol fairness that any of the other high-speed protocols and even TCP Reno. This is because it does not use ACK clocking to time its packet transmissions.

5.5 **THE COMPOUND TCP (CTCP) PROTOCOL**

CTCP was invented by Tan et al. [5,12] from Microsoft Research and serves as the default congestion control algorithm in all operating systems from that company, from Windows Vista onward. In addition to making efficient use of high-speed links, the main design objective of CTCP was to be more TCP friendly compared with the existing alternatives such as HSTCP and CUBIC.

To do so, they came up with an innovative way to combine the fairness of delay-based congestion control approach (as in TCP Vegas) and the aggressiveness of loss-based approaches. Tan et al. [5,12] made the observation that the reason protocols such HSTCP and BIC are not very TCP friendly is that they continue to use the loss-based approach to congestion detection and as a result overload the network. To correct this problem, they suggested that the system should keep track of congestion using the TCP Vegas queue size estimator and use an aggressive window increase rule only when the estimated queue size is less than some threshold. When the estimated queue size exceeds the threshold, then CTCP switches to a less aggressive window increment rule, which approaches the one used by TCP Reno.

To implement their approach, they used the following decomposition for the window size into two components:

$$W(t) = W_c(t) + W_d(t) \tag{42}$$

In equation 42, $W_c(t)$ is the part of the window that reacts to loss-based congestion signals and changes its size according to the rules used by TCP Reno. The component $W_d(t)$, on the other hand, reacts to a delay-based congestion signal and a uses a new set of rules for changing its window size. Specifically, $W_d(t)$ has a rapid window increase rule when the network is sensed to be underutilized and gracefully reduces its size when the bottleneck queue builds up.

Define the following:

$W(t)$: CTCP Window size at time t
$W_c(t)$: Congestion component of the CTCP window size at time t
$W_d(t)$: Delay component of the CTCP window size at time t
T: Base value of the round trip latency
$T_s(t)$: Smoothed estimate of the round trip latency at time t
$R_E(t)$: Expected estimate of the CTCP throughput at time t
$R(t)$: Observed CTCP throughput at time t
$\theta(t)$: Delay-based congestion indicator at time t
γ: Delay threshold, such that the system is considered to b congested if $\theta(t) \geq \gamma$

We briefly recap the calculation of the delay-based congestion indicator from TCP Vegas (see Chapter 1):

$$R_E(t) = \frac{W(t)}{T}$$

$$R(t) = \frac{W(t)}{T_s(t)} \tag{43}$$

$$\theta(t) = (R_E(t) - R(t))T$$

Note that the expression for θ can also be written as

$$\theta(t) = \frac{W(t)}{T_s(t)}(T_s(t) - T) \tag{44}$$

which by Little's law equals the number of queued packets in the network.

CTCP specifies that the congestion window should evolve according to the following equations on a per RTT basis:

$$W \leftarrow W + \alpha W^k, \text{ when there are no packet losses or queuing delays and} \tag{45}$$

$$W \leftarrow (1 - \beta)W \text{ on one or more packet losses during a RTT} \tag{46}$$

Given that the standard TCP congestion window evolves according to (per RTT):

$$W_c \leftarrow W_c + 1 \text{ with no loss, and} \tag{47a}$$

$$W_c \leftarrow \frac{W_c}{2} \text{ with loss} \tag{47b}$$

it follows that the delay-based congestion window W_d should follow the following rules (per RTT):

$$W_d \leftarrow W_d + [\alpha W^k - 1]^+ \quad if \quad \theta \leq \gamma \tag{48a}$$

$$W_d \leftarrow [W_d - \varsigma\theta]^+ \quad if \quad \theta \geq \gamma \tag{48b}$$

$$W_d \leftarrow \left[(1 - \beta)W_d - \frac{W_c}{2}\right]^+ \text{ with loss} \tag{48c}$$

Using the fact that $W = W_c + W_d$, it follows from equations 47a and 47b and 48a to 48c that the CTCP window evolution rules (equations 45 and 46) can be written as

$$W \leftarrow W + \delta \quad if \quad W + \delta < \gamma \tag{49a}$$

$$W \leftarrow W_0 \quad if \quad W + \delta \geq W_0 \quad and \quad W_c < W_0 \tag{49b}$$

$$W \leftarrow W + 1 \quad if \quad W_c \geq W_0 \tag{49c}$$

$$W \leftarrow (1 - \beta)W \text{ with loss} \tag{49c}$$

where $\delta = \max\{\lfloor \alpha W^k \rfloor, 1\}$ and W_0 is given by equation 51.

The shape of the window increase function in equations 49a to 49c (Figures 5.12 and 5.13) is explained as follows: When the network queuing backlog is smaller than γ, the delay-based congestion window grows rapidly as per equation 48a. When the congestion level reaches γ, the congestion window continues to increase at the rate of one packet per round trip time, and the delay window starts to ramp down as per equation 48b. If the rate of increase of the congestion window W_c equals the rate of decrease of the delay window W_d, then the resulting CTCP window W stays constant at W_0 until the size of the congestion window W_c exceeds W_0. At that point, the CTCP window W resumes its increase at the same linear rate as the congestion window, and the delay window dwindles to zero (see equation 49c).

Referring to Figure 5.12, we now derive an expression for the throughput of CTCP using the deterministic sample path–based technique from Section 2.3. The evolution of the window increase is divided into three periods, as explained. Let the duration of these periods be T_{DE}, T_{EF}, and T_{FG} and let N_{DE}, N_{EF} and N_{FG} be the number of packets transmitted over these intervals. Then the average throughput R_{avg} is given by

$$R_{avg} = \frac{N_{DE} + N_{EF} + N_{FG}}{T_{DE} + T_{EF} + T_{FG}} \tag{50}$$

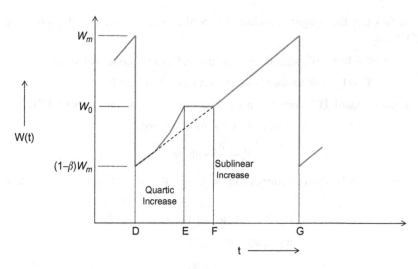

FIGURE 5.12

Evolution of CTCP window size.

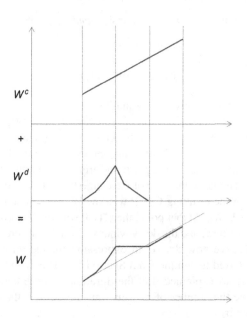

FIGURE 5.13

Evolution of the individual window sizes in CTCP.

Assuming that the CTCP window size at the end of the cycle is given by W_m, so that the window size at the start of the next cycle is given by $(1 - \beta)W_m$, we now proceed to compute the quantities in equation 50. Noting that the queue backlog during the interval T_{EF} is given by γ, it follows from Little's law that

$$\gamma = (T_s - T)\frac{W_0}{T_s}$$

where W_0 is the CTCP window size during this interval. Hence, it follows that

$$W_0 = \gamma\frac{T_s}{T_s - T} \tag{51}$$

During the interval T_{DE}, the CTCP window increases according to

$$\frac{dW}{dt} = \frac{\alpha W^k}{T_s}, \text{ so that} \tag{52}$$

$$\frac{W^{1-k}}{1 - k} = \frac{\alpha t}{T_s} \tag{53}$$

For the case $k = 0.75$, which is the recommended choice for k as we shall see later, it follows from equation 53 that

$$W(t) = \left(\frac{\alpha t}{4T_s}\right)^4, \quad t_D \leq t \leq t_E$$

which illustrates the rapid increase in the window size in this region. Because W increases as a power of 4, we refer to this as quartic increase.

Because the window size increases from $(1 - \beta)W_m$ to W_0 during the interval T_{DE}, from equation 53, it follows that

$$T_{DE} = \frac{T_s}{\alpha(1 - k)}\left[W_0^{1-k} - (1 - \beta)^{1-k}W_m^{1-k}\right] \tag{54}$$

and the number of packets transmitted during this interval is given by (with $T_{DE} = t_D - t_E$)

$$N_{DE} = \int_{t_d}^{t_E} \frac{W}{T_s}dt = \left[\frac{\alpha(1-k)}{T_s}\right]^{\frac{1}{1-k}}\frac{1}{T_s}\int_{t_d}^{t_E} t^{\frac{1}{1-k}}dt$$

$$= \frac{1}{\alpha(2 - k)}\left[W_0^{2-k} - (1 - \beta)^{2-k}W_m^{2-k}\right] \tag{55}$$

Note that the interval T_{EF} comes to an end when the size of the congestion window W^c becomes equal to W_0. Because $\frac{dW^c}{dt} = \frac{1}{T_s}$, by equation 47, it follows that

$$T_{DF} = [W_0 - (1 - \beta)W_m]T_s \quad \text{and} \tag{56}$$

$$T_{EF} = T_{DF} - T_{DE} = [W_0 - (1 - \beta)W_m]T_s - \frac{T_s}{\alpha(1 - k)}\left[W_0^{1-k} - (1 - \beta)^{1-k}W_m^{1-k}\right] \tag{57}$$

$$\text{and } N_{EF} = W_0 T_{EF}. \tag{58}$$

During the interval T_{FG}, the CTCP window increases linearly as for TCP Reno, so that

$$\frac{dW}{dt} = \frac{1}{T_s} \quad \text{so that} \quad \Delta W = \frac{\Delta t}{T_s}.$$

Hence,

$$T_{FG} = (W_m - W_0)T_s \text{ and} \tag{59}$$

$$N_{FG} = \int_{t_F}^{t_G} \frac{W}{T_s} dt = \int_{t_F}^{t_G} \frac{t}{T_s^2} dt = \frac{t_G^2 - t_F^2}{2T_s^2} \tag{60}$$

$$= \frac{W_m^2 - W_0^2}{2}$$

Note that the total number of packets transmitted over the interval T_{DG} is also given by $1/p$, so that

$$\frac{1}{p} = N_{DE} + N_{EF} + N_{FG} \tag{61}$$

Equation 61 can be numerically solved to obtain the value of W_m, which can then be substituted back into equations 54, 57, and 59 to obtain the length of the interval T_{DG}. From equation 50, it follows that

$$R_{avg} = \frac{1/p}{T_{DG}} \tag{62}$$

If we make the assumption that the packet loss rate is high enough to cause the window size to decrease during the interval T_{DE}, it is possible to obtain a closed-form expression for R. In this case, $N_{DE} = 1/p$ so that

$$\frac{1}{\alpha(2-k)} \left[W_m^{2-k} - (1-\beta)^{2-k} W_m^{2-k} \right] = \frac{1}{p} \text{ so that}$$

$$W_m = \left[\frac{\alpha(2-k)}{1-(1-\beta)^{2-k}} \right]^{\frac{1}{2-k}} \frac{1}{p^{\frac{1}{2-k}}} \text{ and} \tag{63}$$

$$T_{DE} = \frac{T_s W_m^{1-k}}{\alpha(1-k)} \left[1 - (1-\beta)^{1-k} \right] \tag{64}$$

The average throughput R_{avg} is then given by

$$R_{avg} = \frac{\frac{1}{p}\alpha(1-k)}{T_s W_m^{1-k}(1 - (1-\beta)^{1-k})}$$

$$= \left(\frac{\alpha}{p} \right)^{\frac{1}{2-k}} \frac{1}{T_s(1 - (1-\beta)^{1-k})} \left[\frac{1-(1-\beta)^{2-k}}{2-k} \right]^{\frac{1-k}{2-k}} \tag{65}$$

To make the variation of the throughput with p the same as that for HSTCP, Tan et al. [5,12] chose k so that $1/(2 - k) = 0.833$, so $k = 0.8$. To make the implementation easier, they used $k = 0.75$ instead.

We can develop some intuition into CTCP's performance with the following considerations: With reference to Figure 5.12, note that the demarcation between the quartic increase portion of the CTCP window and the linear increase portion is governed by the window size parameter W_0 given by

$$W_0 = \gamma \frac{T_s}{T_s - T}.$$

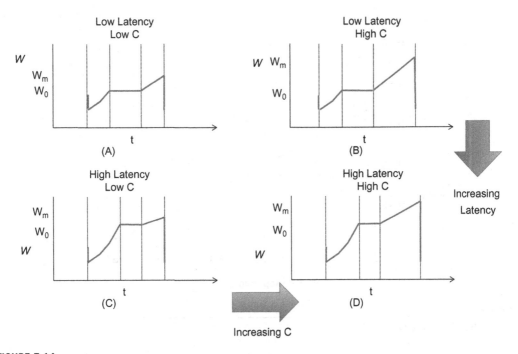

FIGURE 5.14

Variation of TCP window with varying latency and link capacities.

From this equation, it follows that:

- For networks with large latencies, the end-to-end delay is dominated by the propagation delays; hence, $T_s \approx T$. This leads to a large value of W_0.
- For networks with small latencies, the queuing delays may dominate the propagation delays, so that $T_s \gg T$. This leads to small values of W_0.

The interesting fact to note is that W_0 is independent of the link capacity, which we now use to obtain some insights into CTCP behavior. Also note that in the absence of random link errors, the maximum window size W_m is approximately equal to the delay bandwidth product CT.

Based on the values of the link speed C and the threshold W_0, we can have four different scenarios (Figure 5.14):

- As link speed C increases, for a fixed value of end-to-end latency, then W_m increases, and as a result, the number of packets transmitted in the linear portion of window increases (see, e.g., the change from equations 14a to 14b or 14c to 14d). This can also be seen by the formula for N_{FG} in equation 60. As a result, at higher link speeds, the CTCP throughput converges toward that for TCP Reno.
- As the end-to-end latency increases, then W_0 increases as explained above, and the number of packets transmitted in the quartic region of the CTCP window increases (see, e.g., the change

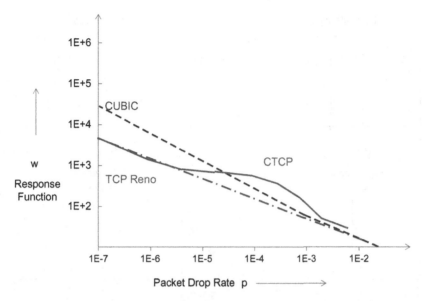

FIGURE 5.15

Response functions for CTCP, CUBIC, and Reno.

from equation 14a to 14c or 14b to 14d). This can also be seen by the formula for N_{DE} in equation 55. As a result, an increase in latency causes the CTCP throughput to increase faster compared with that of Reno. This behavior is reminiscent with that of CUBIC because CUBIC's throughput also increased with respect to Reno as the end-to-end latency increases. However, the CTCP throughput will converge back to that for Reno as the link speed becomes sufficiently large, while the CUBIC throughput keeps diverging.

These two effects are clearly evident in the response function plot in Figure 5.15.

Figure 5.15 plots the response function for CTCP in which the following features are evident: The response functions for Reno and CTCP are close to each other at lower link speeds. Then as the link speed increases, CTCP increases at a faster rate and diverges away from Reno. This can be explained by the fact that the quartic increase portion dominates the linear increase in this region. Finally, when the link speed assumes very large values, to the left part of the graph, CTCP and Reno again converge together. This is because the linear portion of the window increase in CTCP is dominant at high link speeds, as explained earlier.

As the lend-to-end latency increases, we can expect this pattern to persist, with the difference that the portion of the curve where the CTCP response time is bigger will move to the left (because of larger values of W_0).

Figure 5.15 also plots the response function for CUBIC for comparison purposes. Observe that response functions for CUBIC starts diverging away from that of Reno as the link speed increases, and unlike CTCP, the divergence keeps increasing. This implies that at very high link speeds CTCP will be at a disadvantage with respect to CUBIC or Reno, as has been noted by Munir et al. [13].

From the discussion in the previous few sections, we observe that there is a fundamental difference between the response function for HSTCP on one hand and that for CUBIC or CTCP on the other. In the latter case, the response function changes as the round trip latency changes and tends to be more TCP Reno friendly at lower latencies. This is an attractive property to have because lower latencies correspond to LAN environments, in which most transfers still use TCP Reno. On the other hand, at higher latencies, both CUBIC and CTCP response functions diverge from that of TCP Reno (CUBIC more so than CTCP). This is tolerable because Reno is not able to make full use of the available link capacity in high-latency and high-capacity networks and may even become unstable.

5.6 **THE FAST TCP PROTOCOL**

The design of FAST TCP was inspired by that of TCP Vegas, and in contrast to the other high-speed protocols, it uses end-to-end delay as a measure of congestion rather than dropped packets. Given the description of TCP Vegas in Chapter 1, the following equation describes the evolution of TCP Vegas' window size (assuming that the parameters $\alpha = \beta$):

$$W_i(t+1) = W_i(t) + \frac{1}{T_i(t)} \text{sgn}(\alpha_i - R_i(t)\theta_i(t)) \tag{66}$$

where $\theta_i(t)$ is the queuing delay that connection i experiences, such that the round trip latency is given by $T_i(t) = T_i + \theta_i(t)$, where T_i is the fixed part. Hence, $R_i(t)\theta_i(t)$ is a measure of the number of queued packets from the connection in the network. The function $\text{sgn}(z) = -1$ if $z < 0$, 0 if $z = 0$ and 1 if $z > 0$. Hence, TCP Vegas adjusts its window up or down by one packet per RTT depending on whether the number of queued packets is smaller or greater than its target α.

To create a high-speed version of this algorithm, Wei et al. [7]. changed the window size evolution equation to

$$W_i(t+1) = W_i(t) + \gamma_i(\alpha_i - R_i(t)\theta_i(t)) \quad \gamma_i \in (0, 1] \tag{67}$$

As a result, the window adjustments in FAST TCP depend on the magnitude as well as the sign of the difference $\alpha_i - R_i(t)\theta_i(t)$ and are no longer restricted to a change of at most 1 every round trip time. Hence, FAST can adjust its window by a large amount, either up or down, when the number of buffered packets is far away from its target and by a smaller amount when it is closer.

It can be shown that FAST has the following property: The equilibrium throughputs of FAST are the unique optimal vector that maximize the sum $\sum_i \alpha_i \log R_i$ subject to the link constraint that the aggregate flow rate at any link does not exceed the link capacity. This result was obtained using the Primal-Dual solution to a Lagrangian optimization problem using the methodology described in Chapter 3. Furthermore, the equilibrium throughputs are given by

$$R_i^{avg} = \frac{\alpha_i}{\overline{\theta_i}} \tag{68}$$

Just as for TCP Vegas, equation 68 shows that FAST does not penalize flows with large round trip latencies, although in practice, it has been observed that flows with longer RTTs obtain smaller throughput than those with shorter RTTs. Equation 68 also implies that in equilibrium, source i maintains α_i packets in the buffers along its path. Hence, the total amount of buffering in the network is at least $\sum_i \alpha_i$ to reach equilibrium. Wang et al. [14] have also proven a stability result for FAST, which states that it is locally asymptotically stable in general networks when all the sources have a common round trip delay, no matter how large the delay is.

5.7 THE EXPRESS CONTROL PROTOCOL (XCP)

The XCP congestion control algorithm [15] is an example of a "clean slate" design, that is, it is a result of a fundamental rethink of the congestion control problem without worrying about the issue of backward compatibility. As a result, it cannot deployed in a regular TCP/IP network because it requires multi-bit feedback, but it can be used in a self-contained network that is separated from the rest of the Internet (which can done by using the split TCP architecture from Chapter 4, for example).

XCP fundamentally changes the nature of the feedback from the network nodes by having them provide explicit window increase or decrease numbers back to the sources. It reverses TCP's design philosophy in the sense that all congestion control intelligence is now in the network nodes. As a result, the connection windows can be adjusted in a precise manner so that the total throughput at a node matches its available capacity, thus eliminating rate oscillations. This allows the senders to decrease their windows rapidly when the bottleneck is highly congested while performing smaller adjustments when the sending rate is close to the capacity (this is similar to the BIC and CUBIC designs and conforms to the averaging principle). To improve system stability, XCP reduces the rate at which it makes window adjustments as the round trip latency increases.

Another innovation in XCP is the decoupling of efficiency control (the ability to get to high link utilization) from fairness control (the problem of how to allocate bandwidth fairly among competing flows). This is because efficiency control should depend only on the aggregate traffic behavior, but any fair allocation depends on the number of connections passing through the node. Hence, an XCP-based AQM controller has both an efficiency controller (EC) and a fairness controller (FC), which can be modified independently of the other. In regular TCP, the two problems coupled together because the AIMD window increase−decrease mechanism is used to accomplish both objectives, as was shown in the description of the Chiu-Jain theory in Chapter 1.

5.7.1 XCP PROTOCOL DESCRIPTION

The XCP protocol works as follows:

- Traffic source k maintains a congestion window W_k, and keeps track of the round trip latency T_k. It communicates these numbers to the network nodes via a congestion header in every packet. Note that the rate R_k at source k is given by

$$R_k = \frac{W_k}{T_k}$$

Whenever a new ACK arrives, the following equation is used to update the window:

$$W_k \leftarrow W_k + S_k \tag{69}$$

where S_k is explicit window size adjustment that is computed by the bottleneck node and is conveyed back to the source in the ACK packet. Note that S_k can be either positive or negative, depending on the congestion conditions at the bottleneck.

- Network nodes monitor their input traffic rate. Based on the difference between the link capacity C and the aggregate rate Y given by $Y = \sum_{k=1}^{K} R_k$, the node tells the connections sharing the link to increase or decrease their congestion windows, which is done once every average round trip latency, for all the connections passing through the node (this automatically reduces the frequency of updates as the latencies increase). This information is conveyed back to the source by a field in the header. Downstream nodes can reduce this number if they are experiencing greater congestion, so that in the end, the feedback ACK contains information from the bottleneck node along the path.

- **Operation of the Efficiency Controller (EC):** The EC's objective is to maximize link utilization while minimizing packet drops and persistent queues. The aggregate feedback ϕ (in bytes) is computed as follows:

$$\phi = \alpha T_{av} \left(C - \sum_{k=1}^{K} R_k \right) - \beta b \tag{70}$$

where α, β are constants whose values are set based on the stability analysis, T_{av} is the average round trip latency for all connections passing through the node, and b is the minimum queue seen by an arriving packet during the last round trip interval (i.e., it's the queue that does not drain at the end of a round trip interval). The first term on the RHS is proportional to the mismatch between the aggregate rate and the link capacity (multiplied by the round trip latency to convert it into bytes). The second term is required for the following reason: When there is a persistent queue even if the rates in the first term are matching, then the second term helps to reduce this queue size.

From the discussion in Chapter 3, the first term on the RHS in equation 7 is proportional to the derivative of the queue length, and the second term is proportional to the difference between the current queue size and the target size of zero. Hence, the XCP controller is equivalent to the proportional-integral (PI) controller discussed in Chapter 3.

Note that the increase in transmission rates in XCP can be very fast because the increase is directly proportional to the spare link bandwidth as per equation 70, which makes XCP suitable for use in high-speed links. This is in contrast to TCP, in which the increase is by at most one packet per window.

- **Operation of the Fairness Controller (FC):** The job of the FC is to divide up the aggregate feedback among the K connections in a fair manner. It achieves fairness by making use of the AIMD principle, so that:
  - If $\phi > 0$, then the allocation is done so that the increase in throughput for all the connections is the same.
  - If $\phi < 0$, then the allocation is done so that the decrease in throughput of a connection proportional to its current throughput.

When ϕ is approximately zero, then the convergence to fairness comes to a halt. To prevent this, XCP does an artificial deallocation and allocation of bandwidth among the K connections by using the feedback h given by

$$h = \max \left(0, 0.1 \sum_{k=1}^{K} R_k - |\phi| \right), \tag{71}$$

so on every RTT, at least 10% of the traffic is redistributed according to AIMD. This process is called "bandwidth shuffling" and is the principle fairness mechanism in XCP to redistribute bandwidth among connections when a new connection starts up.

The per packet feedback to source k can be written as

$$\phi_k = p_k - n_k \tag{72}$$

where p_k is the positive feedback and n_k is the negative feedback.

First consider the case when $\phi > 0$. This quantity needs to be equally divided among the throughputs of the K connections. The corresponding change in window size of the kth connection is given by $\Delta W_k = \Delta R_k T_k \propto T_k$ because the throughput deltas are equal. This change needs to be split equally among the packets from connection k that pass through the node during time T_k, say m_k. Note that m_k is proportional to W_k/MSS_k and inversely proportional to T_k. It follows that the change in window size per packet for connection k is given by

$$p_k = K_p \frac{T_k^2 MSS_k}{W_k} \tag{73}$$

where K_p is a constant. Because the total increase in aggregate traffic rate is $\frac{h + \max(\phi,0)}{T_{av}}$, it follows that

$$\frac{h + \max(\phi,0)}{T_{av}} = \sum^{L} \frac{p_k}{T_k} \tag{74}$$

where the summation is over the average number of packets seen by the node during an average RTT. Substituting equation 73 into equation 74, we obtain

$$K_p = \frac{h + \max(\phi,0)}{T_{av} \sum^{L} \frac{T_k MSS_k}{W_k}} \tag{75}$$

When $\phi < 0$, then the decrease in throughput should be proportional to the current throughput. It follows that $\Delta W_k = \Delta R_k T_k \propto R_k T_k = W_k$. Splitting up this change in window size among all the m_k packets that pass through the node during an RTT, it follows that

$$n_k = \frac{K_n W_k}{m_k} = K_n T_k MSS_k \tag{76}$$

where the constant K_n is given by

$$K_n = \frac{h + \max(-\phi,0)}{T_{av} \sum^{L} MSS_k} \tag{77}$$

5.7.2 XCP STABILITY ANALYSIS

In this section, we show that the if parameters α, β (that appear in equation 70) satisfy the conditions:

$$0 < \alpha < \frac{\pi}{4\sqrt{2}} \quad \text{and} \quad \beta = \alpha^2 \sqrt{2} \tag{78}$$

then the system is stable, independently of delay, capacity, and number of connections. This analysis is done using the techniques introduced in Chapter 3, whereby the system dynamics with feedback are captured in the fluid limit using ordinary differential equations, to which the Nyquist stability criterion is applied.

In this section, we will assume that the round trip latencies for all the k connections are equal, so that $T_k = T_{av} = T$, $k = 1,\ldots,K$. Using the notation used in the previous section, note that the total traffic input rate into the bottleneck queue is given by

$$Y(t) = \sum_{k=1}^{K} R_k(t) = \sum_{k=1}^{K} \frac{W_k(t)}{T} \tag{79}$$

Because the aggregate feedback ϕ is divided up among the K connections, every T seconds, it follows that the total rate of change in their window sizes is given by ϕ/T bytes/sec. Using equation 70, it follows that

$$\sum_{k=1}^{K} \frac{dW_k}{dt} = \frac{1}{T}[-\alpha T(y(t-T)-C) - \beta b(t-T)] \tag{80}$$

From equations 79 and 80, it follows that

$$\frac{dY(t)}{dt} = \frac{1}{T^2}[-\alpha T(Y(t-T)-C) - \beta b(t-T)] \tag{81}$$

Hence, the equations that govern the input traffic rate and buffer dynamics are the following

$$\frac{db(t)}{dt} = \begin{cases} Y(t) - C & \text{if } b(t) > 0 \\ \max(0, Y(t) - C) & \text{if } b(t) = 0 \end{cases} \tag{82}$$

$$\frac{dY}{dt} = -\frac{\alpha}{T}(Y(t-T)-C) - \frac{\beta}{T^2}b(t-T) \tag{83}$$

These form a feedback loop, as shown in Figure 5.16. In this figure, the queue dynamics are governed by equation 82, and the rate allocation is done via equation 83. These equations have the equilibrium point $b_{eq} = 0$ and $Y_{eq} = C$. If we consider the following linear equations around this equilibrium point, by making the substitution $x(t) = Y(t) - C$, we get

$$\frac{db(t)}{dt} = x(t) \tag{84}$$

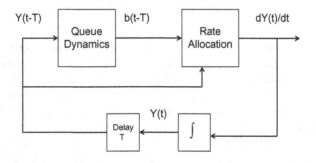

FIGURE 5.16

Rate allocation and queue size dynamics in eXpress Control Protocol (XCP).

$$\frac{dx(t)}{dt} = -K_1 x(t-T) - K_2 b(t-T) \tag{85}$$

where

$$K_1 = \frac{\alpha}{T} \quad and \quad K_2 = \frac{\beta}{T^2} \tag{86}$$

Passing to the Laplace transform space, it follows from equations 84 and 85 that the open loop transfer function for the system is given by

$$G(s) = \frac{sK_1 + K_2}{s^2} e^{-sT} \tag{87}$$

To apply the Nyquist Criterion, we express equation 87 in the complex plane by making the substitution $s = j\omega$, so that

$$G(j\omega) = |G(j\omega)|e^{-\arg(G(j\omega))}$$

where

$$|G(j\omega)| = \frac{\sqrt{\omega^2 K_1^2 + K_2^2}}{\omega^2} \tag{88}$$

and

$$\arg(G(j\omega)) = \pi - \tan^{-1}\frac{\omega K_1}{K_2} + \omega T \tag{89}$$

We now choose the critical frequency ω_c at which $|G(j\omega_c)| = 1$, as a function of the parameters K_1 and K_2 as follows

$$\omega_c = \frac{K_2}{K_1} \tag{90}$$

Using equation 88, it follows that $\frac{K_2}{K_1^2} = \sqrt{2}$, which can be expressed using equation 86 as $\beta = \alpha^2 \sqrt{2}$.

To prove stability of the closed-loop system, the Nyquist criterion requires that $\arg(G(j\omega_c)) < \pi$ radians. Substituting equation 90 into equation 89, it follows that

$$\arg(G(j\omega_c)) = \pi - \frac{\pi}{4} + \frac{\beta}{\alpha} < \pi \quad i.e. \quad \alpha < \frac{\pi}{4\sqrt{2}}$$

which completes the proof.

This analysis shows that unlike for traditional congestion control and AQM schemes, XCP's stability criterion is independent of the link capacity, round trip latency, or number of connections. It was later shown by Balakrishnan et al. [16] that the linearization assumption around the point $b_{eq} = 0$ may not be a good approximation because the system dynamics are clearly nonlinear at this point (see equation 82). They did a more exact stability analysis using Lyapunov functionals and showed that the more exact stability region for α, β varies as a function of T and is in fact much larger than the region given by equation 78. However, it is not an exact superset because there are points near the boundary of the curve $\beta = \alpha^2 \sqrt{2}$ that lie in the stable region as per the linear analysis but actually lie in the unstable region according to the nonlinear analysis (see Balakrishnan et al. [16]).

5.8 **THE RATE CONTROL PROTOCOL (RCP)**

The RCP protocol [17] was inspired by XCP and builds on it to assign traffic rates to connections in a way such that they can quickly get to the ideal Processor Sharing (PS) rate. RCP is an entirely rate-based protocol (i.e., no windows are used). Network nodes compute the ideal PS-based rate and then pass this information back to the source, which immediately changes its rate to the minimum PS rate that was computed by the nodes that lie along its path.

RCP was designed to overcome the following issue with XCP: When a new connection is initiated in XCP and the nodes along its path are already at their maximum link utilizations, then XCP does a gradual redistribution of the link capacity using the bandwidth-shuffling process (see equation 71). Dukkipatti and McKeown [17] have shown that this process can be quite slow because new connections start with a small window and get to a fair allocation of bandwidth in a gradual manner by using the AIMD principle. However, it takes several round trips before convergence happens, and for smaller file sizes, the connection may never get to a fair bandwidth distribution. Hence, one of the main innovations in RCP, compared with XCP, is that the bandwidth reallocation happens in one round trip time, in which a connection gets its equilibrium rate.

The RCP algorithm operates as follows:

- Every network node periodically computes a fair-share rate R(t) that it communicates to all the connections that pass through it. This computation is done approximately once per round trip delay.
- RCP mandates two extra fields in the packet header: Each network node fills field 1 with is fair share value R(t), and when the packet gets to the destination, it copies this field into the ACK packet sends it back to the source. Field 2, as in XCP, is used communicate the current average round trip latency T_k, from a connection to all the network nodes on its path. The nodes use this information to compute the average round trip latency T_{av} of all the connections that pass through it.
- Each source transmits at rate R_k, which is the smallest offered rate along its path.
- Each network node updates its local rate R(t) according to the equation below:

$$R(t) = R(t - T_{av}) + \frac{\left[\alpha(C - Y(t)) - \beta\frac{b(t)}{T_{av}}\right]}{\hat{N}(t)} \tag{91}$$

where $\hat{N}(t)$ is the node's estimate of the number of connections that pass through it and the other variables are as defined for XCP.

The basic idea behind equation 91 is that if there is spare bandwidth available (equal to $C - Y(t)$), then share it equally among all the connections; on the other hand, if $C - Y(t) < 0$, then the link is over subscribed, and each connection is asked to decrease its rate evenly. If there is a queue build-up of b(t), then a rate decrease of $b(t)/T_{av}$ will bring it down to zero within a round trip interval.

RCP replaces the interval at which the node recomputes R(t) to T′, so that it is user configurable and uses the following estimate for the number of connections:

$$\hat{N}(t) = \frac{C}{R(t - T')}$$

so that equation 91 can be written as

$$R(t) = R(t - T') \left| 1 + \frac{\frac{T'}{T_{av}}\left(\alpha(C - Y(t)) - \beta\frac{b(t)}{T_{av}}\right)}{C} \right| \tag{92}$$

where the rate change has been scaled down by T'/T_{av} because it is done more than once per T_{av} seconds.

It can be easily shown that system dynamic equations for RCP are exactly the same as for XCP (see equations 82 and 83). Hence, the stability conditions derived for XCP in the previous section hold in this case as well.

5.9 STABILITY OF HIGH-SPEED TCP ALGORITHMS

The algorithms described in this chapter all operate in the region where regular TCP has been shown to exhibit poor performance because of oscillatory behavior. From the analysis that was described in Chapter 3, the following techniques were found to increase the stability of congestion control algorithms in networks with high link capacity or end-to-end latency:

- Sophisticated AQM schemes that feed back the buffer occupancy value, as well as the first or higher derivatives of the buffer occupancy. Note that the first derivative of the buffer occupancy is given by

$$\frac{db(t)}{dt} = C - \sum_i R_i$$

so that it provides the same information as the difference between the link capacity and the current traffic load (i.e., how close the link is to saturation).
- Window size increment rules that incorporate the Averaging Principle (AP) to reduce the rate of the window size increase as the link approaches saturation

The natural question to ask is how do the algorithms described in this chapter fare in this regard? We have not seen any work that applies control theory to models for HSTCP, BIC, CUBIC, or CTCP, but simulations show that they are much more stable than Reno in the high-link speed and large propagation delay environment.

A reason why this is the case can be gleaned from the principles enunciated earlier. Applying the Averaging Principle, algorithms that reduce the window increment size as the link reaches saturation, are more stable than those that do not do so. BIC, CUBIC, CTCP, and FAST all fall into this category of algorithms. BIC, CUBIC, and FAST reduce their window increment size in proportion to how far they are from the link saturation point while CTCP changes to a linear rate of increase (from quartic) when the queue backlog increases beyond a threshold. XCP and RCP, on the other hand, use a sophisticated AQM scheme in which the network nodes feed back the value of the buffer occupancy as well as the difference between the link capacity and the total traffic load. The Quantum Congestion Notification (QCN) algorithm that we will meet in Chapter 8 uses a combination of the averaging principle and first derivative feedback to achieve stability.

The HSTCP algorithm, on the other hand, does not fall cleanly into one of these categories. But note that HSTCP decreases its window size decrement value (on detecting packet loss) as the window size increases, and in general, algorithms that do a less drastic reduction of their window size compared with Reno have better stability properties (because this has the effect of reducing the rate oscillations). This is also true for TCP Westwood (see Chapter 4), whose window size reduction is proportional to the amount of queuing delay. The Data Center Congestion Control Protocol (DCTCP) algorithm (see Chapter 7) also falls in this class because it reduces its window size in proportion to the amount of time that the queue size exceeds some threshold.

5.10 FURTHER READING

Other TCP algorithms designed for high-speed long latency links include Scalable TCP [18], H-TCP [19], Yeah-TCP [6], TCP Africa [9], and TCP Illinois [4]. All of these are deployed on fewer than 2% of the servers on the Internet, according to the study done by Yang et al. [8].

REFERENCES

[1] Xu L, Harfoush K, Rhee I. Binary increase congestion control (BIC) for fast long distance networks. IEEE INFOCOM 2004;4:2514–24.
[2] Bao W, Wong VWS, Leung VCM. A model for steady state throughput of TCP CUBIC. IEEE Globecom 2010:1–6.
[3] Floyd S., Ratnasamy S., Shenker S. Modifying TCP's congestion control for high speed networks. 2002. http://www.icir.org/floyd/papers/hstcp.pdf
[4] Liu S, Basar T, Srikant R. TCP-Illinois: a loss and delay based congestion control algorithm for high speed networks. VALUETOOLS 2006.
[5] Tan K, Song J, Zhang Q, Sridharan M. A compound TCP approach for high speed and long distance networks. IEEE INFOCOM 2006.
[6] Baiocchi A, Castellani AP, Vacirca F. YeAH-TCP: yet another highspeed TCP. PFLDNet 2007;7:37–42.
[7] Wei DX, Jin C, Low SH, Hegde S. FAST TCP: motivation, architecture, algorithms, performance. IEEE/ACM ToN 2006;14(6):1246–59.
[8] Yang P, Luo W, Xu L, et al. TCP congestion avoidance algorithm identification. International Conference on Distributed Computing Systems 2013;22(4):1311–24.
[9] King R, Baraniuk R, Riedi R. TCP Africa: an adaptive and fair rapid increase rule for scalable TCP. IEEE INFOCOM 2005;3:1838–48.
[10] Floyd S. Highspeed TCP for large congestion windows. RFC 3649.
[11] Ha S, Rhee I, Xu L. CUBIC: a new TCP friendly high speed TCP variant. ACM Sigops Oper Syst Rev 2008;42(5):64–74.
[12] Tan K, Song J, Zhang Q, Sridharan M. Compound TCP: a scalable and TCP friendly congestion control for high speed networks. PFLDNet 2006.
[13] Munir K, Welzl M, Damjanovic D. Linux beats Windows!—or the worrying evolution of TCP in common operating systems. PFLDNet 2007.

[14] Wang J, Wei DX, Low S. Modeling and stability of FAST TCP. INFOCOM 2005;2:938—48.

[15] Katabi D, Handley M, Rohrs C. Congestion control for high bandwidth-delay product networks. ACM SIGCOMM 2002;32(4):89—102.

[16] Balakrishnan H, Dukkipati N, McKeown N, Tomlin CJ. Stability analysis of explicit congestion control protocols. IEEE Commun Mage 2007;11(10):823—5.

[17] Dukkipati N, McKeown N. Processor sharing flows in the Internet. Stanford HPNG TR 2005:271—85.

[18] Kelly T. Scalable TCP: Improving performance in highspeed wide area networks. ACM SIGCOMM CCR 2003;33(2):83—91.

[19] Leith D, Shorten R. H-TCP: TCP for high speed and long distance networks. PFLDNet 2004.

SUGGESTED READING

Blanc A, Collange C, Avrachenkov K. Comparing some high speed TCP versions under Bernoulli losses. INRIA Res Rep 2009:9.

Blanc A, Avrachenkov K, Collange D, Neglia G. Compound TCP with random losses. Networking 2009:482—94.

Carofiglio G, Muscariello L, Rossi D. Rethinking Low Extra Delay Background Transport (LEDBAT) Protocols. Computer Networks 2013;57(8):1838—52.

Li Y, Leith D, Shorten RN. Experimental evaluation of TCP protocols for high-speed networks. IEEE/ACM ToN 2007;15(5):1109—22.

FLOW CONTROL FOR VIDEO APPLICATIONS

6

6.1 INTRODUCTION

Video streaming has grown in popularity as the Internet matures and currently consumes more bandwidth than any other application. Most of this traffic is driven by consumer consumption of video, with services such as Netflix and YouTube leading the pack. Video traffic comes in two flavors, video on demand (VoD) and live-video streaming. VoD traffic is from stored media and is streamed from servers, and it constitutes the majority of the video traffic.

Video has some fundamental differences in transmission requirements compared with traditional data traffic, such as the fact that there are real-time constraints in the delivery of video traffic to the client player. As explained in Section 6.2, this constraint arises because the client video device expects data to be constantly available so that it can keep updating the screen at a constant rate (which is usually 30 frames/s). If there is a hiccup in this process and no data is available, then this results in a temporarily frozen screen while the network catches up.

Most of the early work on packet video transmission focused on providing real-time transmission by means of new techniques that supported resource reservations and QoS (quality of service) provisioning in the network. In the Internet Engineering Task Force (IETF), protocols such as RSVP and IntServ were designed during the 1990s with the intent of using them for provisioning network resources for streaming video delivery. Other protocols that were designed during this era to support real-time streaming included RTP (Real Time Protocol), which served as the packet transport; RTSP (Real Time Streaming Protocol); and RTCP (Real Time Control Protocol), which were used to configure and control the end systems to support the video streams. Even though these protocols are now widely used for supporting real-time video in the Internet, most operators balked at supporting these protocols for consumer video transmission because of the extra complexity and cost involved at both the servers and in the network infrastructure.

During the early years of the Web, the conventional wisdom was that video streaming would have to be done over the User Datagram Protocol (UDP) because video did not require the absolute reliability that TCP provided, and furthermore, TCP retransmissions are not compatible with real-time delivery that video requires. In addition, it was thought that the wide rate variations that are a result of TCP's congestion control algorithm would be too extreme to support video streams whose packet rate is steady and does not vary much. Because of UDP does not come with any congestion control algorithm, there was considerable effort expended in adding this capability to UDP so it could use it for carrying video streams and at the same time coexist with regular TCP traffic. The most significant result from this work was a congestion control algorithm called TCP Friendly Congestion

Control (TFRC) [1]. This was a rate-based algorithm whose design was based on the square-root formula for TCP throughput derived in Chapter 2. The sender kept estimates of the round trip latency and Packet Drop Rate and then used the square root formula to estimate the throughput that a TCP connection would experience under the same conditions. This estimate was then used to control the rate at which the UDP packets were being transmitted into the network.

The video transmission landscape began to change in the early 2000s when researchers realized that perhaps TCP, rather than UDP, could also be used to transmit video. TCP's rate fluctuations, which were thought to be bad for video, could be overcome by using a large receive buffer to dampen them out. Also because most video transmissions were happening over the Web, using the HyperText Transfer Protocol (HTTP) for video was also very convenient. The combination of HTTP/TCP for video delivery had several benefits, including:

- TCP and HTTP are ubiquitous, and most video is accessed over the Web.
- A video server built on top of TCP/HTTP uses commodity HTTP servers and requires no special (and expensive) hardware or software pieces.
- HTTP has built-in Network Address Translation (NAT) traversal capabilities, which provide more ubiquitous reach.
- The use of HTTP means that caches can be used to improve performance. A client can keep playback state and download video segments independently from multiple servers while the servers remain stateless.
- The use of TCP congestion control guarantees that the network will remain stable in the presence of high−bit rate video streams.

The initial implementations of video over HTTP/TCP used a technique called Progressive Download (PD), which basically meant that the entire video file was downloaded as fast as the TCP would allow it into the receiver's buffer. Furthermore, the client video player would start to play the video before the download was complete. This technique was used by YouTube, and even today YouTube uses an improved version of the PD algorithm called Progressive Download with Byte Ranges (PD-BR). This algorithm allows the receiver to request specific byte ranges of the video file from the server, as opposed to the entire file.

A fundamental improvement in HTTP/TCP delivery of video was made in the mid 2000s with the invention of an algorithm called HTTP Adaptive Streaming (HAS), which is also sometimes known by the acronym DASH (Dynamic Adaptive Streaming over HTTP). This algorithm is described in detail in Section 6.3 and was first deployed by Move Networks and then rapidly after that by the other major video providers. Using HAS, the video receiver is able to adaptively change the video rate so that it matches the bandwidth that the network can currently support. From this description, HAS can be considered to be a flow control rather than a congestion control algorithm because its objective is to keep the video receive buffer from getting depleted rather than to keep network queues from getting congested. In this sense, HAS is similar to TCP receive flow control except for the fact that the objective of the latter algorithm is to keep the receive buffer from overflowing. HAS operates on top of TCP congestion control, albeit over longer time scales, and the interaction between the two is rich source of research problems.

HAS remains an area of active research, and the important issues such as the best algorithm to control the video bit rate, the interaction of HAS with TCP, and the interaction of multiple HAS streams at a bottleneck node are still being investigated. There have been several suggestions to improve the original HAS bit rate adaptation algorithm, some of which are covered in Section 6.3.

Today the reliable delivery of even high-quality high-definition (HD) video has become commonplace over the Web, and some of the credit for this achievement can be attributed to the work described in this chapter.

The rest of this chapter is organized as follows: Section 6.2 introduces the fundamentals of video delivery over packet networks, Section 6.3 describes the HAS protocol, Section 6.4 introduces Adaptive Bit Rate (ABR) algorithms, Section 6.5 describes several ABR algorithms that have been proposed in the literature, and Sections 6.6 and 6.7 discuss the TCP throughput measurement problem and the interaction between TCP and ABR.

An initial reading of this chapter can be done in the sequence $6.1 \rightarrow 6.2 \rightarrow 6.3 \rightarrow 6.4 \rightarrow 6.5$ followed by either 6.5.1 or 6.5.2 or 6.5.3 (depending on the particular type of ABR algorithm the reader is interested in). Section 6.6 and 6.7 contain more advanced material and may be skipped during a first reading.

6.2 VIDEO DELIVERY OVER PACKET NETWORKS

Video pictures, or frames, have to be played at a rate of about 30 frames per second (fps) to create the illusion of motion. Video compression is done by using the Discrete Cosine Transform (DCT) on the quantized grey scale and color components of a picture frame, and then transmitting the truncated DCT coefficients instead of the original picture. In addition to the intraframe compression, all compression algorithms also carry out interframe compression, which takes advantage of temporal picture redundancy in coding a frame by taking its delta with respect to a previous frame. Figure 6.1A shows a sequence of video frames, encoded using the Moving Picture Experts Group (MPEG) standard. There are three types of frames shown: I frames are largest because they only use intraframe compression; B and P frames are smaller because they use previous I frames to further reduce their size. This results in a situation in which the encoded bits per frame is a variable quantity, thus leading to Variable Bit Rate (VBR) video. Figure 6.1B shows the bits per frame for a sample sequence of frames.

A number of video coding standards are in use today: The most widely used is an ITU Standard called H.264 or MPEG-4; others include proprietary algorithms such as Google's VP-9. Video coding technology has rapidly advanced in recent years, and today it is possible to send an HD-TV 1080p video using a bit rate of just 2 mbps.

The encoded video results in a VBR stream that is then transmitted into the network (Figure 6.2). Because we are not depending on the network to provide a guaranteed bandwidth for the video stream, there arises the problem of matching the video bit rate with the bandwidth that the network can currently provide on a best-effort basis. If the network bandwidth is not sufficient to support the video bit rate, then the decoder at the receiving end starts to consume the video data at rate that is greater than the rate at which new data is being received from the network. As a result, the decoder ultimately runs out of video data to decode, which results in a screen freeze and the familiar "buffer loading" message that we often see. This is clearly not a good outcome, and to avoid this without having to introduce costly and complex guaranteed bandwidth mechanisms into the network, the following solutions try to match the video bit rate to the available network bandwidth:

• Use of a large receive buffer: As shown in Figure 6.2, the system can smooth out the variations in network throughput by keeping a large receive buffer. As a result, temporary reductions in throughput can be overcome by used the video stored in the receive buffer.

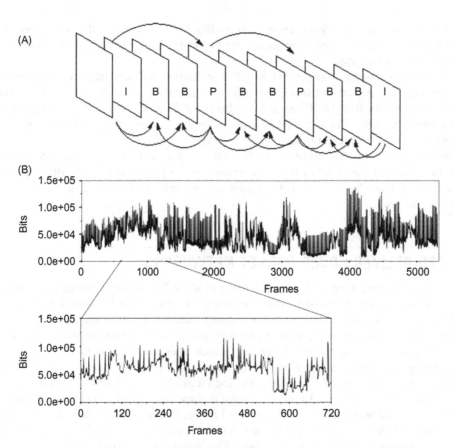

FIGURE 6.1

(A) MPEG-2 frame sequence. (B) Bits generated per frame.

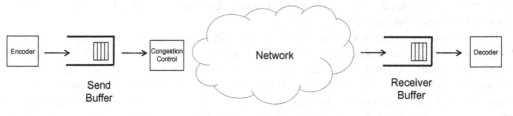

FIGURE 6.2

End-to-end block diagram of a video transmission system.

- Transcoding-based solutions (Figure 6.3A): These algorithms change one or more parameters of the compression algorithm that operates on the raw video data to vary the resulting bit rate. Examples include varying the video resolution, compression ratio, or frame rate. Transcoding is very CPU intensive and requires hardware support to be done at scale, which makes them difficult to deploy in Content Delivery Networks (CDN).

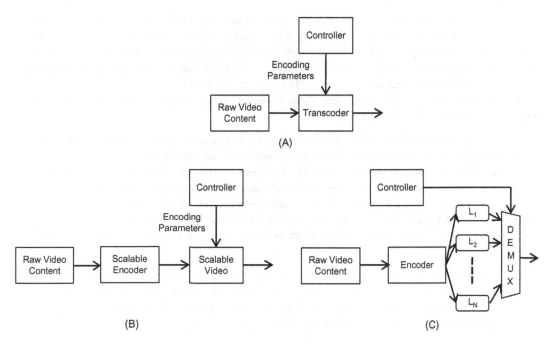

FIGURE 6.3

Adaptive streaming techniques. **(A)** Transcoding based Adaptation, **(B)** Scalable Encoding based Adaptation, and **(C)** Stream Switching based Adaptation.

- Scalable encoding solutions (Figure 6.3B): These can be implemented by processing the encoded video data rather than the raw data. Hence, the raw video can be encoded once and then adapted on the fly by using the scalability features of the encoder. Examples of scalable encoding solutions include adapting the picture resolution or frame rate by exploiting the spatial or temporal scalability in the data. However, even scalable encoding is difficult to implement in CDNs because specialized servers are needed for this.
- Stream switching solutions (Figure 6.3C): This technique is the simplest to implement and can also be used by CDNs. It consists of preprocessing the raw video data to produce multiple encoded streams, each at a different bit rate, resulting in N versions. An algorithm is used at the time of transmission to choose the most appropriate rate given the network conditions. Stream switching algorithms use the least processing power because after the video is encoded, no further operations are needed. The disadvantages of this approach include the fact that more storage is needed and the coarser granularity of the encoded bit rates.

The industry has settled on using a large receive buffer and stream switching as the preferred solution for video transmission. Before the coding rate at the source can be changed, the video server has to be informed about the appropriate rate to use. Clearly, this is not a function that a congestion control protocol such as TCP provides; hence, all video transmissions systems define a protocol operating on top of TCP. In some of the early work on video transport, protocols such as Rate Adaptation Protocol (RAP) [2] and TFRC [1] were defined that put the sender in charge of varying the sending rate (and consequently the video rate) based on feedback being received from either the network or the receiver; hence, they were doing a combination of congestion control and flow control. For example, RAP used an additive increase/multiplicative decrease (AIMD)–type scheme that is reminiscent of TCP congestion control, and TFRC used an additive increase/additive decrease (AIAD) scheme that is based on the TCP square root formula.

The HAS protocol, which dominates video transport today, uses a scheme that differs from these early algorithms in the following ways:

- HAS is built on top of TCP transport, unlike the earlier schemes, which were based on UDP. Some of the reasons for using TCP were mentioned in the Introduction.
- Instead of the transmitter, the receiver in HAS drives the algorithm. It keeps track of the TCP rate of the video stream as well as the receive buffer occupancy level, and then using the HTTP protocol, it informs the transmitter about the appropriate video bit rate to use next.
- Instead of sending the video packets in a continuous stream, HAS breaks up the video into chunks of a few seconds each, each of which is requested by the receiver by means of an HTTP request.

HAS adapts the sending rate, and consequently the video quality, by taking longer term averages of the TCP transmit rate and variations in the receive buffer size. This results in a slower variation in the sending rate, as opposed to TCP congestion control, which varies the sending rate rapidly in reaction to network congestion or packet drops.

6.2.1 CONSTANT BIT RATE (CBR) VIDEO TRANSMISSION OVER TCP

To illustrate the transmission of video over packet networks, we will consider the simplest case of live CBR video transmission over a network with variable congestion (Figure 6.4). Let $S(t) = Kt$ be the number of bits the source encoder has transmitted into the network by time t. If $D(t)$ is the number of bits the receiving decoder has pulled from the receive buffer by time t, then

$$D(t) = \begin{cases} 0 & 0 \le t \le \tau \\ K(t-\tau) & t \ge \tau \end{cases} \tag{1}$$

where τ is the delay before the decoder starts pulling data from the receive buffer. During this initial start-up time, $K\tau$ bits are transmitted by the encoder, which are in transit in the network or waiting to be decoded in the receive buffer.

Let

A(t): The number of bits that have arrived at the receive buffer
N(t): The number of bits in transit through the network
B(t): The number of bits waiting to be decoded in the receive buffer

Then

$$N(t) = S(t) - A(t) = Kt - A(t), \qquad t \ge 0 \tag{2}$$

$$B(t) = \begin{cases} A(t) & 0 \le t \le \tau \\ A(t) - D(t) = A(t) - K(t-\tau) & t \ge \tau \end{cases} \tag{3}$$

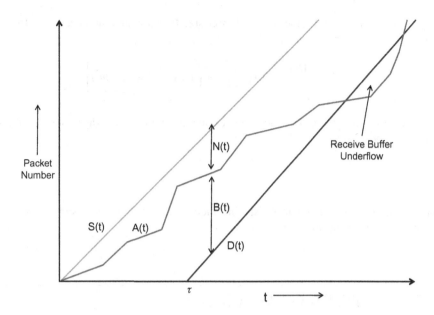

FIGURE 6.4

Time evolution of transmitted bits, received bits, and buffer size.

so that

$$N(t) + B(t) = \begin{cases} Kt & 0 \leq t \leq \tau \\ K\tau & t \geq \tau \end{cases} \tag{4}$$

which is a constant for $t \geq \tau$.

Note that A(t) is dependent on the congestion state of the network, hence

- If the network is congestion free, then A(t) is close to S(t), so that the amount of traffic in the network $N(t) \approx 0$ by equation 2, and the amount of bits in the receiver is approximately given by $B(t) \approx K\tau$ by equation 3, so that the receive buffer is full.
- If the network is congested, then A(t) begins to approach D(t), so that $B(t) \approx 0$ and $N(t) \approx K\tau$ by equations 3 and 4. In this situation, the decoder may run out of bits to decode, resulting in a frame freeze.

If TCP is used to transport the CBR video stream, then to reduce the frequency of buffer underflows at the receiver, the designer can resort to policies such as:

1. Make sure that the network has sufficiently high capacity to support the video stream: Wang et al. [3] have shown that to support a CBR video stream of rate K bps, the throughput of the TCP stream transporting the video should be at least 2K bps. This ensures that the video does not get interrupted too frequently by frame freezes.
2. Use a sufficiently large receive buffer: Kim and Ammar [4] have shown that for a CBR stream of rate K, given a network characterized by a random packet drop rate p, round trip latency T,

and retransmission timeout T_0, the receive buffer size B that results in a desired buffer underrun probability P_u, is lower bounded by

$$B \geq \frac{0.16}{pP_u} \left[1 + 9.4 \left(\frac{T_0}{T} \right)^2 \min \left(1, 3 \sqrt{\frac{3p}{8}} \right) p(1 + 32p^2) \right]$$ (5)

This result assumes that the CBR video rate K coincides with the average data rate that the TCP connection can support, so that

$$K = \frac{1}{T} \sqrt{\frac{3}{2p}}$$

This last assumption is difficult to satisfy in practice, which may be reason why equation 5 is not commonly used to dimension receive buffers.

6.3 HTTP ADAPTIVE STREAMING (HAS)

The discussion in Section 6.2 showed that when TCP is used to transport CBR video, one can reduce the incidence of receive buffer exhaustion, either by overprovisioning the network so that the TCP rate is double the video rate or by using a sufficiently large receive buffer, which averages out the rate fluctuations attributable to TCP congestion control, but this begs the question of whether there are better ways of solving this problem that use less resources.

Most of the video streaming industry has now settled on HAS as the extra ingredient needed to send video over the Internet. HAS was able to improve the system by adding another layer of rate control on top of TCP. However, unlike TCP, the HAS algorithm is video aware and is able to interact with the video application at the sender to adaptively change its sending rate. The result of this interaction is shown in Figure 6.5, where one can see the video rate decreasing if the network congestion increases, and conversely increasing when the congestion reduces. As a result of this, the system is able to stream video without running into frame-freeze conditions and without having to overprovision the network or keep a very large receive buffer (compare Figure 6.5 with Figure 6.4 in which the receiving buffer underflows without bit rate adaptation). Note that Figure 6.5 assumes that the video is encoded at multiple rates, which can be adaptively changed depending on the network conditions.

As mentioned in the Introduction, HAS uses HTTP/TCP for transporting video rather than the traditional RTP/UDP stack. With HAS, a video stream is divided into short segments of a few seconds each, referred to as chunks or fragments. Each chunk is encoded and stored in the server at a number of versions, each with a different bit rate as shown in Figure 6.6. At the start of the video session, a client downloads a manifest file that lists all the relevant information regarding the video streams. The client then proceeds to download the chunks sequentially using HTTP GETs. By observing the rate at which data is arriving to the client and the occupancy of the video decoding buffer, the client chooses the video bit rate of the next chunk. The precise algorithm for doing so is known as the ABR algorithm and is discussed in the next section.

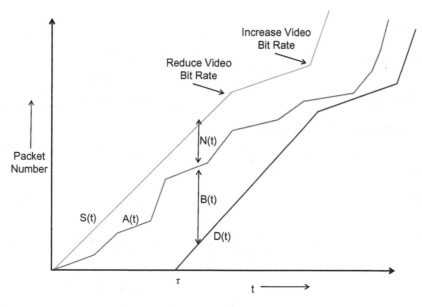

FIGURE 6.5

Illustration of avoidance of buffer underflow caused by HTTP Adaptive Streaming (HAS) bit rate adaptation.

Examples of commercial HAS systems that are in wide use today include the following:

- Microsoft HTTP Smooth Streaming (HSS) [5]: Uses a chunk size of 2 sec and a 30-sec receive buffer at the receiver
- Apple HTTP Live Streaming (HLS)
- Adobe HTTP Dynamic Streaming (HDS) [6]: Uses a receive buffer of size less than 10 sec
- Netflix [7]: Uses a chunk size of 10 sec and a 300-sec receive buffer

These HAS algorithms are proprietary to each vendor, which typically do not reveal details about their schemes. One can obtain some understanding of how they behave by carrying out measurements, and this program was carried out by Akhshabi et al. [8], from whom the numbers quoted here have been taken.

6.4 THE ADAPTIVE BIT RATE (ABR) ALGORITHM

The ABR is the algorithm that HAS uses to adapt the video bit rate. With reference to Figure 6.7, while the TCP inner control loop reacts to network congestion and tries to match the TCP send rate with the rate that the network can support, the ABR outer loop reacts to the rates that TCP decides to use and tries to match the rate of the video stream to the average TCP rate. The TCP control loop operates in order of a time period, which is approximately equal to the

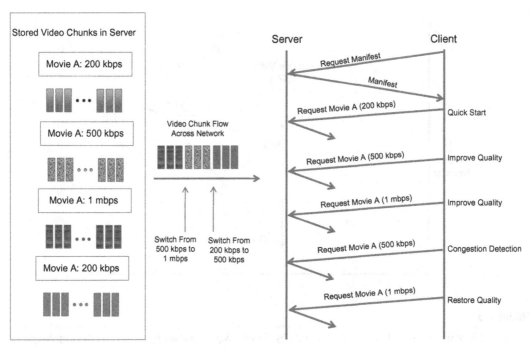

FIGURE 6.6

Illustration of HTTP requests and bit rate adaptation in HTTP Adaptive Streaming (HAS).

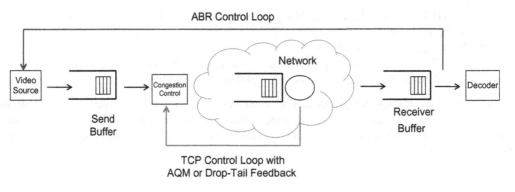

FIGURE 6.7

Illustrating the two control loops: TCP and Adaptive Bit Rate (ABR).

round trip delay (i.e., tens of milliseconds in most cases); the ABR control loop operates over a much larger time period, ranging from a few seconds to tens of seconds depending on the ABR algorithm. This leads to a natural averaging effect because ABR does not attempt to match the fluctuating short-term TCP throughput but rather a smoothed throughput that is averaged over several seconds. Even then, it is a nontrivial problem to estimate the "true" average TCP rate from measurements made at the receiver [9], and we shall see later that ABR's transmission policy can lead to an overestimation of TCP throughput, which results in oscillations in the video rate.

The ABR algorithm controls the following quantities:

- The rate at which the receiver sends HTTP requests back to the video source
- The appropriate video stream to transmit, whose rate most closely matches the rate that can be supported by the network

The objectives of an ideal ABR algorithm include the following:

1. Avoid interruptions of playback caused by buffer underruns.
2. Maximize the quality of the video being transmitted: Fulfilling this objective constitutes a trade-off with objective 1 because it is always possible to minimize the number of interruptions by always transmitting at the lowest rate.
3. Minimize the number of video quality shifts to improve user experience: This leads to a trade-off with objective 2 because the algorithm can maximize the video quality by reacting to the smallest changes in the network bandwidth, which, however, increases the number of quality shifts.
4. Minimize the time between the user making a request for a new video and the video actually starting to play: This objective can also be achieved at the cost of objective 2 by using the lowest bit rate at the start.

Define the following:

$V = \{V(1), \ldots, V(L)\}$ Set of available bit rates for the video stream that are available at the transmitter, with $0 < V(n) < V(m)$ for $n < m$

U_n: The video rate from the set V which is used for the nth chunk, which is an output of the ABR algorithm

τ: Size of a chunk in seconds, in terms of actual time spent in playing the video contained in it

R_n: Throughput for the nth video chunk as measured at the receiver

$\hat{T}_n$: HTPP inter-request interval, between the nth and $(n+1)^{rst}$ requests. This is also an output of the ABR algorithm.

$\tilde{T}_n$: Download duration for the nth chunk

T_n: Actual inter-request time between HTTP requests from the receiver, between the nth and $(n+1)^{rst}$ request, so that

$$T_n = \max(\hat{T}_n, \tilde{T}_n) \tag{6}$$

This is also referred to as the nth download period.

B_n: Duration of the video stored in the video buffer at the end of the n_{th} period

Because the size of the receive buffer is in terms of the duration of video data stored in it, the download of a chunk causes the buffer size to increase by τ seconds irrespective of the rates U_n or R_n. Similarly, it always takes τ seconds to play the video data in a chunk, irrespective of the rate at which the video has been coded.

Most ABR algorithms use the following three steps:

1. Estimation: The throughput during the nth video chunk is estimated using the following equation:

$$R_n = \frac{U_n \tau}{\tilde{T}_n} \qquad (7)$$

The buffer size (in seconds) at the end of the nth download period is computed by

$$B_n = \max(0, B_{n-1} + \tau - T_n) \qquad (8)$$

2. Video rate determination: The ABR algorithm determines the rate U_{n+1} to be used for the next chunk by looking at several pieces of information, including (1) the sequence of rate estimates R_n and (2) the buffer occupancy level B_n. Hence,

$$U_{n+1} = F(B_n, \{R_m : m \le n\}) \qquad (9)$$

where F(.) is a rate determination function.

3. Scheduling: The ABR algorithm determines the time when the next chunk is scheduled to be downloaded at by computing an HTTP inter-request time of $\hat{T}_n$, such that

$$\hat{T}_n = G(B_n, \{R_m : m \le n+1\}) \qquad (10)$$

Note that equation 7 assumes that the video rate is fixed at U_n for the duration of the nth chunk. In reality, it may vary, and we can take this into account by replacing $U_n \tau$ by U_n^τ, which is the number of bits received as part of the nth chunk.

Figure 6.8A shows the downloading of multiple video chunks at the receiver. As noted earlier, the time spent in playing the video contained in a chunk is always τ seconds; however, the time required to transmit a chunk is variable and is given by equation 7. Keeping in mind that

$$\frac{R_n}{U_n} = \frac{\tau}{\tilde{T}_n}$$

it follows that (see Figure 6.8), if

- $R_n = U_n$ (Figure 6.8A): Because the two rates are perfectly matched, it takes exactly τ seconds to transmit the chunk, and there is no change in the buffer size at end of the n_{th} period (by equation 8). This is ideal state for the ABR algorithm because it makes full use of the network capacity, and the buffer size is steady. Note that in practice, this perfect match does not occur because of the quantization in the video bit rates.
- $R_n > U_n$ (Figure 6.8B): In this case, $\tau > \tilde{T}_n$, so the network fills up the buffer faster (two chunks every τ seconds) than the constant rate at which the decoder is draining it (one chunk every τ seconds). This condition needs to be detected by the ABR algorithm so that it can take control action, which consists of increasing the video bit rate so that it can take advantage of the higher network capacity. If the video bit rate is already at a maximum, the ABR algorithm avoids buffer overflow by spacing out the time interval between chunks (see Figure 6.10).
- $R_n < U_n$ (Figure 6.8C): In this case, $\tau < \tilde{T}_n$ so the decoder drains the buffer at a higher rate than the rate at which the network is filling it, which can result in an underflow. This condition also needs to be detected promptly by the ABR algorithm so that it can take control action, which consists of reducing the video bit rate to a value that is lower than the network rate.

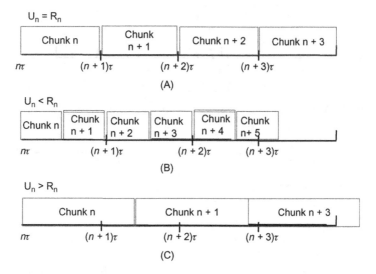

FIGURE 6.8

Illustrating chunk download times as a function of video bit rate and TCP throughput.

To understand the dynamics of ABR algorithms, consider the scenario pictured in Figure 6.9. Assume that the TCP throughput is fixed and is given by R, and furthermore, it lies between the video rates V(m) and V(m + 1).

- If the ABR algorithm chooses rates U_n that are V(m + 1) or larger, then this will result in the scenario shown in Figure 6.9B, in which the decoder drains the buffer faster than the rate at which the network is filling it, resulting in a decreasing buffer size. If left unchecked, then this will eventually result in an underflow of the receive buffer.
- If the ABR algorithm chooses rates U_n that are equal to V(m) or smaller, then this will result in the scenario shown in Figure 6.9C, in which the network fills the buffer faster than the rate at which the decoder can drain it. This will result in an increasing buffer size.

Because of the quantization in video rates, it is impossible to get to $U_n = R$, and this can result in the video rate constantly fluctuating between V(m) and V(m + 1) to keep the buffer from overflowing or underflowing. To avoid this, most ABR algorithms stop increasing the video rate U_n after it gets to V(m) and compensate for the difference between V(m) and R by increasing the gap between successive downloads, as shown next.

The case when the TCP throughput R exceeds the maximum video rate V(L) (Figure 6.10A) will result in the system dynamics shown in Figure 6.9C in which the receive buffer size keeps increasing. If the ABR algorithm observes that the buffer size is increasing even at the maximum video bit rate, then it stabilizes the buffer by increasing the gap between successive downloads, as shown in Figure 6.10B. There are two ways in which it can choose the gap size:

- The gap size is fixed at τ: In this case, during each period, the amount of video data consumed is equal to the data being added, resulting in a stable buffer.
- After the end of the chunk download, the ABR algorithm waits for the buffer to drain until it reaches a target level before starting the next download.

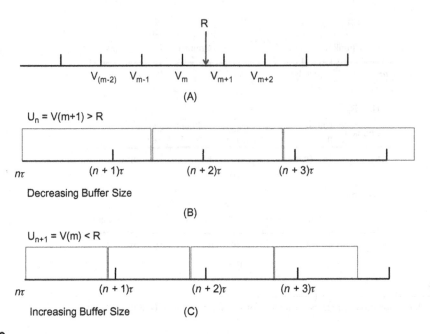

FIGURE 6.9

Scenario 1: The TCP throughput R is less than the highest video bit rate.

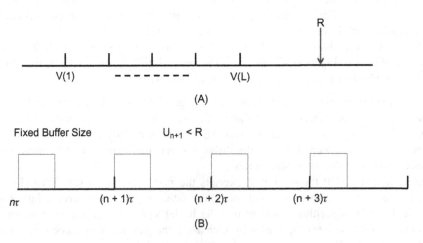

FIGURE 6.10

Scenario 2: The TCP throughput R is larger than the highest video bit rate.

At a high level, the ABR algorithm tries to match the rate at which the receive buffer is being drained by the video decoder (i.e., the sequence $\{U_n\}$), with the rate at which this buffer is being replenished by the network (i.e., the sequence $\{R_n\}$) in a way such that the receive buffer does not become empty. This is difficult problem because the rate at which the buffer is being filled is constantly fluctuating because it is determined by TCP's congestion control algorithm as a function of the congestive state of the network. This problem is made harder because buffer fluctuations may also be caused by the VBR nature of the video stream.

It does not makes sense to constantly keep changing the video bit rate in response to network rate changes because studies have shown that switching back and forth between different video versions significantly degrades the user experience. Hence, one of the objectives of the ABR algorithms is to avoid video rate fluctuations caused by short-term bandwidth variations and TCP throughput estimation errors. In general, it has been observed that whereas algorithms that try to keep the buffer size stable cause larger variations in the video bit rate, algorithms that try to keep the video bit rate stable lead to larger variations in the buffer size. Several techniques are used to smoothen out the video rate fluctuations, such as:

- Use the receive buffer to dampen out temporary fluctuations in TCP bit rate: This is illustrated by the Threshold Based Buffer (TBB) algorithm [10] (see Section 6.5.2.1).
- Use smoothing filters to reduce fluctuations in the TCP bit rate estimates. This is illustrated by the STB algorithm (see Section 6.5.1.3).
- Use fudge factors when making threshold based decisions.

Even though it is not a congestion control algorithm, most ABR designs conform to the AIMD rules. Hence, the video bit rate is incremented smoothly in an additive manner when the available network bandwidth is consistently higher than the current bit rate. Conversely, when the network bandwidth decreases because of congestion, ABR should quickly decrease the video bit rate to avoid playback freezes. Another reason to use multiplicative decrease for the video rate is the following: In case of congestion, the TCP reacts by multiplicatively reducing its own bit rate, and because the objective of the ABR algorithm is to match the video bit rate to the TCP throughput, it follows that it should also try to reduce the video bit rate multiplicatively.

6.5 DESCRIPTION OF SOME ADAPTIVE BIT RATE (ABR) ALGORITHMS

Adaptive Bit Rate or ABR algorithms are an active area of research, and new algorithms are being constantly invented in both academia and industry. These can be broadly classified in the following categories:

1. Algorithms that rely mostly on their estimates of TCP throughput. Algorithms in this category include:
   - Network Throughput Based (NTB)
   - Smoothed Throughput Based (STB) [8]
   - AIMD Based (ATB) [11]
   - The FESTIVE algorithm [12]

2. Algorithms that rely mostly on the receive buffer size. Algorithms in this category include:
  - Threshold Based Buffer (TBB) [10]
  - Buffer Based Rate Selection (BBRS) [13]
3. Control Theory Based (CTB) [14−16]
    These algorithms estimate the best video bit rate to use by solving a control theory problem.

In the research literature, there are algorithms that rely on the Send buffer size to control the video bit rate [17]. These algorithms have some inherent disadvantages compared with the receiver-based algorithms, including that they increase the complexity and cost of the video server. Also, the benefits of caching the content in a distributed fashion are lost. Hence, these types of algorithms are not covered in this chapter.

6.5.1 THROUGHPUT-BASED ADAPTIVE BIT RATE (ABR) ALGORITHMS

This class of algorithms uses estimates of the TCP throughput as the main input to the algorithm. However, all such algorithms also incorporate a safety feature whereby if the receive buffer size falls below a threshold, then the system switches the video bit rate to the minimum value to avoid a buffer underflow.

6.5.1.1 Network Throughput-Based (NTB) Algorithm

This is the simplest type of ABR algorithm. Essentially, the video bit rate for the next download is set equal to the latest value of the TCP throughput estimate, so that

$$U_{n+1} = Q(R_n) \quad where \quad R_n = \frac{U_n \tau}{\tilde{T}_n} \tag{11}$$

The quantization function Q chooses the video bit rate that is smaller than R_n and closest to it. Note that equation 11 cancels out the instantaneous fluctuations in TCP throughput by averaging over an interval, which is typically 2 to 10 seconds long. The NTB algorithm is very effective in avoiding buffer underruns because it reacts instantaneously to fluctuations in TCP throughput. Studies have shown that receive buffer size shows the least amount of variation under NTB compared with the other algorithms [18]. However, on the flip side, it has the largest rate of changes in the video bit rate because it does nothing to dampen any of these fluctuations. As a result, it is not commonly used in practice except as a way to benchmark other ABR algorithms.

Figure 6.11 shows an example a typical sample path of the NTB algorithm. The video rate is typically set to the minimum value V(1) at start-up, but it quickly increases to the maximum bit rate V(L) because of application of equation 11. Downloads are done in a back-to-back manner until the receive buffer is full. When this happens, the download interval is increased to τ seconds to keep the average TCP throughput R equal to V(L). If the TCP throughput falls below V(L), then the receive buffer occupancy starts to reduce, and the algorithm switches to the back-to-back downloads again. This takes the system to the scenario illustrated in Figure 6.9, where in the absence of any smoothing, the algorithm will constantly switch between the bit rates that are above and below R.

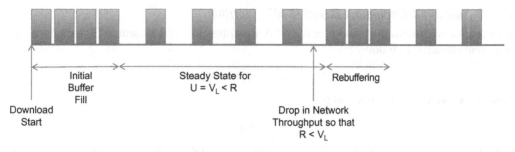

Initial Buffer Fill   Steady State for $U = V_L < R$ Rebuffering

Download Start

Drop in Network Throughput so that $R < V_L$

FIGURE 6.11

Dynamics of the TCP throughput Based (NTB) algorithm.

6.5.1.2 AIMD-Based Algorithm (ATB)

The ATB algorithm [11] makes a number of modifications to the NTB algorithm to smoothen out the bit rate fluctuations. Using the same notation as before, the ATB algorithm keeps track of the ratio μ given by

$$\mu = \frac{\tau}{\tilde{T}_n} \tag{12}$$

Note that because $\mu = \frac{R_n}{U_n}$, if $\mu < 1$, then the video bit rate is larger than the TCP throughput, and the converse is true when $\mu > 1$. Hence, μ serves as a measure of network congestion.

The bit rate increment−decrement rules are as follows:

- If $\mu > 1 + \varepsilon$ (and the buffer size exceeds a threshold) where $\varepsilon = \max\left(\frac{V(i+1)-V(i)}{V(i)}, \forall i \in [1,\ldots,L]\right)$, then the chunk download happens faster than the rate at which the decoder can play that chunk (see Figure 8B). The video bit rate is switched up from V(m) to V(m + 1), which corresponds to an additive increase policy. Hence, in contrast to NTB, the ATB algorithm increases the bit rate using an additive increase policy, which helps to reduce jumps in video quality. Also, the factor ε helps to reduce bit rate oscillations for the case when the TCP throughput lies between two video bit rates (illustrated in Figure 6.9A).

- If $\mu < \gamma_d$, where $\gamma_d < 1$ is the switch-down threshold, then the download of a chunk takes longer than the time required for the decoder to play that chunk, which leads to a reduction in the receive buffer size. Hence, an aggressive switch down is performed, with the reduced video bit rate chosen to be the first rate V(i) such that $V(i) < \mu V(c)$, where V(c) is the current bit rate. This corresponds to a multiplicative decrease policy. The presence of the factor γ_d may lead to the situation in which the buffer drains down slowly. To prevent an underflow, the algorithm switches to the minimum bit rate V(1) if the buffer falls below a threshold.

From this description, the ATB algorithm uses fudge factors in its threshold rules and a less aggressive increase rate to reduce bit rate fluctuations. If the TCP throughput exceeds the maximum video bit rate, then it spaces out the chunk download times to prevent the buffer from overflowing.

6.5.1.3 Smoothed Throughput Based (STB) Algorithm

To reduce the short-term fluctuations in the NTB algorithm, the STB algorithm [8] uses a smoothed throughput estimate, as follows:

$$\hat{R}_n = (1 - \delta)\hat{R}_{n-1} + \delta R_n \tag{13}$$

where R_n is given by (11), followed by

$$U_{n+1} = Q(\hat{R}_n)$$

As a result of the smoothing, the STB algorithm considerably reduces the number of changes to the video bit rate in response to TCP throughput fluctuations. However, if there is a sudden decrease in TCP throughput, STB is not able to respond quickly enough, which can result in buffer underflows. However, if the buffer size is big enough, then STB provides a simple and viable ABR technique. The interval between chunks is controlled in the same way as in the NTB algorithm.

6.5.1.4 The FESTIVE Algorithm

Jiang et al. [12] pointed out the following problems that exist in ABR algorithms that are caused due to their measurements of TCP throughput to control the video bit rates:

- The chunk download start-time instances of the connections may get stuck in suboptimal locations. For example, if there are three active connections, then the chunk download times of two of the connections may overlap, while the third connection gets the entire link capacity. This leads to unfairness in the bit rate allocation.

  Their suggested solution is to randomize the start of the chunk download times; that is, instead of downloading a chunk strictly at intervals of τ seconds (or equivalently when the buffer size reaches a target value), move it randomly either backward or forward by a time equal to the length of download.
- Connections with higher bit rate tend to see a higher estimate of their chunk's TCP throughput. As explained in Section 6.5.2, this is because the chunks of connections with higher bit rates occupy the bottleneck link longer, and as a result, they have a greater chance of experiencing time intervals during which they have access to the entire link capacity.

  To solve this problem, Jiang et al. [12] recommended that the rate of increase of the bit rate for a connection should not be linear but should decrease as the bit rate increases (another instance of the averaging principle!). This policy can be implemented as follows: If the bit rate is at level k, then increase it to level k + 1 only after k chunks have been received. This will lead to a faster convergence between bit rates of two connections that are initially separated from each other.
- Simple averaging of the TCP throughput estimates is biased by outliers if one chunk sees a very high or very low throughput. To avoid this, Jiang et al. [12] implemented a harmonic mean estimate of the last 20 throughput samples, which is less sensitive to outliers.

As a result of these design changes, the HAS design using the FESTIVE algorithm was shown to outperform the commercial HAS players by a wide margin.

6.5.2 BUFFER SIZE-BASED ADAPTIVE BIT RATE ALGORITHMS

This class of algorithms uses receive buffer size as their primary input, although most of them also use the TCP throughput estimate to do fine tuning. It has been recently shown (see Section 6.5.3) that buffer size–based ABR algorithms outperform those based on rate estimates.

6.5.2.1 Threshold Based Buffer (TBB) Algorithm

The following rules are used for adapting the video bit rate in the TBB algorithm [10]:

- Let B(t) be the receive buffer level at time t. Define the following threshold levels for the receive buffer, measured in seconds: $0 \leq B_{min} < B_{low} < B_{high}$. The interval $b_{tar} = [B_{low}, B_{high}]$ is called the target interval, and $B_{opt} = (B_{low} + B_{high})/2$ is the center of the target interval. The TBB algorithm tries to keep the buffer level close to B_{opt}.
- Let V(c) be the current video bit rate. If the buffer level B(t) falls below B_{low} and $V(c) > R_n$, then switch to the next lower bit rate V(c − 1). The algorithm continues to switch to lower bit rates as long as the above conditions are true. Note that if $B(t) < B_{low}$ and $V(c) \leq R_n$, it implies that the buffer level has started to increase, and hence there is no need to switch to a lower rate.
- With the current video bit rate equal to V(c), if the buffer level increases above B_{high} and if $V(c+1) < R_n^{avg}$, then switch to the next higher video bit rate V(c + 1). Note that R_n^{avg} is the average TCP throughput, where the average is taken over the last few chunks (this number is configurable), which helps to dampen temporary network fluctuations.
  If the video bit rate is already at the maximum value V(L) or if

$$V(c + 1) \geq \alpha R_n^{avg}, \tag{14}$$

  then the algorithm does not start the download of the next chunk until the buffer level B(t) falls below $\max(B(t) - \tau, B_{opt})$. Assuming that initially $B(t) - \tau > B_{opt}$, this policy leads to a steady linear decrease in buffer size by τ every τ seconds until it reaches the target operating point B_{opt}. If equation 14 is satisfied, then it means that the bit rates V(c) and V(c + 1) straddle the TCP throughput (as in Figure 6.9A) so that increasing the bit rate to V(c + 1) will cause the buffer to start decreasing.
- If $B(t) \in b_{tar}$, the algorithm does not change the video bit rate to avoid reacting to short-term variations in the TCP throughput. If the bit rate is at maximum value V(L) or if equation 14 is satisfied, then the algorithm does not start the download of the next chunk until the buffer level B(t) falls below $\max(B(t) - \tau, B_{opt})$. This keeps the buffer level at B_{opt} in equilibrium.
- If the buffer level falls below B_{min}, then switch to the lowest video bit rate to V(1).

Simulation results presented by Miller et al. [10] show that the algorithm works quite well and achieves its objectives. Figure 6.12 shows a sample path of the algorithm for the case when $B_{high} = 50$ sec, $B_{low} = 20$ sec (so that $B_{opt} = 30$ sec), and $B_{min} = 10$ sec, with a single video stream passing over a network bottleneck link whose capacity is varied.

- When the link capacity goes up at t1 = 200 sec, the buffer size starts to increase, and when it crosses 50 sec, the algorithm starts to increase the bit rate in multiple steps. When the bit rate reaches the maximum value, the algorithm reduces the buffer size linearly until it reaches B_{opt}.

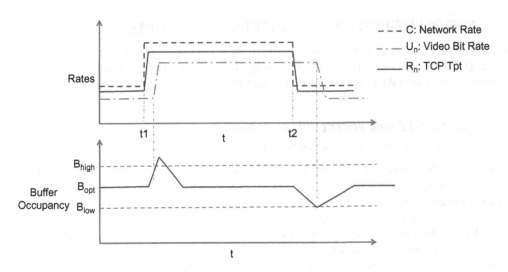

FIGURE 6.12

Illustration of the bit rate and buffer size dynamics for the Threshold Based Buffer (TBB) algorithm.

• When the link capacity is reduced at t2 = 400 sec, it causes the buffer occupancy to decrease, and when it drops below 20 sec, the video bit rate is progressively decreased until it falls below the TCP throughput value. At this point, the buffer starts to fill up again, and when it reaches B_{opt}, the algorithm spaces out the chunks to maintain the buffer at a constant value.

A nice feature of the TBB algorithm is that it enables the designer to explicitly control the trade-off between variation in buffer occupancy and fluctuations in video bit rate in response to varying TCP throughput. This is done by controlling the thresholds B_{high} and B_{low}, such that a large value of the difference $B_{high} - B_{low}$ will reduce video bit rate changes. This aspect of TBB is orthogonal to the features in the FESTIVE algorithm, and a combination of the two will result in a superior system.

6.5.2.2 Buffer Based Rate Selection Algorithm

The BBRS algorithm [13] bases its bit rate selection function entirely on the receive buffer level. This function is illustrated in Figure 6.13. It sets the video bit rate to $Q(U_n)$, where U_n is defined by:

$$U_n = V(1) \quad \text{if} \quad B_{n-1} < r \tag{15a}$$

$$= V(1) + \frac{B_{n-1} - r}{c}(V(L) - V(1)) \quad \text{if} \quad r \le B_{n-1} \le r + c \tag{15b}$$

$$= V(L) \quad \text{if} \quad B_{n-1} > r + c \tag{15c}$$

Note that r and c are free parameters in this algorithm. The algorithm makes the implicit assumption that the maximum TCP throughput is bounded between V(1) and V(L), so that all

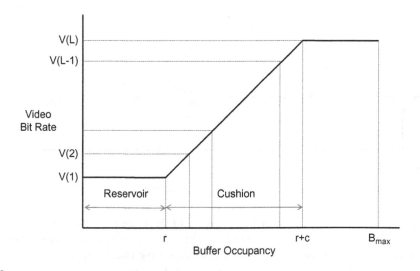

FIGURE 6.13

Video bit rate control function for the Buffer Based Rate Selection (BBRS) algorithm.

chunk downloads always happen in a back-to-back manner. This also implies that if the TCP rate R lies between video bit rate V_m and V_{m+1} (see Figure 6.9), then the buffer occupancy with constantly switch back and forth between $f^{-1}(V_m)$ and $f^{-1}(V_{m+1})$ (where f is the mapping function shown in Figure 6.13), which will result in the video bit rate switching between these two values as well. The TBB algorithm avoids this by keeping track of the TCP throughput in addition to the buffer occupancy, as explained in the previous section.

6.5.3 CONTROL THEORY—BASED ADAPTIVE BIT RATE ALGORITHMS

Inspired by the success of control theory in analyzing congestion control (see Chapter 3), several researchers have attempted to use this theory to derive ABR algorithms [14–16]. The initial work by Tian and Liu [15] and Zhou et al. [16] was based the objective of controlling the receive buffer occupancy to a reference level B_{ref} and then using the difference $(B_n - B_{ref})$ between the current occupancy and the reference value to drive the main control loop as shown in Figure 6.14. (Note the analogy with the TCP case in which the objective of the controller was to regulate the bottleneck buffer occupancy to some reference level.) It is then possible to derive equations for the predicted video bit rate U_n as a function of the buffer size difference and the estimated TCP throughput R_n, which in turn determines the buffer occupancy level in combination with the actual TCP throughput, thus closing the control loop.

In general, it turns out that trying to keep the receive buffer occupancy at the reference level is not the most suitable way to drive the ABR control loop. The reason for this is the fact that from a user point of view, it is more important to get the highest quality video that the network can support while reducing the bit rate fluctuations. The user does not care if the buffer is fluctuating as

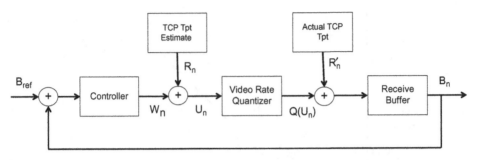

FIGURE 6.14

Application of control theory to the Adaptive Bit Rate (ABR) algorithm.

long as it does not underflow. The model in Figure 6.14 does not take into account the objectives of reducing the bit rate fluctuations or maximizing the video quality. In their algorithms, Tian and Liu [15] and Zhou et al. [16] did include features to reduce the rate fluctuations, but this was done as an add-on to the control loop, not as a consequence of the control model itself.

Recently, Yin et al. [14] have attacked the problem using tools from model predictive control (MPC) theory with much better results, and their work is described in this section. In addition to taking multiple constraints into account in the derivation of the optimal bit rate, the theory also provides a framework within which different algorithms can be compared with the performance of the best possible ABR algorithm, thus enabling us to objectively compare different algorithms.

The MPC optimization problem is defined next. We will use the same notation that was introduced in Section 6.4, with the following additions:

K: Total number of chunks in the video stream so that the duration of the video is $K\tau$ seconds
q(.): $R \rightarrow R_+$ This is a function that maps the selected bit rate U_k to the video quality perceived by the user $q(U_k)$. It is assumed to be monotonically increasing.
B(t): The receive buffer occupancy at time t
R(t): The TCP throughput at time t

The download of chunk k starts at time t_k and finishes at time t_{k+1}, and the download of the next chunk starts at time t_{k+1} (i.e., it is assumed that chunks are downloaded in a back-to-back manner); this implies that the maximum TCP throughput is less than the maximum video bit rate V(L). It follows that

$$t_{k+1} = t_k + \frac{\tau U_k}{R_k} \text{ where} \tag{16}$$

$$R_k = \frac{1}{t_{k+1} - t_k} \int_{t_k}^{t_{k+1}} R(t)dt \tag{17}$$

$$B_{k+1} = \left(B_k - \frac{\tau U_k}{R_k} \right)^+ + \tau \tag{18}$$

where $B_k = B(t_k)$. Note that if $B_k < \frac{\tau U_k}{R_k}$, then the buffer becomes empty before the next download is complete, thus resulting in an underflow.

Define the following Quality of Experience (QoE) elements for the system:

1. Average video quality: $\dfrac{1}{K}\displaystyle\sum_{k=1}^{K} q(U_k)$

2. Average quality variations: $\dfrac{1}{K}\displaystyle\sum_{k=1}^{K-1} |q(U_{k+1}) - q(U_k)|$

3. Total rebuffer time: $\displaystyle\sum_{k=1}^{K}\left(\dfrac{\tau U_k}{R_k} - B_k\right)^{+}$

Or number of rebufferings: $\displaystyle\sum_{k=1}^{K} 1\left(\dfrac{\tau U_k}{R_k} > B_k\right)$

The QoE of video segments 1 through K are defined by a weighted sum of these components

$$QoE_1^K = \sum_{k=1}^{K} q(U_k) - \lambda \sum_{k=1}^{K-1} |q(U_{k+1}) - q(U_k)| - \mu \sum_{k=1}^{K}\left(\dfrac{\tau U_k}{R_k} - B_k\right)^{+} \tag{19}$$

By changing the values of λ and μ, the user can control the relative importance assigned to video quality variability versus the frequency or time spent on rebuffering. Note that this definition of QoE takes user preferences into account and can be extended to incorporate other factors.

The bit rate adaptation problem, called $QoE\_MAX_1^K$, is formulated as follows:

$$\max_{U_1,\dots,U_K} QoE_1^K \tag{20}$$

such that

$$t_{k+1} = t_k + \dfrac{\tau U_k}{R_k}$$

$$B_{k+1} = \left(B_k - \dfrac{\tau U_k}{R_k}\right)^{+} + \tau$$

$$R_k = \dfrac{1}{t_{k+1} - t_k}\int_{t_k}^{t_{k+1}} R(t)dt$$

$$U_k \in V, \quad B_k \in [0, B_{\max}] \quad \forall k = 1, \dots, K$$

The input to the problem is the bandwidth trace $R_t, t \in [t_1, t_{K+1}]$, which is a random sample path realization from the stochastic process that controls TCP throughput variations during the download.

The outputs of $QoE\_MAX_1^K$ are the bit rate decisions $U_1, \dots, U_K$, the download times $t_1, \dots, t_K$ and the buffer occupancies $B_1, \dots, B_K$.

Note that $QoE\_MAX_1^K$ is a finite-horizon stochastic optimal control problem, with the source of the randomness being the TCP throughput R(t). At time t_k when the ABR algorithm is invoked to choose U_k, only the past throughputs $\{R_i, i < k\}$ are known; the future throughputs $\{R_i, i \geq k\}$ are not known. However, algorithms known *bandwidth predictors* can be used to obtain predictions defined as $\{\hat{R}_i, i \geq k\}$. Several bandwidth predictors using filtering techniques such as AR (autoregressive), ARMA (autoregressive moving average), autoregressive integrated moving average

(ARIMA), fractional ARIMA (FARIMA), and so on are known, which are all combinations of moving average and autoregressive filtering [19]. Based on this, the ABR algorithm selects bit rate of the next chunk k as:

$$U_k = f(B_k, \{\hat{R}_i, i \geq k\}). \tag{21}$$

Model predictive control [20] is a subset of this class of algorithms that choose bit rate U_k by looking h steps ahead; that is, they solve the QoE maximization problem $QoE\_MAX_k^{k+h}$ with bandwidth predictions $\{\hat{R}_i, k \leq i \leq k + h\}$ to obtain the bit rate U_k. The bit rate U_k is then applied to the system, and that along with the actual observed TCP throughput R_k is used to iterate the optimization process to the next step $k + 1$.

For a given TCP throughput trace $R_t, t \in [t_1, t_{K+1}]$, we can obtain the offline optimal QoE, denoted as QoE(OPT) (which is obtained by solving $QoE\_MAX_1^K$) because it has perfect knowledge of the future TCP throughputs for the entire duration of the video streaming. This provides a theoretical upper bound for all algorithms for a given throughput trace.

Define QoE(A) to be the QoE for algorithm A and the normalized QoE of A as

$$n - QoE(A) = \frac{QoE(A)}{QoE(OPT)} \tag{22}$$

Yin et al. [14] generated several synthetic TCP throughput traces and used it to compute n-QoE(A) for the MPC algorithm, as well as the BBRS algorithm (as a representative of buffer-based algorithms) and the NTB algorithm (as a representative of throughput-based algorithms). Their results are very interesting and are summarized in Figure 6.15, which graphs the distribution function for n-QoEs from 100 simulation runs. It shows that BBRS performs better than NTB, and both are outperformed by the MPC algorithm, which gets quite close to the optimal.

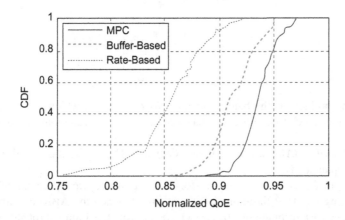

FIGURE 6.15

Comparison of model predictive control (MPC), rate-based, and buffer-based Adaptive Bit Rate (ABR) algorithms.

6.6 **THE PROBLEM WITH TCP THROUGHPUT MEASUREMENTS**

TCP throughput measurements form an essential component of the ABR algorithm. Algorithms such as ATB and STB use these measurements as their main input, and even algorithms such as TBB or BBRS that are based on buffer size measurements are affected by TCP throughput because the transmit time of a chunk (which determines whether the buffer grows or shrinks) is inversely proportional to the TCP throughput.

Recall that the ABR algorithms estimates the per-chunk TCP throughput using the formula

$$R_n = \frac{U_n \tau}{\tilde{T}_n}$$

Consider the case when ABR-controlled video streams pass through a common network bottleneck node with capacity C and assume that the maximum video bit rate $V(L) < C$ and $2V(L) \approx C$. When only one of the video streams is active, it will result in the scenario shown in Figure 6.10 where there is a gap between successive chunks in steady state. When both the video streams become active, then their chunks can get distributed according to one of the scenarios shown in Figure 6.16. In case (A) in the figure, there is no overlap between the chunks at the bottleneck, which implies that each stream gets the full bottleneck bandwidth (i.e., $R_n^1 = R_n^2 = C$). In case (B), there is partial overlap, so that $\frac{C}{2} < R_n^i < C$, $i = 1,2$. In case (C), there is full overlap so that $R_n^1 = R_n^2 = \frac{C}{2}$.

Hence, only in case c does the TCP throughput measurement reflect the ideal allocation of bottleneck bandwidth between the two sources. This effect, which was first pointed out by Akhshabi et al. [9],

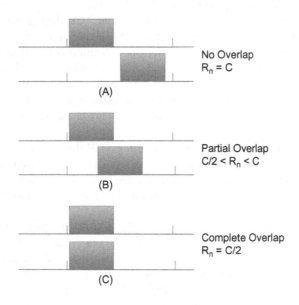

FIGURE 6.16

Overlap of chunks from two video sources at a common bottleneck.

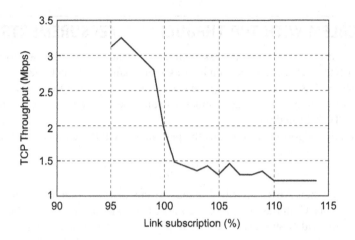

FIGURE 6.17

TCP throughput as a function of link subscription for 100 Adaptive Bit Rate (ABR) sources on a 100-mbps link.

is attributable to the fact that ABR bunches together video packets into chunks for transmission. If the video sources are allowed to transmit continuously, then this effect goes away.

Li et al. [21] carried out a simulation study with 100 sources sharing a bottleneck node of capacity 100 mbps. For the case of an ABR interdownload time of $\tau = 2$ seconds, the transmissions were randomly distributed between 0 and 2 seconds. The TCP throughput was measured using equation 7 using various values of link subscription and is shown in Figure 6.17. It shows the same behavior that we observed for two sources: If the link utilization is less than 100%, then the measured throughput is much higher than the fair bandwidth allocation (about three times the fair-share bandwidth in this example). This causes ABR to increase the video bit rate allocations. As a result of this, the link subscription soon rises above 100%, which causes the TCP throughput to fall precipitously, and the cycle repeats. This behavior has been christened the "bandwidth cliff" effect by Li et al. [21]

Figure 6.18 illustrates the periodic variation in the TCP throughput estimates, the video bit rates and the utilization of the bottleneck link capacity, caused by the bandwidth cliff. Li et al. [21] have recently designed an ABR algorithm called PANDA to avoid the bandwidth cliff effect. The FESTIVE algorithm uses randomization of the chunk download start times to avoid this problem.

By considerations similar to that used for Figure 6.16, it follows that if two HAS sessions are sharing a link and one of them has higher bit rate than the other, then the TCP throughput estimate for the higher bit rate connection will also be higher than that of the lower bit rate connection, which results in unfairness. This is because the higher bit rate connection occupies the link for a longer time, and as a result there are periods when it has access to the entire link bandwidth, thus pushing up its TCP throughput. This problem was first pointed out by Jiang et al. [12], who also proposed a solution for it in their FESTIVE algorithm.

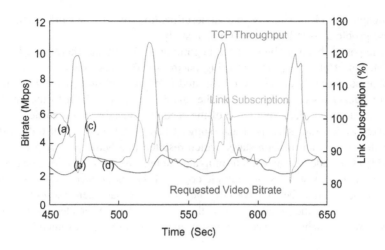

FIGURE 6.18

Video bit rate oscillation as a result of the bandwidth cliff effect.

6.7 INTERACTION BETWEEN TCP AND ABR

In recent years, streaming video has become the dominant form of traffic on the Internet, and as result, video rate control algorithms such as ABR are probably more important than traditional TCP congestion control in understanding the dynamics and evolution of Internet traffic. One of the important issues that researchers have started to investigate only recently is How does ABR rate control interact with TCP congestion control, and how do multiple ABR-controlled streams interact with one another? These topics are discussed in the following two subsections, but in this section, we will describe the consequences of using TCP for transporting individual HAS chunks.

The video stream is sent in a series of individual chunks over TCP, which results in the following issues:

1. The TCP window size that is reached at the end of chunk n serves as the initial window size for chunk (n + 1). As a result, when the chunk (n + 1) transmission starts, up to W TCP segments are transmitted back to back into the network (where W is the TCP window size). For large values of n, this can overwhelm buffers at congested nodes along the path and result in buffer overflows.
2. Assuming that a chunk consists of m packets, all transmission stops after the mth packet is sent. As a result, if one of the last three packets in the chunk is lost (either the $(m-2)^{nd}$, $(m-1)^{rst}$ or m^{th}), then there are not enough duplicate ACKS generated by the receiver to enable the Fast Recovery algorithm. Consequently, this scenario results in TCP Timer (retransmission timeout [RTO]) expiry, which is followed by a reset of the congestion window to its minimum value.

Hence, the interaction between HAS and TCP results in a burst transmission at the start of a chunk and can result in a RTO at the end of a chunk. These can result in a reduction of the resulting throughput of HAS streams and underutilization of the network bandwidth capacity. Mitigating these problems is still an area of active study.

To reduce the packet burst problem at the beginning of the chunk, there have been a couple of suggestions. Esteban et al. [22] proposed using pacing of TCP segments for the entire chunk, so that a window of segments is uniformly transmitted over the duration of a RTT. This did reduce the incidence of packet losses at the start of the chunk but shifted them to the end of the chunk instead. This can lead to a greater incidence of the second issues described earlier, thus making the performance even worse. Liu et al. [23] also suggest using TCP pacing but only restricted to the first RTT after the chunk transmission starts, which resulted in a better performance.

Liu et al. [23] also made a suggestion to mitigate the tail loss issue mentioned earlier. Their technique consists of having the sender send multiple copies of the last packet in the chunk in response to the ACKs that come in after the first copy of the last packet has been transmitted. Hence, if one of the last three packets in the window is lost, then this mechanism creates a duplicate ACK flow from the receiver, which enables the Fast Retransmit mechanism to work as intended.

6.7.1 BANDWIDTH SHARING BETWEEN TCP AND HTTP ADAPTIVE STREAMING

The scenario in which HAS and TCP streams share a bottleneck link is very common in current networks, and hence it is very important to investigate how they share the available bandwidth. This issue was investigated in detail by Huang et al. [24], who carried out a measurement-based study. Their main finding was that HAS streams suffer from what they called a "downward spiral" effect in the presence of a competing TCP flow. This is illustrated in Figure 6.19, in which the

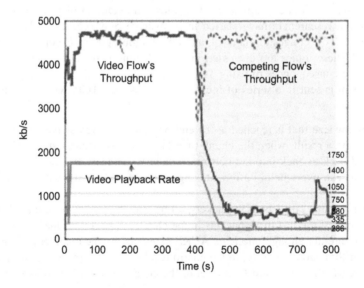

FIGURE 6.19

Loss in video throughput in the presence of a competing TCP flow.

TCP flow is introduced a few minutes after the HAS flow starts up. As soon as this happens, the HAS client picks a video rate that is far below the available bandwidth even though both types of flows share the same round trip latency.

Huang et al. [24] pinpointed the cause of the video rate reduction to step 1 of the ABR algorithm (see Section 6.4), during which the receiver estimates the TCP throughput of the video stream using equation 3). If the computed throughput is an underestimation of the actual available bandwidth, then this can lead to the "downward spiral" shown in Figure 6.19. This indeed turns out to be the case, and the detailed dynamics are as follows:

The following scenario assumes a bottleneck rate of 2.5 mbps.

- In the absence of the competing TCP flow, the HAS stream settles into the usual ON-OFF sequence. During the OFF period, the TCP congestion window times out because of inactivity of greater than 200 ms and resets cwnd to the initial value of 10 packets. Hence, the sender needs to ramp up from slow-start for each new chunk.
- When the competing TCP flow is started, then it fills up the buffer at the bottleneck node during the time the video flow is in its OFF period. As a result, when the video flow turns ON again, it experiences a high packet loss, which results in a decrease in its TCP window size. Also, the chunk transmission finishes before the video streams TCP window has a chance to recover.
- As a result because the ABR estimate of the video rate in equation 7, is actually an estimate of the TCP flow on which the video is riding, and because the TCP throughput suffers in the presence of a competing flow because of the reasons explained earlier, it follows that the ABR algorithm badly underestimates the available link bandwidth.

6.8 FURTHER READING

The YouTube video service from Google does not make use of HAS [25,26]. Instead, it uses a modified form of TCP-based Progressive Download (PD) to transmit the video stream, which operates as follows: At startup, the server transmits the video as fast as it can until the playout buffer (which is 40 sec in size) at the receiver is full. Then it uses rate control to space out the rest of the video transmission, which is also sent in chunks. If the TCP throughput falls, then the send buffer at the server starts to fill up (see Figure 6.2), and this information is used to backpressure the video server.

REFERENCES

[1] Handley M, Floyd S, Padhye J, Widmer J. TCP Friendly Rate Control (TFRC): protocol specification. RFC 2003:3448.
[2] Rejaie R, Handley M, Estrin D. RAP: An end-to-end rate based congestion control mechanism for real-time streams in the Internet. INFOCOM 1999;3:1337–45.
[3] Wang B, Kurose J, Shenoy P, et al. Multimedia streaming via TCP: an analytic performance study. ACM Trans Multimed Comput 2008;4(2):16.
[4] Kim T, Ammar MH. Receiver buffer requirements for video streaming over TCP. 2006;3061–3064.

[5] Zambelli A. IIS smooth streaming technical overview. Redmond, WA: Microsoft Corp., 2009.

[6] Adobe. HTTP dynamic streaming on the Adobe Flash platform. San Jose, CA: Adobe Systems, 2010

[7] Watson M. HTTP adaptive streaming in practice. Netflix Tech. 2011.

[8] Akhshabi S, Begen AC, Dovrolis C. An experimental evaluation of rate-adaptation algorithms in adaptive streaming over HTTP. MMSys 2011:157−68.

[9] Akhshabi A, Anantakrishnan L, Begen AC, et al. What happens when HTTP adaptive streaming players compete for bandwidth. NOSSDAV 2012:9−14.

[10] Miller K, Quacchio E, Gennari G, Wolisz A. Adaptation algorithm for adaptive streaming over HTTP. Packet Video Workshop 2012:173−8.

[11] Liu C, Bouazizi I, Gabbouj M. Rate adaptation for adaptive HTTP streaming. MMSys 2011:169−74.

[12] Jiang J, Sekar V, Zhang H. Improving fairness, efficiency and stability in HTTP based adaptive video streaming with FESTIVE. CoNEXT 2012;22(1):326−40.

[13] Huang T, Johari R, McKeown N., et al. Using the buffer to avoid rebuffers: evidence from a large video streaming service. arXiv preprints 2014.

[14] Yin X., Sekar V., Sinopoli B. Toward a principled framework to design dynamic adaptive streaming algorithms over HTTP. HoTNets−XIII, 2014.

[15] Tian G, Liu Y. Towards agile and smooth video adaptation in dynamic HTTP streaming. CoNEXT 2012:109−20.

[16] Zhou C, Lin CW, Zhang X, Guo Z. Buffer based smooth rate adaptation for dynamic HTTP streaming. IEEE APSIPA 2013:1−9.

[17] De Cicco L, Mascolo S. An experimental investigation of the Akamai adaptive video streaming. Berlin: Springer; 2010.

[18] Thang TC, Le HT, Pham AT, Yong Man Ro. An evaluation of bitrate adaptation methods for HTTP live streaming. IEEE JSAC 2014;32(4):693−705.

[19] Bui N, Michelinakis F, Widmer J. A model for throughput prediction for mobile users. Imdea.org, 2014.

[20] Camacho EF, Alba CF. Model predictive control. Berlin: Springer; 2013.

[21] Li Z, Zhu X, Gahm J, et al. Probe and adapt: rate adaptation for HTTP video streaming at scale. IEEE JSAC 2014;32(4):719−33.

[22] Esteban J, Benno SA, Beck A, et al. Interaction between HTTP adaptive streaming and TCP. NOSSDAV 2012:21−6.

[23] Liu X, Men A, Zhang P. Enhancing TCP to improve throughput of HTTP adaptive streaming. Int J Future Gener Commun Netw 2014;7:1.

[24] Huang T, Handigol N, Heller B, et al. Confused, timid and unstable: picking a video streaming rate is hard. IMC 2012:225−38.

[25] Alcock S, Nelson R. Application flow control in YouTube video systems. ACM SIGCOMM CCR 2011;41(2):24−30.

[26] Ameigeiras P, Munoz JJ, Navarro-Ortiz J, Lopez-Soler JM. Analysis and modeling of YouTube traffic. Trans Emerging Tech 2012;23(4):360−77.

SUGGESTED READING

Akhshabi S, Anantakrishnan L, Dovrolis C, Begen AC. Server based traffic shaping for stabilizing oscillating adaptive streaming players. NOSSDAV 2013:19−24.

Begen AC, Akgul T, Baugher M. Watching video over the web. Part 1: streaming protocols. IEEE Internet Computing 2011;15(2):54−63.

Begen AC, Akgul T, Baugher M. Watching video over the web. Part 2: applications, standardization and open issues. IEEE Internet Comput 2011;15(3):59−63.

Cicco L, Mascolo S, Palmisano V. Feedback control for adaptive live video streaming. MMSys 2011:145−56.

Erman J, Gerber A, Ramadrishnan KK, et al. Over the top video: the gorilla in cellular networks. IMC 2011:127−36.

Gill P, Arlitt M, Li Z, Mahanti A. YouTube traffic characterization: a view from the edge. SIGCOMM 2007:15−28.

Ghobadi M, Cheng Y, Jain A, Mathis M. Trickle: rate limiting YouTube video streaming. USENIX 2012:191−6.

Kim T, Avadhanam N, Subramanian S. Dimensioning receiver buffer requirements for unidirectional VBR video streaming over TCP. INFOCOM 2006:3061−4.

Moving Picture Experts Group. MPEG DASH specification. ISO/IEC DIS 23009-1.2, 2011.

Rao A, Legout A, Lim YS, et al. Network characteristics of video streaming traffic. CoNEXT 2011:25.

CONGESTION CONTROL IN DATA CENTER NETWORKS

7.1 INTRODUCTION

This chapter discusses the topic of congestion control in data center networks (DCN), which have assumed a lot of importance in the networking arena lately. DCNs are used to create "cloud"-based massively parallel information processing systems, which are integral to the way computing is done today. They underlie the massive computing infrastructure that run web sites such as Google and Facebook and constitute a key competitive advantage for these types of companies.

Modern data centers are created by interconnecting together a large number of commodity servers and their associated storage systems, with commodity Ethernet switches. They create a "warehouse-scale" computing infrastructure [1] that scales "horizontally"; that is, we can increase the processing power of the data center by adding more servers as opposed to increasing the processing power of individual servers (which is a more expensive proposition). The job of a DCN in the data center architecture is to interconnect the servers in a way that maximizes the bandwidth between any two servers while minimizing the latency between them. The DCN architecture should also allow the flexibility to easily group together servers that are working on the same application, irrespective of where they are located in the DCN topology.

From the congestion control point of view, DCNs have some unique characteristics compared with the other types of Internet Protocol (IP) networks that we have seen so far in this book:

- The round trip latencies in DCNs are extremely small, usually of the order of a few hundred microseconds, as opposed to tens of milliseconds and larger for other types of networks.
- Applications need very high bandwidths and very low latencies at the same time.
- There is very little statistical multiplexing, with a single flow often dominating a path.
- To keep their costs low, DCN switches have smaller buffers compared with regular switches or routers because vendors implement them using fast (and expensive) static random-access memory (SRAM) to keep up with the high link speeds. Moreover, buffers are shared between ports, so that a single connection can end up consuming the buffers for an entire switch [2].

As a result of these characteristics, normal TCP congestion control (i.e., TCP Reno) does not perform very well because of the following reasons:

- TCP requires large buffers; indeed, the buffer size should be greater than or equal to the delay-bandwidth product of the connection to fully use the full bandwidth of the link as shown in Chapter 2.

- End-to-end delays of connections under TCP are much larger than what can be tolerated in DCNs. The delays are caused by TCP's tendency to fill up link buffers to capacity to fully use the link.

Another special characteristic of DCNs is that they are homogeneous and under a single administrative control. Hence, backward compatibility, incremental deployment, or fairness to legacy protocols are not of major concern. As a result, many of the new DCN congestion control algorithms require fairly major modifications to both the end systems as well as the DCN switches. Their main objective is to minimize end-to-end latency so that it is of the order of a few milliseconds while ensuring high link utilization.

DCN congestion control algorithms fall in two broad categories:

- Algorithms that retain the end-to-end congestion control philosophy of TCP: Data Center TCP (DCTCP) [2], Deadline-Aware Data Center TCP (D^{2}TCP) [3], and High bandwidth Ultra Low Latency (HULL) [4], fall into this category of algorithms. They use a more aggressive form of a Random Early Detection (RED)−like Explicit Congestion Notification (ECN) feedback from congested switches that are then used to modify the congestion window at the transmitter. These new algorithms are necessitated due to the fact that Normal RED or even the more effective form of Active Queue Management (AQM) with the Proportional-Integral (PI) controller (see Chapter 3) is not able to satisfy DCNs' low latency requirements.

- Algorithms that depend on in-network congestion control mechanisms: Some recently proposed DCN congestion control protocols such as D^3 [5], Preemptive Distributed Quick Flow Scheduling (PDQ) [6], DeTail [7], and pFabric [8] fall in this category. They all use additional mechanisms at the switch, such as bandwidth reservations in D^3, priority scheduling in pFabric or packet by packet load balancing in DeTail. The general trend is towards a simplified form of rate control in the end systems coupled with greater support for congestion control in the network because this leads to much faster response to congestion situations. This is a major departure from the legacy congestion control philosophy of putting all the intelligence in the end system.

To communicate at full speed between any two servers, the interconnection network provides multiple paths between them, which is one of the distinguishing features of DCNs. This leads to new open problems in the area of how to load balance the traffic among these paths. Multi-path TCP (MPTCP) [9,10] is one of the approaches that has been suggested to solve this problem, using multiple simultaneous TCP connections between servers, whose windows are weakly interacting with one another.

The Incast problem is a special type of traffic overload situation that occurs in data centers. It is caused by the way in which jobs are scheduled in parallel across multiple servers, which causes their responses to be synchronized with one another, thus overwhelming switch buffers.

The rest of this chapter is organized as follows: Section 7.2 provides a brief overview to the topic of DCN Interconnect networks. We also discuss the traffic generation patterns in DCNs and the origin of the low latency requirement. Section 7.3 discusses the DCTCP algorithm, and Section 7.4 explores Deadline Aware algorithms, including D^{2}TCP and D^3. Section 7.5 is devoted to MPTCP, and Section 7.6 describes the Incast problem in DCNs.

An initial reading of this chapter can be done in the sequence $7.1 \rightarrow 7.2 \rightarrow 7.3 \rightarrow 7.5$, which contains an introduction to data center architectures and a description and analysis of the DCTCP and Multipath TCP algorithms. More advanced readers can venture into Sections 7.4 and 7.6, which discuss deadline aware congestion control algorithms and the Incast problem.

7.2 DATA CENTER ARCHITECTURE AND TRAFFIC PATTERNS

A typical data center consists of thousands of commodity servers that are connected together using a special type of Ethernet network called an Inter-connection Network. An example of a data center using a traditional tree-type interconnection architecture is shown in Figure 7.1, which illustrates the main features of this type of network: Servers are arranged in racks consisting of 20 to 40 devices, each of which is connected to a Top of Rack (ToR) switch. Each ToR is connected to two aggregation switches (ASs) for redundancy, perhaps through an intermediate layer of L2 switches. Each AS is further connected to two aggregation routers (ARs), such that all switches below each pair of ARs form a single Layer 2 domain, connecting several thousand servers. Servers are also partitioned into Virtual Local Area Networks (VLANs) to limit packet flooding and Address Resolution Protocol (ARP) broadcasts and to create a logical server group that can be assigned to a single application. ARs in turn are connected to core routers (CRs) that are responsible for the interconnection of the data center with the outside world.

Some of the problems with this architecture include the following:

- Lack of bisection bandwidth: Bisection bandwidth is defined as the maximum capacity between any two servers. Even though each server may have a 1-Gbps link to its ToR switch and hence to

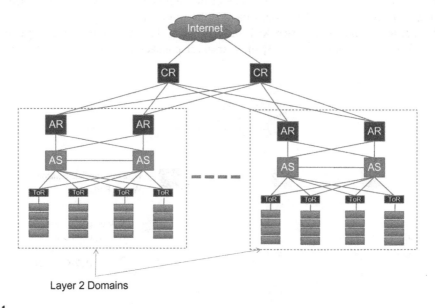

FIGURE 7.1

Traditional tree-type data center network architecture.

other servers in its rack, the links further up in the hierarchy are heavily oversubscribed. For example, only 4 Gbps may be used on the link between the ToR and AS switches, resulting in 1:5 oversubscription when there are 20 servers per rack, and paths through top-most layers of the tree may be as much as 1:240 oversubscribed. As a result of this, designers tend to only user servers that are closer to each other, thus fragmenting the server pool (i.e., there may be idle servers in part of the data center that cannot be used to relieve the congestion in another portion of the system).

Note that bisection bandwidth is a very important consideration in DCNs because the majority of the traffic is between servers, as opposed to between servers and the external network. The reason for this is that large DCNs are used to execute applications such as Web search, analytics, and so on that involve coordination and communication among subtasks running on hundreds of servers using technologies such as map-reduce.

- Configuration complexity: Another factor that constrains designers to use servers in the same Layer 2 domain for a single service is that adding additional servers to scale the service outside the domain requires reconfiguration of IP addresses and VLAN trunks because IP addresses are topologically significant and are used to route traffic to a particular Layer 2 domain. As a result, most designs use a more static policy whereby they keep additional servers idle within the same domain to scale up, thus resulting in server under-utilization.
- Poor reliability and redundancy: Within a Layer 2 domain, the use of Spanning Tree protocol for data forwarding results in only a single path between two servers. Between Layer 2 domains, up to two paths can be used if Equal Cost Multi-Path (ECMP) [11] routing is turned on.

To address these problems, several new data center architectures have been proposed in recent years. Some of the more significant designs include the following:

The VL2 Inter-Connection Network: Instead of using the Tree Architecture, Greenberg et al. [12] proposed using a Clos network [13] of interserver connections (Figure 7.2). As shown, each

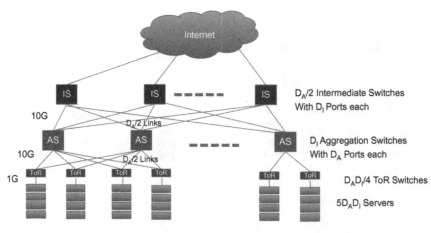

FIGURE 7.2

The VL2 interconnection network.

ToR switch is still connected to two AS switches using 1-Gbps links, but unlike the Tree Architecture, each AS switch is connected to every other AS switch in 2-hops, through a layer of intermediate switches (ISs) using 10 Gbps or higher speed links. As a result, if there are n IS switches, then there are n paths between any two ASs, and if any of the IS fails, then it reduces the bandwidth between 2 AS switches by only 1/n. For the VL2 network shown in Figure 7.2, the total capacity between each layer is given by $D_I D_A/2$ times the link capacity, assuming that there are D_I AS switches with D_A ports each. Also note that the number of ToR switches is given by $D_A D_I/4$, so that if there are M servers attached with a 1-Gbps link to the ToR and the links between the AS and IS are at 10 Gbps, then equating the total bandwidth from the AS to the ToR switches to the total bandwidth in the opposite direction, we obtain

$$M \times \frac{D_A D_I}{4} = 10 \times \frac{D_A D_I}{2} \quad i.e. \quad M = 20$$

servers per ToR, so that the network can support a total of $5D_A D_I$ servers, with a full bisection bandwidth of 1 Gbps between any two servers.

The VL2 architecture uses Valiant Load Balancing (VLB) [14] among flows to spread the traffic through multiple paths. VLB is implemented using ECMP forwarding in the routers. VL2 also enables the system to create multiple Virtual Layer 2 switches (hence the name), such that it is possible to configure a virtual switch with servers that may be located anywhere in the DCN. All the servers in Virtual Switch are able to communicate at the full bisection bandwidth and furthermore are isolated from servers in the other Virtual Switches.

To route packets to a target server, the system uses two sets of IP addresses. Each application is assigned an Application Specific IP Address (AA), and all the interfaces in the DCN switches are assigned a Location Specific IP Address (LA) (a link-state based IP routing protocol is used to disseminate topology information among the switches in the DCN). An application's AA does not change if it migrates from server to server, and each AA is associated with an LA that serves as the identifier of the ToR switch to which it is connected. VL2 has a Directory System (DS) that stores the mapping between the AAs and LAs. When a server sends a packet to its ToR switch, the switch consults the DS to find out the destination ToR and then encapsulates the packet at the IP level, known as tunneling, and forwards it into the DCN. To take advantage of the multiple paths, the system does load balancing at the flow level by randomizing the selection of the Intermediate Switch used for the tunnel. Data center networking—oriented switching protocols such as VxLAN and TRILL use a similar design.

A VL2-based DCN can be implemented using standard switches and routers, the only change required is the addition of a software layer 2.5 shim in the server protocol stack to implement address resolution and tunnel selection functions.

The Fat Tree Architecture: Vahdat et al. [15] proposed another Clos-based DCN architecture called Fat Tree (Figure 7.3). The network is built entirely with k-port 1-Gbps switches and is constructed around k pods, each of which has two layers of switches, with (k/2) switches in each layer. The bottom layer of switches in a pod is connected to the servers, with (k/2) servers connected to each switch. This implies that the system with k pods can connect (k/2) switches/pod * (k/2) server facing ports per switch * k pods = $(k^3/4)$ servers per network. Similarly, it can be shown that there are $k^2/4$ core switches per network, so that the number of equal-cost multipaths between any pair of hosts is also given by $k^2/4$. Because the total bandwidth between the core switch and aggregation

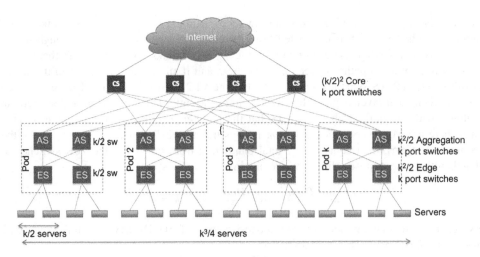

FIGURE 7.3

The Fat Tree interconnection network.

switch layers is given by $k^3/4$, it follows that the network has enough capacity to support a full 1-Gbps bisectional bandwidth between any two servers in the ideal case.

The main distinction compared with VL2 is the fact that the Fat Tree network is built entirely out of lower speed 1 Gbps switches. However, this come at the cost of larger number of interconnections between switches. To take full advantage of the Fat Tree topology and realize the full bisection bandwidth, the traffic between two servers needs to be spread evenly between the $(k/2)^2$ paths that exist between them. It is not possible to do this using the traditional ECMP-based IP routing scheme, so Vahdat et al. designed a special two-level routing table scheme to accomplish this.

Modern data center designs use a simpler form the Clos architecture called Leaf Spine. VL2 is an example of a 3-Layer Leaf Spine design with ToR, AS and IS switches forming the three layers. It is possible to do a 2-Layer Leaf Spine design with just the ToR and IS layers, with each ToR switch directly connected to every one of the IS switches.

As both the VL2 and the Fat Tree interconnections illustrate, the biggest difference between DCNs and more traditional networks is the existence of multiple paths between any two servers in a DCN. This opens the field to new types of congestion control algorithms that can take advantage of this feature.

7.2.1 TRAFFIC GENERATION MODEL AND IMPLICATIONS FOR CONGESTION CONTROL

We provide a short description of a typical online transaction that generates most of the traffic in large DCNs today (Figure 7.4). Applications such as web search, social network content

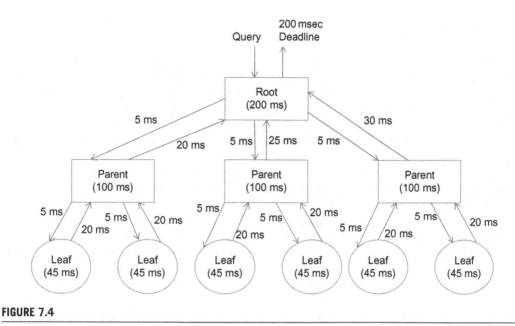

FIGURE 7.4

Map-reduce type data model with deadlines.

composition, and advertisement selection are all based around this design pattern. Each of the nodes in Figure 7.4 represents the processing at a server node; the connector between nodes stands for the transmission of a flow across the interconnection network. A typical online transaction is generated when a user enters a query into a search engine. Studies have shown that the response needs to be generated within a short deadline of 230 to 300 ms. A very large data set is required to answer the query, which is spread among thousands of servers in the DCN, each with its own storage. The way a query progresses through a DCN is shown in Figure 7.4. The query arrives at the root node, which broadcasts it to down to the next level, which in turn generate their own queries one level down until the leaf nodes holding the actual data are reached. Each leaf node sends its response back to its parent, which aggregates the replies from all its child nodes and sends it up to the root. Furthermore, answering a query may involve iteratively invoking this pattern; one to four iterations are typical, but as many as 20 may occur.

This overall architecture is called scatter-gather, partition-aggregate, or map-reduce. The propagation of the request down to the leaves and the responses back to the root must complete within the overall deadline that is allocated to the query; otherwise, the response is discarded. To satisfy this, the system allocates a deadline to each processing node, which gets divided up into two parts: the computation time in the leaf node and the communication latency between the leaf and the parent. The deadlines for individual computational nodes typically vary from about 10 to 100 ms. Some example delay allocations to the nodes and the communications links are shown in Figure 7.4, from which we can see that the deadlines for communications between hosts cannot exceed tens of milliseconds if the system is to be able to meet the overall job deadline.

This model of data center job computation leads to a few different models for congestion control algorithms that are optimized for DCNs, namely:

- Minimization of flow latency becomes a very important requirement in DCNs, which was not the case for other congestion control scenarios. At the same time, other flows in the data center are throughput intensive. For example, large transfers that update the internal data structures at a server node fall into the latter category; hence, throughput maximization and high link utilization cannot be ignored as the congestion control objective. Based on this insight, a number of new congestion control algorithms, such as DCTCP, try to minimize latency with an aggressive form of AQM while not compromising on throughput.
- A second class of algorithms tackles the issue of deadlines for flows directly by using congestion control algorithms that take these deadlines into account. Algorithms such as D^3 [5] and D^2TCP [3] fall in this category.
- A third class of algorithms have adopted a more radical design by parting ways with the "all intelligence should be in the end system" philosophy of the Internet. They contend that end system–based controls have an unsurmountable delay of one round trip before they can react to network congestion, which is too slow for DCNs. Instead they propose to make the network responsible for congestion control while limiting the end system to very simple nonadaptive rate regulation and error recovery functions. Some of these algorithms take advantage of the fact that there are multiple paths between any two servers; hence, the network nodes can quickly route around a congested node on a packet-by-packet basis (e.g., see [7]).

7.3 DATA CENTER TCP (DCTCP)

DCTCP was one of the earliest congestion control algorithms designed for DCNs and is also one of the best known. It was invented by Alizadeh et al. [2], who observed that query and delay sensitive short messages in DCNs experienced long latencies and even packet losses caused by large flows consuming some or all of the buffer in the switches. This effect is exacerbated by the fact that buffers are shared across multiple ports, so that a single large flow on any one of the ports can increase latencies across all ports. As a result, even though the round trip latencies are of the order of a few hundred microseconds, queuing delays caused by congestion can increase these latencies by two orders of magnitude. Hence, they concluded that to meet the requirements for such a diverse mix of short and long flows, switch buffer occupancies need to be persistently low while maintaining high throughput for long flows.

Traditionally, two classes of congestion control algorithms are used to control queuing latencies:

- Delay-based protocols such as TCP Vegas: These use increases in measured Round Trip Latency (RTT) as a sign of growing queue lengths and hence congestion. They rely heavily on accurate RTT measurements, which is a problems in a DCN environment because the RTTs are extremely small, of the order of a few hundred microseconds. Hence, small noise fluctuations in latency become indistinguishable from congestion, which can cause TCP Vegas to react in error.
- AQM algorithms: These use explicit feedback from the congested switches to regulate the transmission rate, RED being the best known member of this class of algorithms. DCTCP falls within this class of algorithms.

Based on a simulation study, Alizadeh et al. [2] came to the conclusion that legacy AQM schemes such as RED and PI do not work well in environments where there is low statistical multiplexing and the traffic is bursty, both of which are present in DCNs. DCTCP is able to do a better job by being more aggressive in reacting to congestion and trading off convergence time to achieve this objective.

DCTCP operates as follows:

1. At the switch: An arriving packet at a switch is marked with Congestion Encountered (CE) codepoint if the queue occupancy is greater than a threshold K at its arrival. A switch that supports RED can be reconfigured to do this by setting both the low and high threshold to K and marking based on instantaneous rather than average queue length.
2. At the receiver: A DCTCP receiver tries to accurately convey the exact sequence of marked packets back to the sender by ACKing every packet and setting the ECN-Echo flag if and only if the data packet has a marked CE codepoint. This algorithm can also be modified to take delayed ACKs into account while not losing the continuous monitoring property at the sender [2].
3. At the sender: The sender maintains an estimate of the fraction of packets that are marked, called α, which is updated once for every window of data as follows:

$$\alpha \leftarrow (1 - g)\alpha + gF \tag{1}$$

where F is the fraction of packets that were marked in the last window of data and $0 < g < 1$ is the smoothing factor. Note that because every packet gets marked, α estimates the probability that the queue size is greater than K.

Features of TCP rate control such as Slow Start, additive increase during congestion avoidance, or recovery from lost packets are left unchanged. However, instead of cutting its window size by 2 in response to a marked ACK, DCTCP applies the following rule once every RTT:

$$W \leftarrow W + 1 \quad \text{if none of the packets are marked in a window} \tag{2}$$

$$W \leftarrow W\left(1 - \frac{\alpha}{2}\right) \quad \text{if one or more packets are marked per window} \tag{3}$$

Thus, a DCTCP sender starts to reduce its window as soon as the queue size exceeds K (rather than wait for a packet loss) and does so in proportion to the average fraction of marked packets. Hence, if very few packets are marked then the window size hardly reduces, and conversely in the worst case if every packet is marked, then the window size reduces by half every RTT (as in Reno).

Following Alizadeh et al. [2,16], we now provide an analysis of DCTCP. It can be shown that in the fluid limit, the DCTCP window size W, the marking estimate α, and the queue size at the bottleneck node b(t) satisfy the following set of delay-differential equations:

$$\frac{dW}{dt} = \frac{1}{T(t)} - \frac{W(t)\alpha(t)}{2T(t)} p(t - T(t)) \tag{4}$$

$$\frac{d\alpha}{dt} = \frac{g}{T(t)}[p(t - T(t)) - \alpha(t)] \tag{5}$$

$$\frac{db}{dt} = N\frac{W(t)}{T(t)} - C \tag{6}$$

where p(t) is the marking probability at the bottleneck node and is given by

$$p(t) = 1_{\{Q(t) > K\}} \tag{7}$$

T(t) is the round trip latency, C is the capacity of the bottleneck node, and N is the number of DCTCP sessions passing through the bottleneck.

Equations 4 to 6 are equivalent to the corresponding equations 54 and 55 for TCP Reno presented in Chapter 3. Equation 5 can be derived as the fluid limit of equation 1, and equation 6 can be derived from the fact that the data rate for each of the N sessions is given by W(t)/T(t), while C is the rate at which the buffer gets drained. To derive equation 4, note that 1/T(t) is the rate at which the window increases (increase of 1 per round-trip), and $-\frac{W(t)\alpha(t)}{2T(t)}$ is the rate at which the window decreases when one or more packets in the window are marked (because $-\frac{W(t)\alpha(t)}{2}$ is the decrease in window size, and this happens once per round trip).

Using the approximation T = D + K/C (where D is the round trip propagation delay), it was shown by Alizadeh et al. [16] that this fluid model agrees quite well with simulations results. Because of the 0-1 type marking function p(t), this system of equations does not have a fixed point and instead converges to a periodic limit-cycle behavior in steady state. It is possible to do a stability analysis of the system using sophisticated tools from Poincare Map theory and thus derive conditions on the parameters C, N, D, K, and g for the system to be stable, which are $g \in (0, 1]$ and (CD + K)/N > 2. They also showed that to attain 100% throughput, the minimum buffer size K at the bottleneck node is given by

$$K > 0.17CD \tag{8}$$

This is a very interesting result if we contrast it with the minimum buffer size required to sustain full throughput for TCP Reno, which from Chapter 2 is given by CD. Hence, DCTCP is able to get to full link utilization using just 17% of the buffers compared with TCP Reno, which accounts for the lower latencies that the flows experience.

Using a simpler model and under the assumption that all N connections are synchronized with each other, it is possible to obtain expressions for the fluctuation of the bottleneck queue size [2], and we do this next (Figure 7.5). This model, called the Sawtooth model by Alizadeh et al. [16], is of the more traditional type that we have analyzed in previous chapters, and the synchronization assumption makes it possible to compute the steady-state fraction of the packets that are marked at a switch. This quantity is assumed to be fixed, which means that the model is only accurate for small values of the smoothing parameter g.

An analysis of the Sawtooth model is done next:

Let $S(W_1, W_2)$ be the number of packets sent by the sender while its window size increases from W_1 to $W_2 > W_1$. Note that this takes $(W_2 - W_1)$ round trip times because the window increases by at most 1 for every round trip. The average window size during this time is given by $(W_1 + W_2)/2$, and because the increase is linear, it follows that

$$S(W_1, W_2) = \frac{W_2^2 - W_1^2}{2} \tag{9}$$

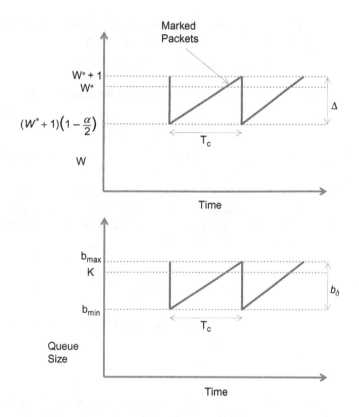

FIGURE 7.5

Window size and bottleneck queue dynamics for DCTCP.

When the window increases to $W^* = (CD + K)/N$, then the queue size reaches K (because $CD + K$ is the maximum number of packets that can be in transit + waiting for service for a buffer size of K and a single source), and the switch starts to mark packets with the congestion codepoint. However, it takes one more round trip delay for this information to get to the source, during which the window size increases to $W^* + 1$. Hence, the steady-state fraction of marked packets is given by

$$\alpha = \frac{S(W^*, W^* + 1)}{S((W^* + 1)(1 - \alpha/2), W^* + 1)} \tag{10}$$

By plugging equations 9 into 10 and simplifying, it follows that

$$\alpha^2 \left(1 - \frac{\alpha}{4}\right) = \frac{2W^* + 1}{(W^* + 1)^2} \approx \frac{2}{W^*} \text{ so that } \alpha \approx \sqrt{\frac{2}{W^*}} \tag{11}$$

To compute the magnitude of oscillations in the queue size, we first compute the magnitude of oscillations in window size of a single connection, which is given by

$$\Delta = (W^* + 1) - (W^* + 1)\left(1 - \frac{\alpha}{2}\right) = (W^* + 1)\frac{\alpha}{2} \tag{12}$$

Because there are N flows, it follows that the oscillation in the queue size b_δ, is given by

$$b_\delta = N\Delta = N(W^* + 1)\frac{\alpha}{2} \approx N\sqrt{\frac{W^*}{2}}$$

$$= \sqrt{\frac{N(CD + K)}{2}} \tag{13}$$

From equation 13, it follows that the amplitude of queue size oscillations in DCTCP is $O(\sqrt{CD})$, which is much smaller than the oscillations in TCP Reno, which are $O(CD)$. This allows for a smaller threshold value K, without the loss of throughput. Indeed, the minimum value of the queue size b_{min}, can also be computed and is given by

$$b_{min} = b_{max} - A$$

$$= K + N - \sqrt{\frac{N(CD + K)}{2}} \tag{14}$$

To find a lower bound on K, we can minimize equation 14 over N and then choose K so that this minimum is larger than zero, which results in

$$K > \frac{CD}{7} = 0.14CD \tag{15}$$

which is close to the value 0.17D derived from the more exact analysis by Alizadeh et al. [16].

Simulation results in Alizadeh et al. [2] show that DCTCP achieves its main objective of reducing the size of the bottleneck queue size; indeed, the queue size with DCTCP is 1/20th the size of the corresponding queue with TCP Reno and RED.

Using this model, it is also possible to derive an expression for the average throughput of DCTCP as a function of the packet drop probability, and we do so next. Using the deterministic approximation technique described in Section 2.3 of Chapter 2, we compute the number of packets transmitted during a window increase–decrease cycle M and the length of the cycle τ to get the average throughput $R_{avg} = \frac{M}{\tau}$, so that

$$R_{avg} = \frac{M}{T\left[W^* - (1 - \frac{\alpha}{2})W^*\right]} = \frac{M}{T(\alpha/2)W^*} = \frac{M}{T}\sqrt{\frac{2}{W^*}} \tag{16}$$

In this equation, $(\alpha/2)W^*$ is the number of round trip latencies in a cycle, and α is approximated by equation 11. Note that M is approximately given by $S((1 - \alpha/2)W^*, W^*$, so that

$$M = \frac{(W^*)^2 - (1 - \frac{\alpha}{2})^2(W^*)^2}{2}$$

$$= \frac{(W^*)^2}{2}\alpha\left(1 - \frac{\alpha}{4}\right)$$

Substituting for α using equation 11, we obtain

$$M = \sqrt{\frac{(W^*)^3}{4}} - \frac{W^*}{4}$$

Following the usual procedure, we equate $M = 1/p$, where p is the packet drop probability, so that

$$\frac{1}{p} = \sqrt{\frac{(W^*)^3}{4}} - \frac{W^*}{4}$$

After some simplifications, we obtain

$$\frac{p^2(W^*)^2}{4} = 1 + \frac{pW^*}{2} + \left(\frac{pW^*}{4}\right)^2 \approx \frac{pW^*}{2} + \left(\frac{pW^*}{4}\right)^2$$

Solving the resulting equation for W^*, we obtain

$$W^* = \frac{p + \sqrt{p^2 + 128p}}{8p} \approx \sqrt{\frac{p^2 + 128p}{8p}} \text{ since } p \ll \sqrt{p^2 + 128p} \text{ for } p \in [0, 1] \tag{17}$$

Substituting for $M = 1/p$ and W^* in equation 16, we obtain

$$R_{avg} = \frac{4}{T\sqrt{p\sqrt{p^2 + 128p}}} = \frac{4}{T\sqrt[4]{p^4 + 128p^3}} \approx \frac{4}{2^{1.75}Tp^{3/4}} = \frac{1.19}{Tp^{0.75}} \tag{18}$$

so that the Response Function for DCTCP is given by (see Chapter 5 for a definition of the Response Function)

$$\log w = 0.07 - 0.75 \log p \tag{19}$$

Equation 18 and 19 imply that DCTCP is comparable to high-speed protocols such as High Speed TCP (HSTCP) in being able to use large link capacities in an efficient manner. Unlike HSTCP or CUBIC, DCTCP does not make allowances to be Reno friendly, so there is no cut-off link capacity below which DCTCP behaves like Reno. The higher throughput of DCTCP compared with Reno can be attributed to DCTCP's less drastic reductions in window size on encountering packet drops. The exponent d of the packet drop probability is given by $d = 0.75$, which points to high degree of intraprotocol RTT unfairness in DCTCP. However Alizadeh et al. [2] have shown by simulations that the RTT unfairness in DCTCP is actually close to that of Reno with RED. Hence, the unfairness predicted by equation 18 is an artifact of the assumption that all the N sessions are synchronized in the Sawtooth model.

7.3.1 THE HULL MODIFICATION TO IMPROVE DCTCP

Alizadeh et al. [4], in a follow-on work, showed that it is possible to reduce the flow latencies across a DCN even further than DCTCP by signaling switch congestion based on link utilizations rather than queue lengths. They came up with an algorithm called HULL (High bandwidth Ultra Low Latency), which implements this idea and works as follows:

Consider a simulated queue called Phantom Queue (PQ), which is a virtual queue associated with each switch egress port, and in series with it as shown in Figure 7.6 (sometimes it is also called a

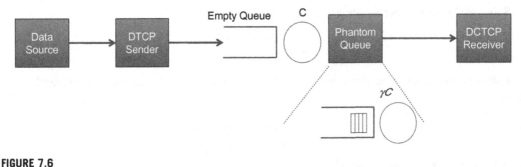

FIGURE 7.6

Implementation of the phantom queue.

Virtual Out Queue [VOQ]). Note that the PQ is not really a queue because it does not store packets; however, it is simply a counter that is updated as packets exit the link to determine the queuing that would have occurred on a slower virtual link (typically about 10% slower). It then marks the ECN for packets that pass through it when the simulated queue is above a fixed threshold. The PQ attempts to keep the aggregate transmission rate for the congestion-controlled flows to be strictly less than the link capacity, which keeps the switch buffers mostly empty. The system also uses DCTCP as its congestion control algorithm to take advantage of its low latency properties.

To further reduce the queue build-up in the switches, HULL also implements Packet Pacing at the sender. The pacer should be implemented in hardware in the server Network Interface Card (NIC) to smooth out the burstiness caused by the data transfer mechanism between the main memory and the NIC.

As a result of these enhancements, HULL has been shown achieve 46% to 58% lower average latency compared with DCTCP, and 69% to 78% slower 99th percentile latency.

7.4 DEADLINE-AWARE CONGESTION CONTROL ALGORITHMS

Section 7.2.1 showed that flows in DCNs come with real-time constraints on their completion times, typically of the order of tens of milliseconds. One of the issues with DCTCP is that it does not take these deadlines into account; instead, because of its TCP heritage, it tries to assign link bandwidth fairly to all flows irrespective of their deadlines. As a result, it has been shown [5] that as much as 7% of flows may miss their deadlines with DCTCP. A number of recent DCN conges-tion control proposals seek to address this shortcoming. All of them try to incorporate the flow deadline information into the congestion control algorithm in some way and in the process have a varying impact on the implementation at the sender, the receiver, and the switches. In this subsection, we will describe two of these algorithms, namely, Deadline Aware Datacenter TCP (D^2TCP) [3] and D^3 [5], in order of increasing difference from the DCTCP design.

7.4.1 DEADLINE AWARE DATACENTER TCP

Historically, the D^3 algorithm came first, but we will start with D^2TCP because it is closer in design to DCTCP and unlike D^3 does not impact the switches or make fundamental changes to

TCP's additive increase/multiplicative decrease (AIMD) scheme. In fact, just like DCTCP, it is able to make use of existing ECN-enabled Ethernet switches.

The basic idea behind D^2TCP is to modulate the congestion window size based on both deadline information and the extent of congestion. The algorithm works as follows:

- As in DCTCP, each switch marks the CE bit in a packet if its queue size exceeds a threshold K. This information is fed back to the source by the receiver though ACK packets.
- Also as in DCTCP, each sender maintains a weighted average of the extent of congestion α, given by

$$\alpha \leftarrow (1 - g)\alpha + gF \tag{20}$$

  where F is the fraction of marked packets in the most recent window and g is the weight given to new samples.
- DCTCP introduces a new variable that is computed at the sender, called the deadline imminence factor d, which is a function of a flows deadline value, and such that the resulting congestion behavior allows the flow to safely complete within its deadline. Define T_c as the time needed for a flow to complete transmitting all its data under a deadline agnostic behavior, and δ as the time remaining until its deadline expires. If $T_c > \delta$, then the flow should be given higher priority in the network because it has a tight deadline and vice versa. Accordingly, the factor d is defined as

$$d = \frac{T_c}{\delta} \tag{21}$$

Note that δ is known at the source. To compute T_c, consider the following: Let X be the amount of data (in packets) that remain to be transmitted and let W_m be the current maximum window size. Recall from Section 7.3 that the number of packets transmitted per window cycle N is given by

$$N = S\left((W_m + 1)\left(1 - \frac{\alpha}{2}\right), W_m + 1\right) = \frac{W_m^2}{2}\alpha\left(1 - \frac{\alpha}{4}\right) = \sqrt{\frac{W_m^3}{4} - \frac{W_m}{4}} \text{ packets/cycle}$$

so that $N \approx \frac{W_m^{1.5}}{2}$

Hence, the number round trip latencies M in a window increase–decrease cycle is given by

$$M = \frac{X}{N} \approx \frac{2X}{W_m^{1.5}}$$

Again from Section 7.3, the length τ of a cycle is given by

$$\tau = TW_m\frac{\alpha}{2} \approx T\sqrt{\frac{W_m}{2}}$$

where T = D + K/C. It follows that T_c is given by

$$T_c = M\tau = \frac{X\sqrt{2}}{W_m}T$$

so that

$$d = \frac{X\sqrt{2}}{W_m\delta}T \tag{22}$$

- Based on α and d, the sender computes a penalty function p applied to the window size, given by

$$p = \alpha^d \tag{23}$$

The following rule is then used for varying the window size once every round trip

$$W \leftarrow \begin{cases} W + 1 & \text{if } p = 0 \\ W\left(1 - \dfrac{1}{p}\right) & \text{if } p > 0 \end{cases} \tag{24}$$

When $\alpha = 0$ then $p = 0$, and the window size increases by one on every round trip. At the other extreme, when $\alpha = 1$, then $p = 1$, and the window size is halved just as in regular TCP or DCTCP. For $0 < \alpha < 1$, the algorithm behaves differently compared with DCTCP, and depending on the value of d, the window size gets modulated as a function of the deadlines. In Figure 7.7, we plot p as a function of α, for $d < 1$, $d = 1$ and $d > 1$. Note than when $d = 1$, then $p = \alpha$, so that the system matches DCTCP. If $d > 1$, then from equation 21, it follows that the time required to transmit the remaining data is larger than allowed by the deadline; hence, the flow should be given higher priority by the network. Equation 23 brings this about by reducing the value of p for such a flow, resulting in a larger window size by equation 24. Conversely, if $d < 1$, equation 24 leads to a smaller window size and hence lower priority for the flow. Hence, the net effect of these window change rules is that far-deadline flows relinquish bandwidth so that near-deadline flows can have greater short-term share to meet their deadlines. If the network congestion keeps increasing despite the far-deadline flows backing off, then Figure 7.7 shows that the curves for $d < 1$ converges toward that for $d > 1$, which implies that in this situation even the near-deadline flows reduce their aggressively.

Vamanan et al. [3] simulated D^2TCP and showed that the algorithm reduces the fraction of missed deadlines by 75% when compared to DCTCP and 50% compared with D^3. It is also able to coexist with TCP flows without degrading their performance.

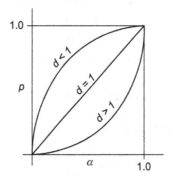

FIGURE 7.7

Deadline-Aware Data Center TCP (D^2TCP) correction function.

7.4.2 THE D³ ALGORITHM

Both the DCTCP and D²TCP algorithms are designed to make use of regular Ethernet switches, albeit those that support RED. In this section, we describe the D³ algorithm that requires significantly enhanced switch functionalities [5]. D³ was the first algorithm that attempted to directly adapt the classical EDF scheduling algorithm to DCNs, and later another algorithm called PDQ [6] built upon it to significantly and improved its performance by adding preemptive scheduling of flows. Indeed, both of these algorithms take us out of the province of AIMD-type window increment−decrement algorithms that have dominated congestion control designs since the 1980s. Note that both of these algorithms are based on the use of First In First Out (FIFO) scheduling at the network nodes. These algorithms are able to simulate the effect of node level EDF scheduling by controlling the rate (in D³) or the admission of packets into the network (in PDQ).

A traditional EDF scheduler operates as follows: All packets arriving into the queue carry an extra piece of information in their headers, which is the deadline by which they have to be finish transmission. The EDF scheduler prioritizes transmissions, such that packets with the smallest or earliest deadline are transmitted first. EDF scheduling can be done either on a nonpreemptive or preemptive basis. In non-preemptive scheduling, after a transmission is started, it finishes to completion; in preemptive scheduling, a packet with a smaller deadline can preempt the transmission of a packet with a longer deadline. A preemptive EDF scheduler can be proven to be optimal [17] in the sense that if the link utilization is under 100%, then all packets under EDF scheduling will meet their deadlines.

A straightforward application of EDF to a DCN runs into the following problems: (1) It is difficult to do EDF on a packet-by-packet basis at switches because packets do not carry any information about their deadlines, and (2) DCN switches do not incorporate priority-based transmission such that packets with closer deadlines could be transmitted earlier. The D³ algorithm solves the first problem by assigning deadlines on a flow basis rather than on a packet basis. Furthermore, it solves the second problem by translating the flow deadline requirement into an equivalent bandwidth requirement, and then reserving this bandwidth, on a per round trip basis at all switches along the path. PDQ, on the other hand, attaches extra fields to the packet header with information about flow deadlines and size among other quantities and lets the switches make priority decisions regarding the flows, which are communicated back to the sources.

We now provide a brief description of the D³ algorithm:

- Applications communicate their size and deadline information when initiating a flow. The sending server uses this information to request a desired rate r given by $r = s/d$, where s is the flow size and d is the deadline. Note that both s and d change as a flow progresses, and these are update by the sender.
- The rate request r is carried in the packet header as it traverses the switches on its path to the receiver. Each switch assigns an allocated rate that is fed back in the form of a vector of bandwidth grants to the sender though an ACK packet on the reverse path. Note that a switch allocates rates on an First Come First Served (FCFS) basis, so that if it has spare capacity after satisfying rate requests for all the deadline flows, then it distributes it fairly to all current flows. Hence, each deadline flow gets allocated a rate a, where $a = r + f_s$ and f_s is the fair share of the spare capacity (Note that f_s can be computed using the techniques described for the RCP algorithm in Chapter 5.)

- On receiving the ACK, the source sets the sending rate to the minimum of the allocated rates. It uses this rate for a RTT (rather than using an AIMD-type algorithm to determine the rate) while piggybacking a rate request for the next RTT on one of the data packets. Note that D^3 does not require a reservation for a specific sending rate for the duration of the entire flow, so the switches do not have to keep state of their rate allocation decisions. Also, D^3 does not require priority scheduling in the switches and can work with FIFO scheduled queues.

The D^3 protocol suffers from the following issues:

- Because switches allocate bandwidth on a FCFS basis, it may result in bandwidth going to flows whose deadlines are further away but whose packets arrive at the switch earlier. It has been shown [3] that this inverts the priorities of 24% to 33% of requests, thus contributing to missed deadlines.
- D^3 requires custom switching sets to handle requests at line rates, which precludes the use of commodity Ethernet switches.
- It is not clear whether the D^3 rate allocation strategy can coexist with legacy TCP because TCP flows do not recognize D^3's honor based bandwidth allocation. This means that a TCP flow can grab a lot of bandwidth so that the switch will not be able to meet the rate allocation promise it made to a D^3 source.

The PDQ [6] scheduler was designed to improve upon D^3 by providing a distributed flow scheduling layer, which allows for flow preemption, while using only FIFO tail-drop queues. This, in addition to other enhancements, improves the performance considerably, and it was shown that PDQ can reduce the average flow completion time compared with TCP and D^3 by 30% and can support three times as many concurrent senders as D^3 while meeting flow deadlines. PDQ is able to implement sophisticated strategies such as EDF or SJF (Shortest Job First) in a distributed manner, using only FIFO drop-tail queues, by explicitly controlling the flow sending rate and retaining packets from low-priority flows at senders.

7.5 LOAD BALANCING OVER MULTIPLE PATHS WITH MULTIPATH TCP (MPTCP)

One of the features that differentiates a DCN from other types of networks is the presence of multiple paths between end points. As explained in Section 7.2, these multiple paths are integral to realizing the full bisection bandwidth between servers in DCN architectures such as a Clos-based Fat Tree or VL2 networks. To accomplish this, the system should be able to spread its traffic among the multiple paths while at the same time providing congestion control along each of the paths.

The traditional way of doing load balancing is to do it on a flow basis, with each flow mapped randomly to one of the available paths. This is usually done with the help of routing protocols, such as ECMP, that use a hash of the address, port number and other fields to do the randomization. However, randomized load balancing cannot achieve the full bisectional bandwidth in most topologies because often a random selection causes a few links to be overloaded and other links to have little load. To address this issue, researchers have proposed the use of centralized schedulers such as Hedera [18]. This algorithm detects large flows, which are then assigned to lightly loaded paths, while existing flows may be reassigned to maximize overall throughput. The issue with centralized schedulers such as this is that the scheduler has to run often (100 ms or faster) to keep up with the flow arrivals. It has been shown by Raiciu et al. [9] that even if a scheduler runs every 500 ms, its performance is no better than that of a randomized load-balancing system.

To address these shortcomings in existing load balancers, Raiciu et al. [9] and Wischik et al. [10] designed a combined load-balancing plus congestion control algorithm called Multipath TCP (MPTCP), which is able to establish multiple subflows on different paths between the end systems for a single TCP connection. It uses a simple yet effective mechanism to link the congestion control dynamics on the multiple subflows, which results in the movement of traffic away from more congested paths and on to less congested ones. It works in conjunction with ECMP, such that if ECMP's random selection causes congestion along certain links, then the MPTCP algorithm takes effect and balances out the traffic.

The MPTCP algorithm operates as follows:

- MPTCP support is negotiated during the initial SYN exchange when clients learn about additional IP addresses that the server may have. Additional subflows can then be opened with IP addresses or in their absence by using different ports on a single pair of IP addresses. MPTCP then relies on ECMP routing to hash the subflows to different paths.
- After the multiple subflows have been established, the sender's TCP stack stripes data across all the subflows. The MPTCP running at the receiver reconstructs the receive data in the original order. Note that there is no requirement for an application to be aware that MPTCP is being used in place of TCP.
- Each MPTCP subflow have its own sequence space and maintains its own congestion window so that it can adapt independently to conditions along the path. Define the following:

    W_r: Window size for the rth subflow
    W_T: Sum of the windows on all the subflows
    T_r: Round trip delay for the rth subflow

The following window increment−decrement rules are used by MPTCP:

For each ACK received on path r, increase the window as per

$$W_r \leftarrow W_r + \min\left(\frac{a}{W_T}, \frac{1}{W_r}\right) \tag{25}$$

where

$$a = W_T \frac{\max_r \frac{W_r}{T_r^2}}{\left(\sum_r \frac{W_r}{T_r}\right)^2} \tag{26}$$

On detecting a dropped packet on subflow r, decrease its window according to

$$W_r \leftarrow \frac{W_r}{2} \tag{27}$$

Hence, MPTCP links the behavior of the subflows by adapting the additive increase constant. These rules enable MPTCP to automatically move traffic from more congested paths and place it on less congested ones. Wischik et al. [10] used heuristic arguments to justify these rules, which we explain next:

- Note that if the TCP window is increased by a/W per ack, then the flow gets a window size that is proportional to $\sqrt{a}$ (see equation 68 in Section 2.3.1 of Chapter 2). Hence, the most straightforward way to split up the flows is by choosing $\alpha = 1/n^2$ and assuming equal round trip delays, resulting in an equilibrium window size of W/n for each subflow. However, this algorithm can result in suboptimal allocations of the subflows through the network because it uses static splitting of the source traffic instead of adaptively trying to shift traffic to routes that are less congested.
- Adaptive shifting of traffic to less congested routes can be done by the using the following rules:

$$W_r \leftarrow W_r + \frac{1}{W_T} \text{ on every ACK, and} \tag{28}$$

$$W_r \leftarrow \frac{W_T}{2} \text{ on detecting packet loss} \tag{29}$$

Consider the case when the packet drop rates are not equal. As a result of equations 28 and 29, the window increment and decrement amounts are the same for all paths; hence, it follows that the paths with higher drop rate will see more window decreases, and in equilibrium, the window size on these paths will go to zero.

Assuming that each of the paths have the same packet loss rate p and using the argument that in equilibrium, the increases and decreases of the window size must balance out, it follows that

$$\left\lfloor \frac{W_r}{T_r}(1-p) \right\rfloor \frac{1}{W_T} = \left\lfloor \frac{W_r}{T_r} p \right\rfloor \frac{W_T}{2} \tag{30}$$

so that

$$W_T = \sqrt{\frac{2(1-p)}{p}} \approx \sqrt{\frac{2}{p}} \tag{31}$$

It follows that the total window size W_T, is the same as for the case when all the traffic was carried on a single path. Hence, unlike the case of static splitting, the adaptive splitting rule does not use more bandwidth by virtue of the fact that it is using multiple paths.

- The window increment–decrement rules (equations 28 and 29) lead to the situation where there is no traffic directed to links with higher packet drop rates. If there is no traffic going to a path for a subflow, then this can be a problem because if the drop rate for that link decreases, then there is no way for the subflow to get restarted on that path. To avoid this, it is advisable to have traffic flow even on links with higher loss rates, and this can be accomplished by using the following rules:

$$W_r \leftarrow W_r + \frac{a}{W_T} \text{ on every ACK and} \tag{32}$$

$$W_r \leftarrow \frac{W_r}{2} \text{ on detecting packet loss} \tag{33}$$

Note that equation 33 causes a decrease in the rate at which the window decreases for higher loss rate links, and the factor a in equation 32 increases the rate of increase. We now derive an expression for W_r for the case when the packet drop rates are different but the round trip latencies are same across all flows.

Define the following:

W_r^m: Maximum window size for the rth subflow
τ_r: Length of a window increase−decrease cycle for the rth subflow
M_r: Multiple of RTTs contained in an increase−decrease cycle
N_r: Number of packets transmitted an increase−decrease cycle for the rth subflow
p_r: Packet drop rate for the rth subflow
T: The common round trip latency for all subflows

We will use the fluid flow model of the system (see Section 7.3). Because the window size increases by aW_r/W_T for every RTT and the total increase in window size during a cycle is $W_r/2$, it follows that

$$M_r = \frac{W_r/2}{aW_r/W_T} = \frac{W_T}{2a}$$

so that

$$\tau_r = M_rT = \frac{W_TT}{2a}$$

Also

$$N_r = \frac{1}{T}\int_0^{\tau_r} W(t)dt = \frac{1}{T}\left[\frac{\tau_rW_r^m}{2} + \frac{\tau_rW_r^m}{4}\right] = \frac{3W_TW_r^m}{8a} \tag{34}$$

Using the deterministic approximation technique, it follows that

$$\frac{3W_TW_r^m}{8a} = \frac{1}{p_r} \tag{35}$$

From equation 35, it follows that

$$W_T = \sum_s W_s^m = W_r^m \sum_s \frac{p_r}{p_s} \tag{36}$$

Substituting equation 36 back into equation 35, we finally obtain

$$W_r^m = \sqrt{\frac{8a}{3}} \frac{1/p_r}{\sqrt{\sum_s 1/p_s}} \tag{37}$$

Hence, unlike the previous iteration of the algorithm, this algorithm allocates a nonzero window size to flows with larger packet drop rates.

- The window increment−decrement rules (equations 32 and 33) are effective in guiding traffic toward links with lower loss rates; however, they do not work very well if the paths have differing round trip delays. This is because the path with the higher round trip delay will experience a lower rate of increase of window size, resulting in a lower throughput even if the packet loss rates are the same. Wischik et al. [10] solved this problem as follows: First, they noted that if

$$\sum_r \frac{W_r}{T_r} = \max_r \frac{W_r^{TCP}}{T_r} \tag{38}$$

is satisfied, where W_r^{TCP} is the window size attained by a single-path TCP experiencing path r's loss rate, then we can conclude the following: (1) The multipath flow takes at least as much capacity as a single path TCP flow on the best of the paths, and (2) the multipath flow takes no more capacity on any single path (or collection of paths) than if it was a single path TCP using the best of those paths. They also changed the window increment−decrement rules to the following:

$$W_r \leftarrow W_r + \min\left(\frac{a}{W_T}, \frac{1}{W_r}\right) \quad \text{on each ACK} \tag{39}$$

$$W_r \leftarrow \frac{W_r}{2} \quad \text{on packet drop} \tag{40}$$

where a is given by

$$a = W_T^m \frac{\max_r \dfrac{W_r^m}{T_r^2}}{\left(\sum_r \dfrac{W_r^m}{T_r}\right)^2} \tag{41}$$

The difference between this algorithm and the previous one is that window increase is capped at $1/W_r$, which means that the multipath flows can take no more capacity on any path than a single-path TCP flow would.

The expression for a in equation 41 can be derived by combining equations 39 and 40 with the condition (equation 38), and we proceed to do this next.

Using the same notation as before, note that the window size for the rth subflow increases by $\min(\frac{aW_r}{W_T}, 1)$ in each round trip. Hence, it follows that

$$M_r \min\left(\frac{aW_r^m}{W_T^m}, 1\right) = \frac{W_r^m}{2} \quad \text{so that}$$

$$M_r = \begin{cases} \dfrac{W_T^m}{2a} & \text{if} \quad aW_r^m < W_T^m \\ \dfrac{W_r^m}{2} & \text{otherwise} \end{cases} \tag{42}$$

It follows that

$$\tau_r = M_r T_r \quad \text{and} \quad N_r = \frac{3}{4T_r} W_r^m \tau_r \tag{43}$$

Using the deterministic approximation technique, it follows that

$$\frac{3}{4T_r} W_r^m \tau_r = \frac{1}{p_r} \tag{44}$$

In equation 38, note that

$$W_r^{TCP} = \sqrt{\frac{8}{3p_r}} \text{ so that}$$

$$\left(\sum_r \frac{W_r^m}{T_r}\right)^2 = \max_r \frac{1}{T_r^2} * \frac{8}{3p_r} \tag{45}$$

Substituting for p_r from (44) and τ_r from (43), it follows that

$$\left(\sum_r \frac{W_r^m}{T_r}\right)^2 = \max_r \frac{2}{T_r^2} W_r^m \tau_r = \max_r \frac{2}{T_r^2} W_r^m T_r \frac{W_T^m}{2a},$$

from which (41) follows.

Raiciu et al. [9] have carried out extensive simulations of MPTCP and have shown that it leads to appreciable improvement in DCN performance. For example, for an eight-path Fat Tree CLOS network, regular TCP with an ECMP-type load balancing scheme only realized 50% of the total bandwidth between two servers, but MPTCP with eight subflows realized about 90% of the total bandwidth. Moreover, the use of MPTCP can lead to new interconnection topologies that are not feasible under regular TCP. Raiciu et al. [9] suggested a modified form of Fat Tree, which they call Dual-Homed Fat Tree (DHFT), which requires a server to have two interfaces to the ToR switch. They showed that DHFT has significant benefits over the regular Fat Tree topology.

7.6 THE INCAST PROBLEM IN DATA CENTER NETWORKS

The Incast problem in DCNs is caused by the temporal dependency created on message traffic that is generated as a result of the Map-Reduce type parallel execution illustrated in Figure 7.4. The parent node sends queries in parallel to multiple leaf nodes, and the subsequent responses from the leaf nodes also tend to be bunched together, as shown in Figure 7.8. This pattern is referred to as Incast [19,20].

The response size not very large on the average, usually a few kilobytes, but even then it has been observed that they suffer from a large packet loss rate. The reason for this has to do with the hardware design of the DCN switches, which tend to have shallow buffers, which are shared among all the ports in switch. As a result, the Incast pattern can lead to a packet drop in one of the following scenarios: (1) because of multiple query responses overflowing a port buffer, (2) because of buffer exhaustion as a result of long background flows on the same port as the Incast packets, and (3) because of buffer exhaustion as a result of long background flows on a different port than the Incast packets.

To solve the Incast problem, researchers do one of the following: (1) try to avoid packet loss or reduce the rate of packet loss or (2) quickly recover from lost packets.

In the first category are techniques such as increasing the switch buffer size and adding a random delay to query responses from the leaf nodes. The latter technique reduces the occurrence of Incast-generated timeouts but at the cost of an increase in the median Job response time. The use of a DCN-specific congestion control protocol such as DCTCP also falls in this category because

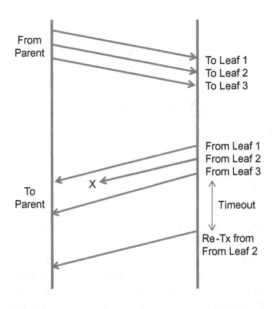

FIGURE 7.8

Illustration of the Incast problem.

they are mode effective in keeping buffer occupancy low compared with regular TCP. In the second category are techniques such as reducing the TCP packet lost timer RTO from the default value of a few 100 ms to less than 1 ms. This has been very effective in improving Incast performance.

7.7 FURTHER READING

Congestion control in DCNs is an extremely active area, with researchers exploring new ideas without being constrained by legacy compatibility issues. One such idea is that of in-network congestion control in which the switches bear the burden of managing traffic. The justification for this is that traditional TCP congestion control requires at least one RTT to react to congestion that is too slow for DCNs because congestion builds very quickly, in less than RTT seconds. The in-network schemes go hand in hand with the multipath nature of modern datacenter architecture, and a good example of this category is the Detail protocol [7]. Routing within the network is done on a packet-by-packet basis and is combined with load balancing, such that a packet from an input queue in a switch is forwarded to the output interface with the smallest buffer occupancy (thus taking advantage of the fact that there are multiple paths between the source and destination). This means that packets arrive at the destination out of order and have to be resequenced before being delivered to the application. This mechanism is called Adaptive Load Balancing (ALB). Furthermore, if an output queue in a switch is congested, then this may result in input queues becoming full as well, at which point the switch backpressures the upstream switch by using the IEEE 802.1Qbb Priority based Flow Control (PFC) mechanism.

The pFabric [8] is another protocol with highly simplified end system algorithm and with the switches using priority-based scheduling to reduce latency for selected flows. Unlike in D^2TCP, D^3 or PDQ, pFabric decouples flow priority scheduling from rate control. Each packet carries its priority in its header, which is set by the source based on information such the deadline for the flow. Switches implement priority-based scheduling by choosing the packet with the high priority number for transmission. If a packet arrives to a full buffer, then to accommodate it, the switch drops a packet whose priority is lower. pFabric uses a simplified form of TCP at the source without congestion avoidance, fast retransmits, dupACKs, and so on. All transmissions are done in the Slow Start mode, and congestion is detected by the occurrence of excessive packet drops, in which case the system enters into probe mode in which it transmits minimum size packets. Hence, pFabric does away with the need to do adaptive rate (or window) control at the source.

Computing services such as Amazon EC2 are a fast-growing category of DCN applications. These systems use Virtual Machines (VMs), which share the servers by using a Processor Sharing (PS) type scheduling discipline to make more efficient use of the available computing resources. Wang and Ng [21] studied the impact of VMs on TCP performance by using network measurements and obtained some interesting results: They found out that PS causes a very unstable TCP throughput, which can fluctuate between 1 Gbps and 0 even at about tens of milliseconds in granularity. Furthermore, even in a lightly congested network, they observed abnormally large packet delay variations, which were much larger than the delay variations caused by network congestion. They attributed these problems to the implementation of the PS scheduler that is used for scheduling VMs. They concluded that TCP models for applications running on VMs should incorporate an additional delay in their round trip latency formula (i.e., the delay caused by end host virtualization).

REFERENCES

[1] Barroso LA, Clidaras J, Holzle U. The datacenter as a computer: an introduction to the design of warehouse scale machines. San Rafael, CA: Morgan and Claypool, 2013.
[2] Alizadeh M, Greenberg A, Maltz DA, et al. Data Center TCP (DCTCP). ACM SIGCOMM 2011;41(4):63−74.
[3] Vamanan B, Hasan J, Vijaykumar TN. Deadline aware Datacenter TCP (D^2TCP). ACM SIGCOMM 2012;42(4):115−26.
[4] Alizadeh M, Kabbani A, Edsall T, et al. Less is more: trading a little bandwidth for ultra-low latency in the data center. NSDI 2012:19.
[5] Wilson C, Ballani H, Karagiannis T, Rowtron A. Better never than late: meeting deadlines in datacenter networks. ACM SIGCOMM 2011;41(4):50−61.
[6] Hong C, Caesar M, Godfrey P. Finishing flows quickly with preemptive scheduling. ACM SIGCOMM 2012;42(4):127−38.
[7] Zats D, Das T, Mohan P, Katz R. DeTail: reducing the flow completion time tail in datacenter networks. ACM SIGCOMM 2012;42(4):139−50.
[8] Alizadeh M, Yang S, Sharif M, et al. pFabric: minimal near optimal datacenter transport. ACM SIGCOMM 2013;43(4):435−46.
[9] Raiciu C, Barre S, Pluntke C, et al. Improving datacenter performance and robustness with multipath TCP. ACM SIGCOMM 2011;41(4):266−77.

[10] Wischik D, Raiciu C, Greenhalgh A, et al. Design, implementation and evaluation of congestion control for multipath TCP. NSDI 2011;11:8.

[11] Hopps CE. IETF RFC 2992: analysis of equal cost multi-path routing. 2000.

[12] Greenberg A, Hamilton JR, Jain N, et al. VL2: a scalable and flexible data center network. ACM SIGCOMM 2009;39(4):51−62.

[13] Clos C. A study of non-blocking switching networks. Bell Syst Tech J 1953;32(2):406−24.

[14] Kodialam M, Lakshman TV, Sengupta S. Efficient and robust routing of highly variable traffic. Hotnets 2004.

[15] Al-Fares, Loukissas A, Vahdat A. A scalable, commodity data center network architecture. ACM SIGCOMM 2008;38(4):63−74.

[16] Alizadeh M, Greenberg A, Maltz DA, et al. Analysis of DCTCP: stability, convergence and fairness. ACM SIGMETRICS 2011;41(4):63−74.

[17] Liu CL, Layland JW. Scheduling algorithms for multiprogramming in a hard real time environment. J ACM 1973;20(1):46−61.

[18] Al-Fares, Radhakrishnan S, Raghavan B, et al. Hedera: dynamic flow scheduling for data center networks. NSDI 2010;10:19.

[19] Chen Y, Griffith R, Liu J, et al. Understanding TCP Incast through collapse in datacenter networks. WREN 2009:73−82.

[20] Yongmao R, Ren, Y, Zhao, Y, et al. A survey on TCP Incast in data center networks. Int J Commun Syst 2012;27(8):1160−72.

[21] Wang G, Ng TS. The impact of virtualization on network performance of Amazon EC2 data center. IEEE INFOCOM 2010:1−9.

SUGGESTED READING

Alizadeh M, Edsall T, Dharmapurikar S, et al. CONGA: distributed congestion aware load balancing for datacenters. ACM SIGCOMM 2014:503−14.

Benson T, Akella A, Maltz D. Network traffic characteristics of data centers in the wild. IMC 2010:267−80.

Chen L, Hu S, Chen K, et al. Towards minimal delay deadline driven datacenter TCP. Hotnets 2013:21.

Honda M, Nishida Y, Eggert L, et al. Multipath congestion control for shared bottlenecks. Proc PFLDNet Workshop 2009:19−24.

Kandula S, Sengupta S, Greenberg A, et al. The nature of datacenter traffic: measurements and analysis. IMC 2009:202−8.

Liu S, Xu H, Cai Z. Low latency datacenter networking: a short survey. arXiv preprint 2014.

Perry J, Ousterhout A, Balakrishnan H, et al. Fastpass: a centralized "zero-queue" datacenter network. ACM SIGCOMM 2014.

CONGESTION CONTROL IN ETHERNET NETWORKS

8

8.1 INTRODUCTION

Ethernet is the most prevalent Layer 2 technology used in Internet Protocol (IP) networks; it is almost as old as IP itself. Traditionally, Ethernet left the job of congestion control to IP while providing basic medium access control (its original purpose in shared media links) and later Layer 2 bridging and switching functionalities. This state of affairs started to change in the past 10 to 15 years as the use of Ethernet expanded to wider domains. One of these domains is data center networking, and Chapter 7 discusses server-to-server networking in DCNs using Ethernet as the switching fabric with TCP running on top.

An aspect of data center networks (DCNs) not discussed in Chapter 7 is that of communications between the servers and storage devices. The networks that are used to interconnect them together are known as Storage Area Networks (SANs). Fiber Channel (FC) is a Layer 1−2 high-speed point-to-point interconnect technology that is used to create SANs. A very strong requirement in SAN networks is that the packet drop rate caused by buffer overflows should be zero. FC networks use a hop-by-hop congestion control method to accomplish this goal, whereby a node that is running out of buffers sends a signal to the node upstream from it to stop it from transmitting.

Link speeds in FC increased over time, but they were not able to keep pace with the more rapid increases in Ethernet link speeds that have gone from 1 to 10 Gbps and then to 100 Gbps in the past decade and a half. In addition, Ethernet adaptors and switches come at a lower cost because of their wider adoption in the industry. Motivated by these considerations, the industry created a FC over Ethernet (FCoE) standard, in which Ethernet is used as the Layer 1−2 substrate in SANs. However, using TCP as the congestion control mechanism will not work in an FCoE SAN because TCP does drop packets during the course of its normal operation. As a result, an effort was started in the Institute of Electrical and Electronics Engineers (IEEE) 802.2 Standards Body to make modifications to Ethernet so that it is suitable for deployment in a SAN (or a DCN in general), called Data Center Bridging (DCB) [1]. One of the outcomes of this effort is a congestion control protocol called IEEE 802.1Qau [2], also known as Quantum Congestion Notification (QCN), which operates at the Ethernet layer and aims to satisfy the special requirements in DCB networks [3].

There is more design latitude in the design of QCN compared with TCP because Ethernet provides 6 bits of congestion feedback (as opposed to 1 bit in TCP), and the QCN design takes advantage of this by implementing a proportional-integral (PI) controller at the Ethernet switch, which we know to be superior than Random Early Detection (RED) controllers. The QCN increase−decrease protocol has some novel features described in Section 8.4. Alizadeh et al. [4]

carried out a comprehensive control theoretic analysis of the fluid model of the QCN algorithm that forms the subject matter of Section 8.5.

8.2 DIFFERENCES BETWEEN SWITCHED ETHERNET AND IP NETWORKS

Alizadeh et al. listed the following contrasts between switched Ethernet networks and IP networks [3]. We already mentioned one of them in the Introduction (i.e., packets should not be dropped); the others are:

- Ethernet does not use per-packet ACKs: This means that (1) packet transmissions are not self-clocked, (2) round trip latencies are unknown, and (3) congestion has to be signaled directly by the switches back to the source.
- There are no Packet Sequence Numbers in Ethernet.
- Sources start at Line Rate because there is no equivalent of the TCP Slow-Start mechanism. Because Ethernet implements its congestion control in hardware, a Slow-Start–like algorithm would have required a rate limiter, which are few in number and used up by the main congestion control algorithm.

The next three differences are more specific to DCNs in general and served as constraints in the design of a transport level congestion control algorithm as well:

- Very shallow buffers: Ethernet switch buffers are of the order of 100s of kilobytes in size.
- Small number of simultaneously active connections.
- Multipathing: Traditional Layer 2 networks used Spanning Trees for routing, which restricted the number of paths to one. The use of Equal Cost Multi-Path (ECMP) opens up the system to using more than 1 path.

8.3 OBJECTIVES OF THE QUANTUM CONGESTION NOTIFICATION ALGORITHM

The QCN algorithm was designed based on all the learning from the design and modeling of TCP congestion control algorithms over the previous 2 decades. As a result, it incorporates features that keep it from falling into performance and stability traps that TCP often runs into. Some of the objectives that it seeks to satisfy include the following:

- Stability: We will use this term in the same sense as in the rest of this book, that is, the bottleneck queue length in a stable system should not fluctuate widely, thus causing overflows and underflows. Whereas the former leads to excessive packet drops, the latter causes link underutilization.
- Responsiveness to link bandwidth fluctuations
- Fairness
- Implementation simplicity: Because the algorithm is implemented entirely in hardware, simplicity is a must.

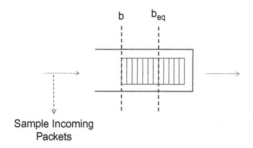

b b_{eq}

Sample Incoming
Packets

FIGURE 8.1

Congestion detection at the Control Point (CP).

8.4 QUANTUM CONGESTION NOTIFICATION ALGORITHM DESCRIPTION

The algorithm is composed of two main parts: Switch or Control Point (CP) Dynamics and Rate Limiter or Reaction Point (RP) Dynamics.

8.4.1 THE CONTROL POINT OR CP ALGORITHM

The CP algorithm runs at the network nodes, and its objective is to maintain the node's buffer occupancy at the operating point b_{eq} (Figure 8.1). It computes a congestion measure F_b and randomly samples an incoming packet with a probability that that depends on the severity of the congestion (Figure 8.2). It sends the value of F_b back to the source of the sampled packet after quantizing it to 6 bits.

Define the following:

b: Value of the current queue length
b_{old}: Value of the buffer occupancy when the last feedback message was generated
$b_{off}: = b - b_{eq}$
$b_d: = b - b_{old}$

Then F_b is given by the formula:

$$F_b = b_{off} + wb_d \tag{1}$$

where w is a non-negative constant, set equal to 2 for the baseline implementation. Note that equation 1 is basically the PI Active Queue Management AQM controller from Chapter 3. The first term on the RHS is the offset from the target operating point (i.e., the buffer oversubscription), and the second term is proportional to the rate at which the queue size is changing. As per equation 55 in Chapter 3, this is proportional to the difference between the link capacity and the total traffic rate flowing through the link (i.e., the link oversubscription).

When $F_b < 0$, there is no congestion, and no feedback messages are sent. When $F_b \geq 0$, then either the buffers or the link or both are oversubscribed, and control action needs to be taken. An incoming packet is sampled with probability $p_s = \phi(F_b)$ (see Figure 8.2), and if $p_s = 1$ and $F_b \geq 0$, then a congestion feedback message is sent back to the source.

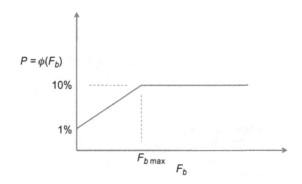

FIGURE 8.2

Sampling probability at the Control Point (CP) as a function of |Fb|.

8.4.2 THE REACTION POINT OR RP ALGORITHM

The RP algorithm runs at the end systems and controls the rate at which Ethernet packets are transmitted in to the network. Unlike TCP, the RP algorithm does not get positive ACKs from the network and hence needs alternative mechanisms for increasing its sending rate. Define the following:

Current rate (R_C): The transmission rate of the source

Target rate (R_T): The transmission rate of the source just before the arrival of the last feedback message

Byte counter: A counter at the RP for counting transmitted bytes; it is used to time rate increases

Timer: A clock at the RP that is used for timing rate increases. It allows the source to rapidly increase its sending rate from a low value when a lot of bandwidth becomes available.

Initially assuming only the Byte Counter is available, RP uses the following rules for increasing and decreasing its rate.

8.4.2.1 Rate Decreases

A rate decrease is only done when a feedback message is received, and in this case, CR and TR are updates as follows:

$$R_T \leftarrow R_C \tag{2}$$

$$R_C \leftarrow R_C(1 - G_d|F_b|) \tag{3}$$

The constant G_d is chosen so that $G_d|F_{b\ max}| = \frac{1}{2}$ (i.e., the rate can decrease by at most 50%). Because only 6 bits are available for feedback, it follows that $F_{b_{max}} = 64$, so that $G_d = 1/128$ accomplishes this objective.

8.4.2.2 Rate Increases

Rate Increase is done in two phases: Fast Recovery and Active Increase (Figure 8.3)

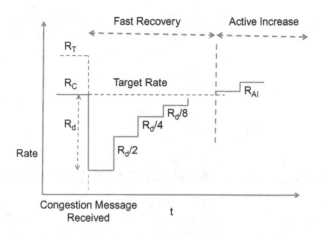

FIGURE 8.3

Quantum Congestion Notification (QCN) Control Point (CP) operation.

Fast Recovery (FR): The source enters the FR state immediately after a rate decrease event, at which point the Byte Counter is reset. FR consists of 5 cycles, in each of which 150 Kbytes of data are transmitted (100 packets of 1500 bytes each), as counted by the Byte Counter. At the end of each cycle, R_T remains unchanged, and R_C is updated as follows:

$$R_C \leftarrow \frac{R_C + R_T}{2} \qquad (4)$$

The rationale behind this rule is if the source is able to transmit 100 packets without receiving another Rate Decrease message (which are sent by the CP once every 100 packets on the average since $p_s = 0.01$), then it can conclude that the CP is uncongested, and therefore it increases its rate. Note that FR is similar to the way in which a Binary Increase Congestion Control (BIC) TCP source increases its window size after a packet drop (see Chapter 5). This mechanism was discovered independently by Alizadeh et al. [3].

Active Increase (AI): After 5 cycles of FR, the source enters the AI state, where it probes for extra bandwidth. AI consists of multiple cycles of 50 packets each. During this phase, R_T and R_C are updates as follows:

$$R_T \leftarrow R_T + R_{AI} \qquad (5)$$

$$R_C \leftarrow \frac{R_C + R_T}{2} \qquad (6)$$

where R_{AI} is a constant, set to 5 mbps by default.

When R_C is extremely small after a rate decrease, then the time required to send out 150 Kbyes can be excessive. To speed this up, the source also uses a Timer, which is used as follows: The Timer is reset when the rate decrease message arrives. The source then enters FR and counts out 5 cycles of T ms duration (T = 10 ms in the baseline implementation), and in the AI state, each cycle is T/2 ms long.

- In the AI state, the R_C is updated when either the Bye Counter or the Timer completes a cycle.
- The source is in the AI state if and only if either the Byte Counter or the Timer is in the AI state. In this case, when either completes a cycle, R_T and R_C are updated according to equations 5 and 6.

- The source is in the Hyper-Active Increase (HAI) state if both the Bye Counter and the Timer are in AI. In this case, at the completion of the ith Byte Counter or Timer cycle, R_T and R_C are updated as follows:

$$R_T \leftarrow R_T + iR_{HAI} \tag{7}$$

$$R_C \leftarrow \frac{R_C + R_T}{2} \tag{8}$$

where R_{HAI} is set to 50 mbps in the baseline.

8.5 QUANTUM CONGESTION NOTIFICATION STABILITY ANALYSIS

The stability analysis is done on a simplified model of the type shown in Chapter 3, Figure 3.2, with N connections with the same round trip latency, passing through a single bottleneck node with capacity C [4]. Following the usual recipe, we will first write down the differential equations in the fluid limit and then linearize them around an operating point, which allows us to analyze their stability using tools such as the Nyquist stability criterion. We will assume that p_s is fixed at $p_s = 1\%$ in this section to simplify the analysis. Also, all connections are assumed to have the same round trip latency equal to τ seconds.

In contrast to other congestion control protocols, two variables $R_C(t)$ and $R_T(t)$, are needed to describe the source behavior:

$$\frac{dR_C}{dt} = -G_d F_b(t-\tau)R_C(t)R_C(t-\tau)p_r(t-\tau) + \left(\frac{R_T(t)-R_C(t)}{2}\right)\frac{R_C(t-\tau)p_r(t-\tau)}{(1-p_r(t-\tau))^{-100}-1} \tag{9}$$

$$\frac{dR_T}{dt} = -(R_T(t)-R_C(t))R_C(t-\tau)p_r(t-\tau) + R_{AI}R_C(t-\tau)\frac{p_r(t-\tau)}{(1-p_r(t-\tau))^{-500}-1} \tag{10}$$

$$\frac{db}{dt} = \begin{cases} NR_C(t)-C & if \quad b(t)>0 \\ \max\{NR_C(t)-C,0\} & if \quad b(t)=0 \end{cases} \tag{11}$$

$$F_b(t) = b(t)-b_{eq} + \frac{w}{Cp_s}(NR_C(t)-C) \tag{12}$$

$$p_r(t) = p_s 1_{[F_b(t)>0]} \tag{13}$$

To justify the negative first terms in equations 9 and 10, note that $R_C(t-\tau)p_r(t-\tau)$ is the rate at which negative ACKs are arriving at the source. Each of these causes R_C to decrease by $R_C(t)G_d F_b(t-\tau)$ and RT to decrease by $R_T(t)-R_C(t)$.

To derive the positive second term in equation 9, consider the following: The rate R_C is increased on the transmission of 150 Kbytes, or 100 packets of 1500 bytes each, if no negative ACK is received in the interim. The change in R_C when this happens is given by

$$\Delta R_C(t) = \frac{R_C(t)+R_T(t)}{2} - R_C(t)$$

$$= \frac{R_T(t)-R_C(t)}{2}$$

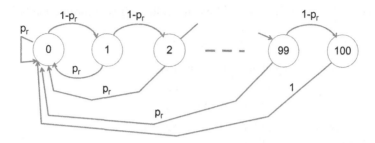

FIGURE 8.4

Markov chain governing the rate R_C.

To compute the rate at which the R_C rate increase events occur, consider the Markov chain in Figure 8.4: It is in state k if k packets have been transmitted back to back without the receipt of a single negative ACK. Starting from state 0, in general, the system may undergo several cycles where it returns back to state 0 before it finally transmits 100 packets back to back and gets to state 100. It can be shown that the average number of packets transmitted to get to state 100 when starting from state 0, is given by

$$E_0(T_{100}) = \frac{(1-p_r)^{-100} - 1}{p_r} \tag{14}$$

This can be derived as follows: Define $u_i = E_i(T_{100}), 0 \le i \le 99$ as the average number of packets transmitted to get to state 100 when starting from state i. Based on the Markov chain in Figure 8.4, the sequence u_i satisfies the following set of equations (with $q_r = 1 - p_r$):

$$u_0 = (1 + u_1)q_r + (1 + u_0)p_r$$
$$u_1 = (1 + u_2)q_r + (1 + u_0)p_r$$
$$\cdots$$
$$u_{98} = (1 + u_{99})q_r + (1 + u_0)p_r$$
$$u_{99} = q_r + (1 + u_0)p_r$$

This set of equations can be solved recursively for u_0, and results in equation 14.

Because the average time between packet transmissions is given by $\frac{1}{R_C(t-\tau)}$, it follows that the average time between increase events is given by

$$\Delta T = \frac{(1-p_r(t-\tau))^{-100} - 1}{R_C(t-\tau)p_r(t-\tau)} \tag{15}$$

The second term on the RHS of equation 9 follows by dividing equation 14 by equation 15. The second term on the RHS of equation 10 is derived using similar considerations. In this case, R_T increments by R_{AI} when 500 packets are transmitted back to back without returning to state 0, which results in a Markov chain just like that in Figure 8.4, except that it extends up to state 500.

We now compute the equilibrium values of the variables in equations 9 to 13. In equilibrium, we replace p_r by p_s throughout.

Define

$$\eta(p_s) = \frac{p_s}{(1-p_s)^{-100} - 1}, \quad \zeta(p_s) = \frac{p_s}{(1-p_s)^{-500} - 1}$$

The fluid flow model in equations 9 to 13 has the following equilibrium points:

$$R_C^* = \frac{C}{N} \tag{16}$$

Equation 16 follows by setting db/dt = 0 in equation 11.

$$R_T^* = \frac{C}{N} + \frac{\varsigma(p_s)R_{AI}}{p_s} \tag{17}$$

Equation 17 follows by setting $dR_T/dt = 0$ in equation 10.
Note that from equation 12, it follows that

$$b^* = b_{eq} + F_b^* \tag{18}$$

and equation 9 implies that

$$F_b^* = \frac{(R_T^* - R_C^*)}{2R_C^*((1-p_s)^{-100} - 1)} \tag{19}$$

Substituting for R_C^* and R_T^* from equations 16 and 17 into equation 19, we finally obtain

$$b^* = b_{eq} + \frac{\eta(p_s)\varsigma(p_s)NR_{AI}}{2p_s^2 G_d C} \tag{20}$$

We now proceed to linearize the equations 9 to 11 around the equilibrium points (R_C^*, R_T^*, b^*). Define the following deltas around the equilibrium:

$$\delta R_C(t) = R_C(t) - R_C^*, \quad \delta R_T(t) = R_T(t) - R_T^*, \quad \delta b(t) = b(t) - b^*$$

Using the Linearization procedure described in Appendix 3.A of Chapter 3, it can be shown that the following equations result:

$$\frac{d\delta R_C}{dt} = -a_1\delta R_C(t) + a_2\delta R_T(t) - a_3\delta R_C(t - \tau) - a_4\delta b(t - \tau) \tag{21}$$

$$\frac{d\delta R_T}{dt} = g\delta R_C(t) - g\delta R_T(t) \tag{22}$$

$$\frac{d\delta b}{dt} = N\delta R_C(t)$$

where

$$a_1 = \frac{\eta(p_s)}{2}R_C^* + \frac{\eta(p_s)\varsigma(p_s)}{2p_s}R_{AI}$$

$$a_2 = \frac{\eta(p_s)}{2}R_C^*, \quad a_3 = G_d w R_C^*, \quad a_4 = p_s G_d (R_C^*)^2, \quad g = p_s R_C^*$$

This system of equations can be shown to have the following characteristic function:

$$1 + G(s) = 0 \tag{23}$$

where

$$G(s) = e^{-s\tau} \frac{a_3(s + g)(s + \gamma)}{s(s^2 + \beta s + \alpha)} \tag{24}$$

with

$$\gamma = \frac{Cp_s}{w}, \quad \beta = g + a_1, \quad \alpha = g(a_1 - a_2).$$

We now state the stability result for QCN. Let

$$\tau^* = \frac{1}{\omega^*}\left(\tan^{-1}\frac{\omega^*}{g} - \tan^{-1}\frac{\omega^*}{\beta} + \tan^{-1}\frac{\omega^*}{\gamma}\right) \tag{25}$$

where

$$\omega^* = \sqrt{\frac{a_3^2}{2} + \sqrt{\frac{a_3^4}{4} + \gamma^2 a_3^2}} \tag{26}$$

Then $\tau^* > 0$, and the system in equations 21 and 22 is stable for all $\tau \le \tau^*$.
To prove $\tau^* > 0$, note that because $\beta > g$, it follows that $\tan^{-1}\frac{\omega^*}{g} > \tan^{-1}\frac{\omega^*}{\beta}$.
To apply the Nyquist criterion, we pass to the frequency domain and write equation 24 as

$$G(j\omega) = |G(j\omega)|e^{-j \arg(G(j\omega))}$$

where

$$|G(j\omega)|^2 = \frac{a_3^2(\omega^2 + g^2)(\omega^2 + \gamma^2)}{\omega^2((\omega^2 - \alpha)^2 + \beta^2\omega^2)}$$

$$< \frac{a_3^2(\omega^2 + g^2)(\omega^2 + \gamma^2)}{\omega^4(\omega^2 + \beta^2 - 2\alpha)}$$

$$< \frac{a_3^2(\omega^2 + \gamma^2)}{\omega^4}$$

The last inequality follows from the fact that $\beta^2 - 2\alpha > g^2$, which can verified by substituting $\beta = g + a_1, \alpha = g(a_1 - a_2)$. Note that setting $\frac{a_3^2(\omega^2 + \gamma^2)}{\omega^4} = 1$, implies that $\omega = \omega^*$. Hence, it follows that $|G(j\omega^*)| < 1$. Because $|G(j\omega)|$ is a monotonically decreasing function of ω, it follows that the critical frequency ω_c at which $|G(j\omega_c)| = 1$, is such that $\omega_c < \omega^*$. By the Nyquist criterion, if we can show that $\arg(G(j\omega)) < \pi$ for all $0 \le \omega < \omega^*$, then the system is stable. This can be done as follows:

$$\arg(G(j\omega)) = \frac{\pi}{2} + \omega\tau + \tan^{-1}\left(\frac{\beta\omega}{\alpha - \omega^2}\right) - \tan^{-1}\frac{\omega}{g} - \tan^{-1}\frac{\omega}{\gamma}$$

$$= \frac{\pi}{2} + \omega\tau + \frac{\pi}{2} - \tan^{-1}\left(\frac{\alpha - \omega^2}{\beta\omega}\right) - \tan^{-1}\frac{\omega}{g} - \tan^{-1}\frac{\omega}{\gamma}$$

$$= \pi + \omega\tau + \tan^{-1}\left(\frac{\omega^2 - \alpha}{\beta\omega}\right) - \tan^{-1}\frac{\omega}{g} - \tan^{-1}\frac{\omega}{\gamma}$$

Because $\alpha > 0$, it follows that

$$\arg(G(j\omega)) < \pi + \omega\tau + \tan^{-1}\frac{\omega}{\beta} - \tan^{-1}\frac{\omega}{g} - \tan^{-1}\frac{\omega}{\gamma}$$

$$= \pi + \omega\tau - \tan^{-1}\left(\frac{(\beta-g)\omega}{\beta g + \omega^2}\right) - \tan^{-1}\frac{\omega}{\gamma} \tag{27}$$

$$\leq \pi + \omega\tau - \tan^{-1}\left(\frac{(\beta-g)\omega}{\beta g + (\omega^*)^2}\right) - \tan^{-1}\frac{\omega}{\gamma}$$

The last inequality follows from the fact that $\omega \leq \omega^*$. Defining

$$\Psi(\omega) = \pi + \omega\tau - \tan^{-1}\left(\frac{(\beta-g)\omega}{\beta g + (\omega^*)^2}\right) - \tan^{-1}\frac{\omega}{\gamma}$$

note that $\Psi(0) = 0$ and for $\tau \leq \tau^*$, $\Psi(\omega^*) \leq \pi$. Moreover $\Psi(\omega)$ is convex for $0 \leq \omega \leq \omega^*$, which implies that $\Psi(\omega) \leq \pi$ for $\omega \in [0, \omega^*]$, and from equation 27, it follows that $\arg(G(j\omega)) < \pi$ in this range, so that the Nyquist stability criterion is satisfied.

8.5.1 DISCUSSION OF THE STABILITY RESULT

Writing out the formula for $|G(j\omega)|$ in detail, we get

$$|G(j\omega)|^2 = \frac{\left(\frac{G_d wC}{N}\right)^2\left(\omega^2 + \left(\frac{p_s C}{N}\right)^2\right)\left(\omega^2 + \left(\frac{p_s C}{w}\right)^2\right)}{\omega^2\left(\left(\omega^2 - \frac{g\eta(p_s)\zeta(p_s)R_{AI}}{2p_s}\right)^2 + \omega^2\left(\frac{p_s C}{N} + \frac{\eta(p_s)C}{2N} + \frac{\eta(p_s)\zeta(p_s)R_{AI}}{2p_s}\right)^2\right)} \tag{28}$$

From equation 28, we can see that the loop gain K for the system is of the order given by

$$K \sim O\left(\frac{C^2}{N}\right) \tag{29}$$

This is in contrast to TCP Reno (see Chapter 3, Section 3.4), whose loop gain (without RED) is of the order

$$K_{RENO} \sim O\left(\frac{C^3\tau^3}{N^2}\right)$$

The absence of the round trip latency from the loop gain in equation 29 is attributable to the fact that QCN is not a window-based congestion control algorithm. In both cases, an increase in link capacity C or a decrease in number of connections drives the system toward instability. Because $\tau \ll 1$, the window based feedback loop plays a role in stabilizing Reno compared with QCN by reducing the system loop gain.

Also note that the critical frequency can be written as

$$\omega^* = a_3\sqrt{\frac{1}{2} + \sqrt{\frac{1}{4} + \left(\frac{\gamma}{a_3}\right)^2}}$$

$$= \frac{G_d wC}{N}\sqrt{0.5 + \sqrt{0.25 + \left(\frac{Np_s}{G_d w^2}\right)^2}} \tag{30}$$

It follows that

$$\frac{\omega^*}{\gamma} = \frac{G_d w^2}{N p_s} \sqrt{0.5 + \sqrt{0.25 + \left(\frac{N p_s}{G_d w^2}\right)^2}} \tag{31}$$

$$\frac{\omega^*}{g} = \frac{G_d w}{p_s} \sqrt{0.5 + \sqrt{0.25 + \left(\frac{N p_s}{G_d w^2}\right)^2}} \text{ and} \tag{32}$$

$$\frac{\omega^*}{\beta} = \frac{G_d w}{\left[p_s + \frac{\eta(p_s)}{2} + \frac{\eta(p_s)s(p_s)NR_{Al}}{2Cp_s}\right]} \sqrt{0.5 + \sqrt{0.25 + \left(\frac{N p_s}{G_d w^2}\right)^2}} \tag{33}$$

The last two terms in the denominator of equation 33 are much smaller than the first term. As a result, it follows that $\frac{\omega^*}{g} \approx \frac{\omega^*}{\beta}$, so that the stability threshold for latency is given by

$$\tau^* \approx \frac{\tan^{-1}\left|\frac{G_d w^2}{N p_s}\sqrt{0.5 + \sqrt{0.25 + \left(\frac{N p_s}{G_d w^2}\right)^2}}\right|}{\frac{G_d w C}{N}\sqrt{0.5 + \sqrt{0.25 + \left(\frac{N p_s}{G_d w^2}\right)^2}}} \tag{34}$$

Substituting $G_d = 1/128$, $w = 2$ and $p_s = 0.01$, we obtain

$$\omega^* = \frac{C}{64N}\sqrt{0.5 + \sqrt{0.25 + 0.1024N^2}} \tag{35}$$

and

$$\tau^* \approx \frac{64N}{C\sqrt{0.5 + \sqrt{0.25 + 0.1024N^2}}} \tan^{-1}\left|\frac{3.125}{N}\sqrt{0.5 + \sqrt{0.25 + 0.1024N^2}}\right| \tag{36}$$

Hence, the stability threshold for the round trip latency is inversely proportional to C and directly proportional to $\sqrt{N}$. For example, substituting C = 1 Gbps (= 83,333 packets/s) and N = 10 yields $\tau^* \approx 2.158$ ms.

8.6 FURTHER READING

In addition to QCN, there were two other algorithms that were considered as candidates for the IEEE802.1Qau protocol. The algorithm by Jiang et al. [5] uses an AQM scheme with explicit rate calculation at the network nodes that is fed back to the source. This scheme has some similarities to the RCP algorithm from Chapter 5. The algorithm by Bergamasco and Pan [6] has some similarities to QCN because it is also based on an AQM scheme that provides PI feedback back to the source using a quantized congestion number F_b. The source nodes then use this number to adjust the parameters of their additive increase/multiplicative decrease (AIMD) scheme, such that the rate is additively increased if $F_b > 0$ and multiplicatively decreased if $F_b < 0$.

REFERENCES

[1] Ethernet Alliance. Data Center Bridging Whitepaper. 2010.

[2] IEEEP802.1Qau. Virtual bridges local area networks—Amendment: Congestion Notification. 2009.

[3] Alizadeh M, Atikoglu B, Kabbani A, et al. Data center transport mechanisms: congestion control theory and IEEE standardization. 46th Annual Allerton Conference 2008:1270–1277.

[4] Alizadeh M, Kabbani A, Atikoglu B, Prabhakar B. Stability analysis of QCN: the averaging principle. ACM SIGMETRICS 2011:49–60.

[5] Jiang J, Jain R, So-In C. An explicit rate control framework for lossless Ethernet operation. Proceedings of the ICC 2008:5914–5918.

[6] Bargamasco D, Pan R. Backward congestion notification, Version 2.0. IEEE 802.1 Meeting, 2005.

EMERGING TOPICS IN CONGESTION CONTROL

9.1 INTRODUCTION

In this chapter, our objective is to provide a brief survey of some emerging topics in congestion control. There has been renewed interest in the topic of congestion control in recent years, driven mostly by applications to data center networks and video streaming. Meanwhile, broader trends in networking, such as the emergence of Software Defined Networks (SDNs), are beginning to have their influence felt on this topic as well. Other advances in technology, such as the progress that has been made in artificial intelligence (AI) and Machine Learning (ML) algorithms, are also having an impact on our subject.

In Section 9.2, we describe Project Remy from Massachusetts Institute of Technology (MIT), which uses ML to automatically generate congestion control algorithms; these have been shown to perform better than their human-designed counterparts. These algorithms are based on the theory developed in Chapter 3 in which congestion control rules are derived as a solution to a distributed optimization problem. Unlike the window increase–decrease rules that we have encountered so far, these rules number in the hundreds and are a function of the specific point in the feedback space. The framework of Project Remy also helps us to explore the delay versus throughput tradeoff in congestion control, as well as provide bounds on how well the best performing algorithm can do.

In Section 9.3, we give a brief description of the field of SDNs. They have been used to facilitate routing and switching level functionality, but they may have a significant impact on congestion control as well. We describe a couple of topics in congestion control that can benefit from the centralized control point that SDNs provide. The first topic is on the use of SDNs to choose an appropriate Active Queue Management (AQM) algorithm at a switch as a function of the application running on top of the connection. For example, drop-tail queues are good enough for applications that prioritize throughput over latency, but more sophisticated AQM is needed for applications for which low latency is important. The second topic is on the use of SDNs to set appropriate parameters for the AQM algorithm.

Section 9.4 is on the Google Congestion Control (GCC) algorithm, which was designed for transmitting real-time video streams and is part of the Web Real-Time Communication (WebRTC) project of the Internet Engineering Task Force (IETF). There are some interesting new ideas in GCC, such as the active participation of the receiver in the congestion control algorithm, which are sure to influence the future direction of this subject. The GCC algorithm does not run on top of TCP but instead uses the Real Time Transport protocol (RTP) for sending data and its accompanying Real Time Control Protocol (RTCP) for obtaining feedback from the receiver. The receiver analyzes the pattern of packet inter-arrival times and then uses a Kalman filter to estimate whether the bottleneck queue is changing in size. It chooses a rate based on this information and feeds this information back to the source, which bases the sending rate on this and some other pieces of information.

9.2 MACHINE LEARNING AND CONGESTION CONTROL: PROJECT REMY

In this section, we describe the work carried out by Winstein et al. at MIT in which they did a fundamental rethink on how to solve the congestion control problem, based on which they came up with an algorithm called Remy that is radically different from all existing work in this area [1–4]. This algorithm is based on applying ideas from partially observable Markov decision processes (POMDPs) to the congestion control problem.

The basic idea behind the derivation of this algorithm is something that we discovered in Chapter 3, that is, the congestion control problem can be regarded as the solution to the distributed optimization of a network wide utility function (see Section 3.2 and Appendix 3.E in Chapter 3). By using POMDP/ML techniques, the algorithm learns the best possible congestion control action, in the sense of minimizing this utility function, based on its observations of the partial network state at each source.

The system uses a simple ON-OFF model for the traffic generation process at each source. The sender is OFF for a duration that is drawn from an exponential distribution. Then it switches to the ON state, where it generates a certain number of bytes that are drawn from an empirical distribution of flow sizes or a closed form distribution.

The important ingredients that go into the algorithm include:

- The form of the utility function that is being minimized
- The observations of the network state at each source
- The control action that the algorithm takes based on these observations

We describe each of these in turn:

1. **Utility function:** Define the function

$$U_\alpha(x) = \frac{x^{1-\alpha}}{1-\alpha} \tag{1}$$

then the form of the network utility function for a connection that Remy uses is given by

$$U_{\alpha\beta\delta}(r, T_s) = U_\alpha(r) - \delta U_\beta(T_s) \tag{2}$$

Given a network trace, r is estimated as the average throughput for the connection (total number of bytes sent divided by the total time that the connection was "ON"), and T_s is estimated as the average round-trip delay. Note that the parameters α and β express the fairness vs efficiency tradeoffs for the throughput and delay, respectively (see Appendix 3.E in Chapter 3), and δ expresses the relative importance of delay versus throughput. By varying the parameter δ, equation 2 enables us to explicitly control the trade-off between throughput and delay for the algorithm. The reader may recall from the section on Controlled Delay (CoDel) in Chapter 4 that legacy protocols such as Reno or Cubic try to maximize the throughput without worrying about the end-to-end latency. To realize the throughput–delay tradeoff, legacy protocols have to use an AQM such as Random Early Detection (RED) or CoDel, which sacrifice some the throughput to achieve a lower delay. Remy, on the other hand, with the help of the utility function in equation 2, is able to attain this trade-off without making use of an in-network AQM scheme.

2. **Network state observations:** Remy tracks the following features of the network history, which are updated every time it receives an ACK:
   a. ack_ewma: This is an exponentially weighted moving average of the inter-arrival time between new ACKs received, where each new sample contributes 1/8 of the weight of the moving average.
   b. send_ewma: This is an exponentially weighted moving average of the time between TCP sender timestamps reflected in those ACKs, with the same weight 1/8 for new samples.
   c. rtt_ratio: This is the ratio between the most recent Round Trip Latency (RTT) and the minimum RTT seen during the current connection.

Winstein et al. [3] arrived at this set of observations by doing a comprehensive test of other types of feedback measurements that are possible at a source. Traditional measurements, such as most recent RTT sample or a smoothed estimate of the RTT sample, were tested and discarded because it was observed that they did not improve the performance of the resulting protocol. In particular, Remy does not make use of two variables that almost every other TCP algorithm uses: the packet drop rate p and the round trip latency T. The packet drop rate is not used because a well-functioning algorithm should naturally lead to networks with small queues and very few losses. The round trip latency T was intentionally kept out because the designers did not want the algorithm to take T into account in figuring out the optimal action to take.

Note that Remy does not keep memory from one busy period to the next at a source, so that all the estimates are reset every time a busy period starts.

3. **Control actions:** Every time an ACK arrives, Remy updates its observation variables and then does a look-up from a precomputed table for the action that corresponds to the new state. A Remy action has the following three components:
   a. Multiply the current congestion window by b, i.e., $W \leftarrow bW$.
   b. Increment the current congestion window by a, i.e., $W \leftarrow W + a$.
   c. Choose a minimum of $\tau > 0$ ms as the time between successive packet sends.

Hence, in addition to the traditional multiplicative decrease/additive decrease actions, Remy implements a combination of window + rate-based transmission policy, where the interval between transmissions does not exceed τ seconds.

At a high level, Remy Congestion Control (RemyCC) consists of a set of piecewise constant rules, called the Rule Table, where each rule maps a rectangular region of the observation space to a three dimensional action. On receiving an ACK, RemyCC updates its values for (ack_ewma, send_ewma, rtt_ratio) and then executes the corresponding action (b, a, τ).

We now describe how these rules are generated:

Remy randomly generates millions of different network configurations by picking up random values (within a range) for the link rates, delays, the number of connections, and the on-off traffic distributions for the connections. At each evaluation step, 16 to 100 sample networks are drawn and then simulated for an extended period of time using the RemyCC algorithm. At the end of the simulation, the objective function given by equation 2 is evaluated by summing up the contribution from each connection to produce a network-wide number. The following two special cases were considered:

$$U = \log R - \delta \log T,$$

(3)

corresponding to proportional throughput and delay fairness and

$$U = -\frac{1}{R}$$

(4)

which corresponds to minimizing the potential delay of a fixed-length transfer.

RemyCC is initialized with the following default rule that applies to all states: $b = 1$, $a = 1$, $\tau = 0.01$. This means that initially there is a single cube that contains all the states. Each entry in the rule table has an "epoch," and Remy maintains a global epoch number initialized to zero.

The following offline automated design procedure is used to come up with the rule table:

1. Set all rules to the current epoch.
2. Find the most used rule in this epoch: This is done by simulating the current RemyCC and tracking the rule that receives the most use. At initialization because there is only a single cube with the default rule, it gets chosen as the most used rule. If we run out of rules to improve, then go to step 4.
3. Improve the action for the most used rules until it cannot be improved further: This is done by drawing at least 16 network specimens and then evaluating about 100 candidate increments to the current action, which increases geometrically in granularity as they get further from the current value. For example, evaluate $\tau \pm 0.01, \tau \pm 0.08, \tau \pm 0.64, \ldots$, while taking the Cartesian product with the choices for a and b. The modified actions are used by all sources while using the same random seed and the same set of specimen networks while simulating each candidate action.

If any of the candidate actions lead to an improvement, then replace the original action by the improved action and repeat the search, with the same set of networks and random seed. Otherwise, increment the epoch number of the current rule and go back to step 2. At the first iteration, this will result in the legacy additive increase/multiplicative decrease (AIMD)−type algorithm because the value of the parameters a, b are the same for every state.

4. If we run out of rules in this epoch: Increment the global epoch. If the new epoch is a multiple of a parameters K, set to K=4, then go to step 5; otherwise, go to step 1.
5. Subdivide the most-used rule: Subdivide the most used rule at its center point, thus resulting in 8 new rules, each with the same action as before. Then return to step 1.

An application of this algorithm results in a process whereby areas of the state space that are more likely to occur receive more attention from the optimizer and get subdivided into smaller cubes, thus leading to a more granular action.

Figure 9.1 shows the results of a comparison of TCP Remy with legacy congestion control protocols (the figure plots the throughput averaged over all sources on the y-axis and the average queuing delay at the bottleneck on the x-axis). A 15-mbps dumbbell topology with a round

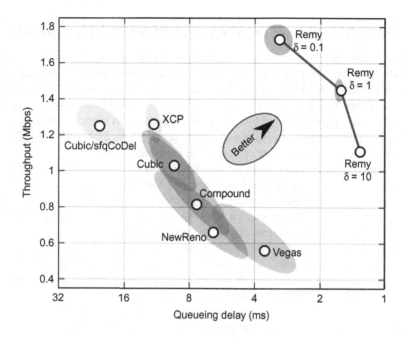

FIGURE 9.1

Comparison of the performance of Remy Congestion Control (RemyCC) with legacy protocols.

trip of 150 ms and $n=8$ connections was used, with each source alternating between a busy period that generates an exponentially distributed byte length of 100 Kbytes and an exponentially distributed off time of 0.5 sec. RemyCC is simulated with the utility function in equation 3 and with three different values of δ, with higher values corresponding to more importance given to delay. The RemyCC algorithm that was generated for this system had between 162 and 204 rules.

The results in Figure 9.1 show that RemyCC outperformed all the legacy algorithms, even those that have an AQM component, such as CUBIC over CoDel with stochastic fair queuing. Further experimental results can be found in Winstein [3].

Figure 9.1 also illustrates that existing congestion control algorithms can be classified by their throughput versus delay performance. Algorithms that prioritize delay over throughput, such as Vegas, lie in lower right hand corner, and those that prioritize throughput over delay lie in the upper left-hand part of the graph. The performance numbers for RemyCC trace an outer arc, which corresponds to the best throughput that can be achieved, for a particular value of the delay constraint. Thus, this framework provides a convenient way of measuring the performance of a congestion control algorithm and how close they are to the ideal performance limit.

Because of the complexity of the rules that RemyCC uses, so far the reasons of its superior performance are not well understood and are still being actively investigated.

9.3 SOFTWARE DEFINED NETWORKS AND CONGESTION CONTROL

Software Defined Networks were invented with the objective of simplifying and increasing the flexibility of the network control plane (NCP) algorithms such as routing and switching. In general, these algorithms are notoriously difficult to change because they involve the creation and maintenance of a network-wide distributed system model that maintains a current map of the network state and is capable of functioning under uncertain conditions in a wide variety of scenarios. Rather than running an instance of the NCP in every node, as is done in legacy networks, an SDN centralizes this function in a controller node. This leads to a number of benefits as explained below.

Figure 9.2 shows the basic architecture for an SDN network, which is made up of two principal components, namely OpenFlow-controlled switches and the SDN controller. Note that the NCP located in the controller is centralized and exists separately from the data plane located in the network switches. The controller communicates with the switches using an out-of-band communication network (shown with the dotted line) using the OpenFlow protocol.

The SDN controller can be implemented in software on a standard server platform. It is implemented using a layered architecture, with the bottom layer called the Network Operating System (NOS) and the upper layer consisting of one or more applications, such as routing, that are used to control the OpenFlow switches. The NOS layer is responsible for managing the communications between the controller and the switches. In addition it also responsible for creating and maintaining a current topology map of the network. This topology map is exposed to the applications running in the controller on its

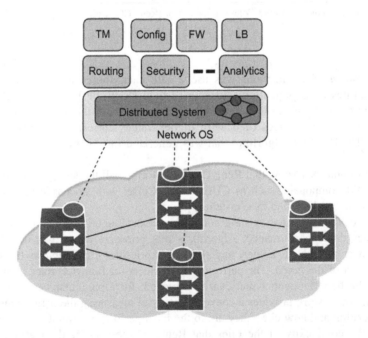

FIGURE 9.2

An example of an open flow—controlled Software Defined Network.

northbound interface (Figure 9.2 shows some example applications running in the SDN network, such as Traffic Management (TM), Network Configuration (Config), Packet Forwarding (FW), and Load Balancing (LB)). As a result of this design, every control application shares a common Distributed System, unlike in current networks, where every application needs to implement its own Distributed System (e.g., the network map maintained by Layer 3 protocol such as OSPF is different from that maintained by a Layer 2 protocol such as Spanning Tree). Moreover, the problem of designing a distributed control algorithm is reduced to a pure software problem because the control algorithm can operate on the network abstraction created by the NOS rather than the real network.

Even though most of the initial work in SDNs has gone into the investigation of its impact on the NCP, researchers have begun to investigate ways in which it might be used to improve the operation of the data plane as well. We describe a couple of ways in which this can be done in Sections 3.1 and 3.2.

9.3.1 USING SOFTWARE DEFINED NETWORKS TO CHOOSE ACTIVE QUEUE MANAGEMENT ALGORITHMS ON A PER-APPLICATION BASIS

In the discussion of the CoDel AQM algorithm in Chapter 4, we first introduced the notion that the most appropriate AQM algorithm is a function of the application, and this line of reasoning is developed further here. In general, based on their performance requirements, applications fall into the following three categories:

1. Throughput maximization: Applications in this category, such as File Transfer Protocol (FTP), are only interested in maximizing their data throughput, regardless of the latency.
2. Power maximization: Recall that the power of a connection was defined as a function of the average throughput R_{av}, and average latency T_s as

$$Power = \frac{R_{av}}{T_s} \tag{5}$$

   Applications such as video conferencing are interested in achieving a high throughput, but at the same time, they like to keep their latencies low. Hence, they belong to the power maximization category.
3. Minimization of Flow Completion Time (FCT): Web surfing (or HTTP transfer) is a typical application in this category, in which the transfer size is smaller compared with FTPs and the user is interested in minimizing the total time needed to complete a page download.

Note that throughput maximization for a connection also leads to FCT minimization; hence, the first and third categories are related. In the context of a network where both types of connections pass through a common link, the presence of the FTP connection can severely downgrade the FCT of a web page download if they both share a buffer at the bottleneck node. Ways in which this problem can be avoided are:

a. By using an AQM scheme such as CoDel to control the queue size at the bottleneck node: CoDel will keep the buffer occupancy and hence the latency low but at the expense of a reduction in the throughput in both the FTP and HTTP connection. This is not an ideal situation because the FTP connection has to give up some of its throughput to keep the latency for the HTTP connection down.

b. By isolating the FTP and HTTP connections at the bottleneck node into their own subqueues, by using a queue scheduling algorithm such as Fair Queuing: In this case, neither subqueue requires an AQM controller. The HTTP connection will only see the contribution to its latency caused by its own queue, which will keep it low, and the FTP connection can maintain a large subqueue at the bottleneck to keep its throughput up without having to worry about the latency. This is clearly a better solution than a).

If an FTP and video conferencing flow (as representatives of categories 1 and 2) share a bottleneck node buffer, then again we run into the same problem, that is, the queuing delay attributable to the FTP will degrade the video conferencing session. Again, we can use an AQM scheme at the node to keep the queuing delay low, but this will be at a cost of decrease in FTP throughput of 50% or more (see Sivaraman et al. [5]). A better solution would be to isolate the two flows using Fair Queuing and then use an AQM scheme such as CoDel only on the video conferencing connection.

From this discussion, it follows that the most appropriate AQM scheme at a node is a function of the application that is running on top of the TCP connection. By using fair queuing, a node can isolate each connection into its own subqueue and then apply a (potentially) different AQM scheme to each subqueue. Sivaraman et al. [5] propose that this allocation of an AQM algorithm to a connection can be done using the SDN infrastructure. Hence, the SDN controller can match the type of application using the TCP connection to the most appropriate AQM algorithm at each node that the connection passes through. Using the OpenFlow protocol, it can then configure the queue management logic to the selected algorithm.

The capability of dynamically reconfiguring the AQM algorithm at a switch does not currently exist in the current generation of switches and routers. These are somewhat inflexible because the queue management logic is implemented in hardware to be able to function at high speeds. Sivaraman et al. [5] propose that the queue management logic be implemented in an Field Programmable Gate Array (FPGA), so that it can be reconfigured by the SDN controller. They actually implemented the CoDel and RED AQM algorithms in a Xilinx FPGA, which was able to support a link speed of 10 Gbps, to show the feasibility of this approach. The other hurdle in implementing this system is that currently there is no way for applications to signal their performance requirements to the SDN controller.

9.3.2 USING SOFTWARE DEFINED NETWORKS TO ADAPT RANDOM EARLY DETECTION PARAMETERS

Recall from the analysis in Chapter 3 that a RED algorithm is stable (in the sense of not causing large queue fluctuations) for number of connections greater than N^- and round trip latency less than T^+, if the following conditions are satisfied:

$$\frac{L_{red}(T^+C)^3}{(2N^-)^2} \le \sqrt{\frac{\omega_c^2}{K^2} + 1} \quad \text{where} \tag{6}$$

$$\omega_c = 0.1 \min\left\{\frac{2N^-}{(T^+)^2 C}, \frac{1}{T^+}\right\}, \quad L_{red} = \frac{\max_p}{\max_{th} - \min_{th}}, \quad K = -\frac{\log_e(1 - w_q)}{\delta}$$

Hence, a RED algorithm can become unstable if

- The number of connections passing through the link becomes too small, or
- The round trip latency for the connection becomes too big, or
- The link capacity becomes too large.

One way in which instability can be avoided was described in Chapter 4, which is by using the Adaptive RED (ARED) algorithm that changes the parameter max_p as a function of the observed queue size at the node. We propose that another way of adapting RED is by making direct use of equation 6 and using the SDN controller to change RED parameters as the link conditions change.

Note that the number of connections N and the link capacity C are the two link parameters that influence the stability condition (equation 6), and the end-to-end latency T is a property of the connection path. As explained in Chapter 4, C is subject to large fluctuations in cellular wireless links; however, it may not be possible to do real-time monitoring of this quantity from the SDN controller. On the other hand, for wireline connections, C is fixed, and the only variables are N and T, which change relatively slowly. Moreover, the SDN controller tracks all active connections in the network as part of its base function, and hence it can easily figure out the number of active connections passing through each node. The round trip latency can be reported by applications to the SDN controller using a yet to be defined interface between the two.

Using these two pieces of information, the SDN controller can then use equation 6 to compute the values of L_{red} and K to achieve stability and thereby set the RED parameters max_p, max_{th}, min_{th}, and w_q. Following ARED, it can choose to vary only max_p while keeping the other parameters fixed, but it has more flexibility in this regard.

Another example of this is the use of the equation

$$\tau^* \approx \frac{\tan^{-1}\left[\frac{G_d w^2}{Np_s}\sqrt{0.5 + \sqrt{0.25 + \left(\frac{Np_s}{G_d w^2}\right)^2}}\right]}{\frac{G_d wC}{N}\sqrt{0.5 + \sqrt{0.25 + \left(\frac{Np_s}{G_d w^2}\right)^2}}}$$

which gives the stability threshold for the QCN algorithm in Ethernet networks as a function of the link speed C, number of connections N and algorithm parameters (p_s, w, G_d) (see Chapter 8, Section 8.5). As the number of connections N varies, the SDN controller can vary the algorithm parameters to maintain the stability threshold in the desired range.

9.4 THE GOOGLE CONGESTION CONTROL (GCC) ALGORITHM

The GCC algorithm [6,7] belongs to the category of congestion control algorithms that are used for real-time streams such as telephony and video conferencing. Delivery of real-time media is actually a fairly large subcategory in itself that is characterized the by following:

- Rather than TCP, real-time streams make use of the Real Time Transport Protocol (RTP) for transport, which is implemented on top of UDP. This is because reliable delivery is not as important as additional services provided by RTP, such as jitter compensation and detection of out-of-sequence frames.

- Unlike TCP, every RTP packet is not ACK'd. Instead, the receiver provides feedback by using the Real Time Control Protocol (RTCP). It generates periodic RTCP Receiver Report (RR) packets that are sent back to the source. These contain information such as number of received packets, lost packets, jitter, round trip delay time, and so on.

The information in the RTCP RR report is then used by the source to control its transmission rate. Traditionally, the TCP Friendly Rate Control Algorithm (TFRC) has been used for this purpose (see Floyd et al. [8] for a description of TFRC). This algorithm controls the transmit rate as a function of the loss event rate statistic that is reported by the receiver.

There are a number of problems in using TFRC in modern cellular networks, including:

- The packet loss rate in these networks is close to zero, as explained in Chapter 4, because of the powerful ARQ and channel coding techniques that they use. The only losses may be due to buffer overflow, but even these are very infrequent because of the large buffers in the base stations. Loss-based protocols such as TFRC tend to fill up the buffer, leading to unacceptably large delays.
- Cellular links are subject to large capacity variations, which lead to congestion in the form of the bufferbloat problem described in Chapter 4, which are not taken into account by TFRC.

The GCC algorithm is designed to address these shortcomings. It is part of the RTCWeb project within the IETF, which also includes other specifications to enable real-time audio and video communication within web browsers without the need for installing any plug-in or additional third-party software. GCC is available in the latest versions of the web browser Google Chrome.

The GCC algorithm tries to fully use the bottleneck link while keeping the queuing delay small. We came across the problem of minimizing queuing delays on a variable capacity link in the context of TCP in Chapter 4, where the solutions included using AQM techniques such as CoDel or end-to-end algorithms such as Low Extra Delay Background Transport (LEDBAT). The GCC algorithm belongs to the latter category since it does not require any AQM at the intermediate nodes. (Note that LEDBAT is not directly applicable here because it relies on the regular flow of TCP ACKs for feedback.) GCC uses a sophisticated technique using Kalman filters to figure out if the bottleneck queue is increasing or decreasing and uses this information to compute a number called the Receive Rate. It sends the Receive Rate back to the source in a special control packet called REMB, which then combines it with other information such as the packet loss rate to determine the final transmit rate.

The GCC algorithm is composed of two modules, one of which runs at the sender and the other at the receiver. These are described in the next two sections.

9.4.1 SENDER SIDE RATE COMPUTATION

The sender combines several pieces of information to come up with the transmit rate, including the packet loss rate (as conveyed by the RTCP RR packets), the rate of an equivalent TFRC source, and the rates coming from the receiver in the REMB packets.

Define the following:

t_k: Arrival time of the kth RTCP RR packet
t_r: Arrival time of the rth REMB packet
$R_s(t_k)$: Sender transmit rate at time $t = t_k$
$R_r(t_r)$: Receiver computed rate in the REMB message received $t = t_r$

$X(t_k)$: Sending rate as computed using the TFRC algorithm at time $t = t_k$
$f_l(t_k)$: Fraction of lost packets at $t = t_k$

On receipt of the kth RTCP RR packet, the sender uses the following formula to compute its rate:

$$R_s(t_k) = \begin{cases} \max\{X(t_k), R_s(t_{k-1})(1 - 0.5f_l(t_k))\} & f_l(t_k) > 0.1 \\ 1.05(R_s(t_{k-1}) + 1kbps) & f_l(t_k) < 0.02 \\ R_s(t_{k-1}) & otherwise \end{cases} \quad (7)$$

The reasoning behind these rules is the following:

- When the fraction of lost packets exceeds 10%, then the rate is multiplicatively decreased but not below the equivalent TFRC rate.
- When the fraction of lost packets is less than 2%, then the rate is multiplicatively increased.
- When the packet loss rate is between 2% and 10%, then the rate is kept constant.

Hence, in contrast to TCP, the GCC sender does not decrease its rate even for loss rates as high as 10%, and actually increases the rate for loss rates under 2%. This is done because video streams are capable of hiding the artifacts created because of smaller packet loss rates.

When the sender receives the rth REMB packet, it modifies its sending rate as per the following equation:

$$R_s(t_r) \leftarrow \min\{R_s(t_r), R_r(t_r)\} \quad (8)$$

9.4.2 RECEIVER SIDE RATE COMPUTATION

The novelty of the GCC algorithm lies in its receiver side rate computation algorithm. By filtering the stream of received packets, it tries to detect variations in the bottleneck queue size and uses this information to set the receive rate. It can be decomposed into three parts: an arrival time filter, an overuse detector, and a remote rate control.

9.4.2.1 Arrival Time Model and Filter

In the RTCWeb protocol, packets are grouped into frames, such that all packets in a frame share the same timestamp.

Define the following:

t_i: Time when all the packets in the ith frame have been received
τ_i: RTP timestamp for the ith frame
$L(t_i)$: Size of the ith frame
$C(t_i)$: Estimate of the bottleneck link capacity at $t = t_i$
$b(t_i)$: Queuing time variation at $t = t_i$

Note that a frame is delayed relative to its predecessor if $t_i - \tau_i > t_{i-1} - \tau_{i-1}$. We define the sequence d_i to be the difference between these two sequences, so that

$$d_i = t_i - t_{i-1} - (\tau_i - \tau_{i-1}) \quad (9)$$

Variations in d_i can be caused by the following factors: (1) changes in the bottleneck link capacity C, (2) changes in the size of the video frame L, (3) changes in bottleneck queue size b, or (4) network jitter. All of these factors are captured in the following model for d_i:

$$d_i = \frac{L(t_i) - L(t_{i-1})}{C(t_i)} + b(t_i) + n(t_i) \tag{10}$$

Note that the network jitter process $n(t_i)$ has zero mean because the drift in queue size is captured in the previous term $b(t_i)$.

Using equation 10, GCC uses a Kalman filter (see Appendix 9.A) to obtain estimates of the sequences $C(t_i)$ and $b(t_i)$ and then uses these values to find out if the bottleneck queue is oversubscribed (the queue length is increasing) or undersubscribed. The calculations are as follows:

Define $\xi_i = [1/C(t_i) \quad b(t_i)]^T$ as the "hidden" state of the system, which obeys the following state evolution equation:

$$\xi_{i+1} = \xi_i + u_i \tag{11}$$

where u_i is a white Gaussian noise process with zero mean and covariance Q_i.

From equation 10, it follows that the observation process d_i obeys the following equation

$$d_i = h_i \xi_i + v_i \tag{12}$$

where $h_i = [L(t_i) - L(t_{i-1}) \quad 1]$ and v_i is a white Gaussian noise process with zero mean and variance S_i.

Let $\hat{\xi}_i = [1/\hat{C}(t_i) \quad \hat{b}(t_i)]^T$ be the sequence representing the estimate for ξ_i. From Kalman filtering theory, it follows that

$$\hat{\xi}_i = \hat{\xi}_{i-1} + K_i(d_i - h_i \hat{\xi}_{i-1}) \tag{13}$$

where K_i is the Kalman gain given by

$$K_i = \frac{E_{i-1} h_i^T}{\hat{S}_i + h_i E_{i-1} h_i^T} \quad and \quad E_i = (I - K_i h_i) E_{i-1} + Q_i \tag{14}$$

The variance S_i is estimated using an exponential averaging filter modified for variable sampling rate, as

$$\hat{S}_i^2 = \beta \hat{S}_{i-1}^2 + (1 - \beta)(d_i - h_i \hat{\xi}_{i-1})^2 \text{ and}$$

$$\beta = (1 - \alpha)^{\frac{30}{1000 f_{max}}} \quad where \quad f_{max} = \max \left\{ \frac{1}{\tau_j - \tau_{j-1}} \right\} \text{ for}$$

$$j = i - K + 1, \ldots, i \quad \alpha \in [0.1, 0.001]$$

Q_i is chosen to be a diagonal matrix with the main diagonal elements given by

$$diag(Q(i)) = \frac{30}{1000 f_{max}} [10^{-10} \quad 10^{-2}]^T.$$

These filter parameters are scaled with the frame rate to make the detector respond as quickly to low frame rates as at high frame rates.

9.4.2.2 Remote Rate Control

Assuming that the last packet in the ith frame is received at time t_i, the receiver computes the rate $R_r(t_i)$ according to the following formula:

$$R_r(t_i) = \begin{cases} \eta R_r(t_{i-1}) & if \quad state = Increase \\ \alpha A(t_i) & if \quad state = Decrease \\ R_r(t_{i-1}) & if \quad state = Hold \end{cases} \quad (15)$$

where $\eta \in [1.005, 1.3]$, $\alpha \in [0.8, 0.95]$ and $A(t_i)$ is the receiving rate measured in the last 500 ms. Also, the $R_r(t_i)$ cannot exceed $1.5*A(t_i)$ in order to prevent the receiver from requesting a bitrate that the sender cannot satisfy.

Note that the rates are controlled by the state of the Finite State Machine (FSM) in Figure 9.3, which is called the Remote Rate Controller. The state of this FSM is changed according to the signal produced by the Overuse Detector, which is based on the output of the Arrival Time Filter, as follows:

- If $\hat{b}(t_i)$ increases above a threshold and keeps increasing for a certain amount of time or for a certain amount of consecutive frames, it is assumed that the network is congested because the bottleneck queue is filling up, and the "overuse" signal is triggered.
- If $\hat{b}(t_i)$ decreases below a threshold, this means that the bottleneck queue is being emptied. Hence, the network is considered underused, and the "underuse" signal is generated. Upon this signal, the FSM enters the Hold state, where the available bandwidth estimate is held constant while waiting for the queues to stabilize at a lower level.
- When $\hat{b}(t_i)$ is close to zero, the network is considered stable, and the "normal" signal is generated.

The REMB messages that carry the value of R_r from the receiver to the sender are sent either every 1 sec if R_r is decreasing or immediately if R_r decreases more than 3%.

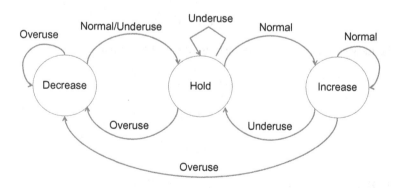

FIGURE 9.3

Finite state machine that controls the remote rate.

APPENDIX 9.A **KALMAN FILTERING**

Consider a linear system, with an $n \times 1$ dimensional state variable x_t, which evolves in time according to the following equation:

$$x_t = A_t x_{t-1} + B_t u_t + \varepsilon_t \tag{F1}$$

where u_t is a $m \times 1$ dimensional control vector driving x_t, A_t is a square matrix of size $n \times n$, B_t is $n \times m$ matrix, and ε_t is a $n \times 1$ Gaussian random vector with mean 0 and covariance given by R_t. A state transition of the type (F1) is known as linear Gaussian to reflect the fact that it is linear in its arguments with additive Gaussian noise.

The system state x_t is not observable directly; its value has to be inferred through the $k \times 1$ dimensional state observation process z_t given by

$$z_t = C_t x_t + \delta_t \tag{F2}$$

where C_t is $k \times n$ dimensional matrix and δ_t is the observation (or measurement) noise process. The distribution of δ_t is assumed to be multivariate Gaussian with zero mean and covariance Q_t.

The Kalman filter is used to obtain estimates of the state variable x_t at time t, given the control sequence u_t and output sequence z_t. Because x_t is a Gaussian random variable, the estimates are actually estimates for its mean μ_t and covariance Σ_t at time t.

The Kalman filter uses an iterative scheme, which works as follows:

1. At time t = 0, start with initial estimates for the mean and covariance of x_t given by (μ_0, Σ_0).
2. At time t−1, assume that the estimates for the mean and covariance of x_{t-1} have been computed to be $(\mu_{t-1}, \Sigma_{t-1})$. Given the control u_t and output z_t at time t, the estimates (μ_t, Σ_t) are computed recursively as follows, in two steps.
3. In step a, the control u_t is incorporated (but not the measurement z_t), to obtain the intermediate estimates $(\overline{\mu}_t, \overline{\Sigma}_t)$ given by

$$\overline{\mu}_t = A_t \mu_{t-1} + B_t u_t \tag{F3}$$

$$\overline{\Sigma}_t = A_t \Sigma_{t-1} A_t^T + R_t \tag{F4}$$

4. In step b, the measurement z_t is incorporated to obtain the estimates (μ_t, Σ_t) at time t, given by

$$K_t = \overline{\Sigma}_t C_t^T (C_t \overline{\Sigma}_t C_t^T + Q_t)^{-1} \tag{F5}$$

$$\mu_t = \overline{\mu}_t + K_t(z_t - C_t \overline{\mu}_t) \tag{F6}$$

$$\Sigma_t = (I - K_t C_t)\overline{\Sigma}_t \tag{F7}$$

The variable K_t computed in equation F6 is called the Kalman gain, and it specifies the degree to which the new measurement is incorporated into the new state estimate.

REFERENCES

[1] Winstein K, Balakrishnan H. End-to-end transmission control by modeling uncertainty about the network state. Hotnets 2011:19.

[2] Winstein K, Balakrishnan H. TCP ex machina: computer generated congestion control. ACM SIGCOMM 2013;43(4):123−34.

[3] Winstein K. Transport architectures for an evolving Internet. PhD thesis, Massachusetts Institute of Technology, 2014.

[4] Sivaraman A, Winstein K, Thaker P, Balakrishnan H. An experimental study of the learnability of congestion control. ACM SIGCOMM 2014:479−90.

[5] Sivaraman A, Winstein K, Subramanian S, Balakrishnan H. No silver bullet: extending SDN to the data plane. Hotnets 2013:19.

[6] Lundin H, et al. Google congestion control algorithm for real time communications on the world wide web. IETF Draft, 2013.

[7] de Cicco L, Carlucci G, Mascolo S. Experimental investigation of the Google congestion control for real-time flows. ACM SIGCOMM 2013:21−6.

[8] Floyd S, Handley M, Padhye J. Equation based congestion control for unicast applications. ICSI TR-00-003 2000;30(4):43−56.

SUGGESTED READING

Ghobadi M, Yeganeh SH, Ganjali Y. Re-thinking end-to-end congestion control in software defined networks. Hotnets 2012:61−6.

Singh V, Lozano AA, Ott J. Performance analysis of receive side real-time congestion control for WebRTC. Packet Video Workshop, 2013.

Winstein K, Sivaraman A, Balakrishnan H. Stochastic forecasts achieve high throughput and low delay over cellular networks. USENIX NSDI Conference, 2013.

Index

Note: Page numbers followed by "*f*" refer to figures.

Printed in the United States
By Bookmasters